IN
AND
OUT
OF
VOGUE

GRACE MIRABELLA

WITH JUDITH WARNER

DOUBLEDAY   NEW YORK   LONDON   TORONTO   SYDNEY   AUCKLAND

IN AND OUT OF VOGUE

PUBLISHED BY DOUBLEDAY

a division of Bantam Doubleday Dell Publishing Group, Inc.
1540 Broadway, New York, New York 10036

D O U B L E D A Y and the portrayal of an anchor with a
dolphin are trademarks of Doubleday, a division of Bantam
Doubleday Dell Publishing Group, Inc.

Book design by Marysarah Quinn

Library of Congress Cataloging-in-Publication Data
Mirabella, Grace, 1929–
    In and out of Vogue / by Grace Mirabella with Judith Warner. —
1st ed.
        p.   cm.
      1. Mirabella, Grace, 1929–   .   2. Vogue.   3. Editors—United
States—Biography.   4. Periodical editors—United States—Biography.
I. Warner, Judith.   II. Title.
PN149.9.M48A3   1995
070.4′1′092—dc20
      [B]   95-16378
                                                                          CIP

ISBN 0-385-42613-5
Copyright © 1995 by Grace Mirabella
All Rights Reserved
Printed in the United States of America
September 1995

10   9   8   7   6   5   4   3   2   1

FIRST EDITION

To Bill—

Without you, there'd be very little!

—*g*

ACKNOWLEDGMENTS

Letitia Baldrige
William Cahan, archivist
Condé Nast Library
Betty Dorso
Amy Gross
Jade Hobson
Despina Messinesi
Dawn Mello
Priscilla Rattazzi
Babs Simpson
Paul Sinclaire
Alexander Vreeland
And, of course, Judy Warner, who was heroic.

Naturally, when one is "at it" as long as I have been in the fashion maga-zine world, there are so many people, big talents, who make up the weave and woof of one's life; but there is a special cluster whose talent and integrity I'll always admire:

Giorgio Armani
Geoffrey Beene
Manolo Blahnik
Bill Blass
Rose Marie Bravo
Donna Karan
Calvin Klein
Diego Della Valle
Arthur Elgort
Carla Fendi
Ralph Lauren
Rosita and Tai Missoni
Issey Miyake
Isaac Mizrahi
Helmut Newton
Irving Penn
Yves Saint Laurent
Emanuel Ungaro

IN
AND
OUT
OF
VOGUE

INTRODUCTION

1950. My mother and I sit in a coffee shop in East Orange, New Jersey. I've invited her to lunch. I'm wearing jeans, with a camel's hair jacket. The jacket is from the boy's department. The shoes are penny loafers. The stitching is coming out of their seams. That's my look. Casual and American. I think that it's great.

My mother, who works in an upscale dress shop on East Orange Avenue, thinks otherwise. She darts nervous glances over her shoulder, fearful that someone who knows her will come along and ask to be introduced to this *person* sitting across from her.

Finally, she lets me have it.

"Do you plan to go around all the time looking like that?" she asks. "If you want to have a career in fashion, Grace, you'd better learn how to dress."

1971. As the newly named editor of American *Vogue*, I attend the couture in Paris for the first time. I am wearing Halston separate pieces of a beige cashmere sweater and his pants plus a wonderful white cashmere men's scarf, an outfit Halston planned carefully for me and made in his custom order department months in advance. I have the misfortune of sitting next to fashion doyenne Hebe Dorsey, the reporter for the *International Herald-Tribune* who was then the ruling voice of the European fashion press. The next day Dorsey reports that I came to the couture in a "sweater," looking "like the girl next door"—Main Street, U.S.A. It's not a compliment. Neither is her appraisal of my prospects at the top of the illustrious *Vogue* masthead: "Fashion will never be the same."

This is the story of my life.

I didn't spend my years moving up through the ranks at *Vogue* and then founding my own magazine in a boy's department store jacket and ripped loafers. I haven't lunched in jeans in recent history. My jackets and pants, for the past few decades, have been Saint Laurent's, Halston's, Geoffrey Beene's. But my attitude toward clothes is the same as it was ten or twenty or maybe forty-five years ago.

I am not a fashion maven. I never have been and never will be. You'll never catch me saying things like "Think Pink," and you'll never see me wearing dark sunglasses during lunch at The '21' Club. I don't play the fashion game; I don't lunch, wine-and-dine with the fashion-y crowd, and I've never perfected the art of going backstage after a bad fashion show and telling the designer that it was "fabulous." I'm not a Diana Vreeland, or a Carrie Donovan, or an Anna Wintour, playing the movie version of a fashion editor à la *Lady in the Dark*. I've always been something of an outsider to the fashion world. I'm an outsider by birth, by taste, and by choice.

Going back to first causes, I'm from Newark. *New Jersey*. For people in Manhattan, where I've spent my entire adult life, New Jersey is more than a place; it's an adjective, and what it describes is just about anything Manhattanites find aesthetically or morally undesirable. This was never made clearer to me than in a cartoon that ran recently in the *New Yorker*. It showed an unfashionable, overweight matron walking in the street of a city (I suspect Newark) that overlooked the New York skyline. She was wearing a T-shirt that read, "DKNJ." And the caption read, "Donna Karan's Nightmare." Enough said.

The fact of my being from New Jersey has at times been taken to have a certain charm, but the fact of my being from *Newark* is generally viewed as so unconscionable that most people who have written about me at various points in my career have literally struck it from the record. According to them, I was born either in South Orange or Maplewood, towns where I did live or go to school at some point in my life, and I've never seen fit to correct them. For I've seen the dangerous effect that "New Jersey" can have on unsuspecting people. New York socialite Marietta Tree, for one, nearly dropped dead when she first heard I was from the Garden State.

I remember the scene all too well. It was 1976, and my husband, Bill Cahan, and I were guests at a party in Andy Warhol's god-awful Factory that Françoise de Langlade, then fashion editor of *Vogue* and soon-to-be wife of Oscar de la Renta, had thrown for Yves Saint Laurent chairman Pierre Bergé. It was the usual mid-seventies scene: Warhol's Skull paintings hung on the walls, and red votive candles lit our tables, shining upon the presence of such social luminaries as Diana Vreeland, Diane von Furstenberg, Helene Rochas, Nan Kempner, and Lally Weymouth. Marietta, whose younger daughter, Penelope, had been one of *Vogue*'s top models in the late 1960s and who was considered quite a good friend of my husband's, was sitting at our table. Just as we were finishing with dinner, in a loud, horsey voice that resonated with the breeding of the generations of New England Peabodys that had produced her, she drew the attention of our table to me, and shouted, "Grace!! Where are you from?"

"New Jersey," I answered.

"New Jersey!" she gasped, feigning shortness of breath as all our dinner companions looked up. "Can you *imagine?* The editor of *Vogue* from *New Jersey?"*

It's possible that I may have taken it the wrong way.

But I really do think that Marietta Tree, by falling into her suburbia-induced swoon, was making a larger point. For the Dorseys and Trees of this world, I wasn't just the "girl next door" because of my cashmere sweaters and ignominious state of birth. Tree's *"New Jersey!"* really meant something quite different: that I wasn't issued from the same, well, *class* as most *Vogue* editors of my era. Similarly, Dorsey's "sweater" was a code word, if not a war cry, that suggested that I perhaps wasn't "fashion-y" enough to be taken seriously as a fashion magazine editor.

That charge, that I am not, somehow, a *real* fashion person, has dogged me throughout the greater portion of my professional life, through my years as editor in chief at *Vogue*, and through my tenure as founder and director of *Mirabella*. It's a criticism that I have always claimed as a badge of honor. Not fashion-y enough? That suits me fine, if being the opposite means accepting with open arms every backless and frontless and topless and see-through thing that clomps its way down the runway in combat boots. I've never been one for that. I don't like glitz and I don't like trendy things and I don't like slapdash and silly fashion games. All of which has, at times, led some very influential people to conclude that I don't like or appreciate *fashion* at all.

And that's a point with which I beg to differ.

Fashion is what you define it to be. For me, fashion is about women. It's about what their lives are like and what they are striving to be. There's a quote from Anatole France which, I think, sums this up in a marvelous way. J. C. Flugel cites it in the preface to his book *The Psychology of Clothes*. It reads: "If I were permitted to choose amongst the collection of books which will be published a hundred years after my death, do you know which one I should choose? Not a novel in this future library, nor a book of history. I would simply take, my friend, a fashion magazine to see how the women would dress a century after my decease. And these furbelows would tell me more about future humanity than all the philosophers, novelists, preachers or scholars."

To me, fashion has always been a vehicle—a fascinating, sometimes magnificent vehicle—for helping women enjoy and delight in their lives. Fashion to me isn't, and never has been, an end in and of itself. You'll never find me getting excited about shoulder pads or caring deeply, one way or the other, if hemlines went up or down. And you won't find a magazine that bears my name going on about it either.

What I've always cared about, *passionately*, is style. Style is how a woman carries herself and approaches the world. It's about how she wears her clothes and it's more: an attitude about living. Dressing up in the most expensive thing around has nothing to do with style. Style transcends money, fashion trends, "prettiness."

I've always cared about style because I care about women, and women, especially working women in our time, need good style. Women who in other decades "dressed up" to go out to lunch or to dinner or to cocktails or who dressed for work in a world where their job options were extremely limited placed an entirely different demand on their clothing than most women do today. Women today lead exceedingly jam-packed, complex lives which require that they spend as little time as possible doing their hair, choosing their clothes, and making sure that once they're dressed, nothing is coming undone, or creasing badly, or digging its stays into their ribs.

And yet, women *need* to look good. They need this even more urgently now that they dress for board meetings than they did in the days when they dressed to be decorative, because now the stakes are so much higher. As Naomi Wolf pointed out, disturbingly, in *The Beauty Myth*, what a woman wears and how she wears it can directly affect whether she's hired, fired, or promoted.

And beyond looking good, a woman has to *feel* good in her
clothes. They have to move with her when she walks and sits and
runs board meetings. They have to help her make her points, not
strike points against her. A woman can't relax and give her job her
all if she's worrying that her suit is too short or her heels too high.
She can't attend a business lunch in a see-through blouse or a pouf
skirt. Looking good—and dressing appropriately—gives women
the confidence they need to succeed. It also, objectively, gives them
a leg up in a competitive market.

I took part in a panel discussion on American Style this winter
at the Metropolitan Museum of Art. My role was to speak for the
fashion industry, to add a Seventh Avenue-eye view to the very
academic proceedings. A woman in the audience, I recall, asked
me to define a wonderful moment in American style. I said, "I'll
tell you what my *ideal* would be. My idea of a great American style
moment would be a woman going in the rain to a big dinner, or
running to catch a taxi, not worried the least about her hair or her
dress because she doesn't *have* to worry anymore. She's not wearing some great beehive hairdo. She's not wearing six-inch heels.
Her hair is so well cut and her clothes move with such ease that
suddenly being caught in the rain is not a major drama: she's not
going to be ruined, and she's not in a mess."

My male fellow panelists were puzzled. But the other woman
on the panel and those in the audience were delighted. They knew
what I meant. The picture I had in my mind was about more than
how a woman dresses or does her hair. What it was really about
was an image of how a woman lives her life. It was about imagining a comfortable, active life, an unencumbered life. I've devoted
my life in fashion to trying to help women achieve this kind of
style.

American style, when it's at its best—as in the clothing of Calvin Klein or Ralph Lauren or Bill Blass or Geoffrey Beene—
captures just this vision. It's filled with a spirit of mobility, a spirit
of freedom. It announces to the world that the American woman is
a distinct breed, that she's on the move and there's no holding her

back. It's an endangered species these days, that sort of style, but when you can find it, it can shock you with its greatness.

It's no mystery why I'm such a fan of American style. I came of age on Seventh Avenue in the 1950s, at the very same time that the American sportswear and separates markets were coming into their own, growing bigger and bigger and eventually displacing the old top-of-the-line labels as the center of the fashion industry. Ready-to-wear was an outgrowth, in a sense, of the Second World War, which had isolated Seventh Avenue from the couture salons of Europe and paved the way to the development of a uniquely American way of designing and producing clothing.

The 1950s in American fashion were about breaking down barriers, about mobility, about bridging the gap between the hundred or so women who could afford to buy at the couture and the vast numbers who had no access to high-quality design at all. Through mass production, ready-to-wear democratized access. Yet, unlike Levittown, it also did so with style.

The rise of ready-to-wear democratized not only women's access to good clothes, but it also changed the balance of power within the fashion industry. Before its time, couturiers creating fashions for society women dictated the looks that prevailed each season, and lower-priced manufacturers—invisible to fashion magazines like *Vogue*—copied those designs and sold them to the masses in department stores. Since only a tiny portion of women had the buying power to purchase clothes from the best manufacturers (one talked of manufacturers, not designers, in those days), the vast majority of women were just ignored by the industry. Working women didn't even enter the equation. They didn't exist in great numbers and certainly didn't matter in fashion terms; they didn't have the buying power. Fashion magazines like *Vogue*, which was always semijokingly referred to as a final finishing school for girls who had already completed Emma Willard or Miss Porter's, were publications about the rich, produced by the rich for the rich.

The rise of ready-to-wear after the Second World War meant

that a larger quantity of better clothing was available to many more women. The availability of this clothing, and the increased buying power of middle-class women in the post-war boom period, meant that the fashion industry had to start to widen its sights and design for a greater portion of the population than the ladies who lunched. It's no accident, I think, that this development coincided with the emergence of sportswear. Sportswear was a freer, easier, less-is-more, more popular way of dressing, and it embodied, as fashion never had in this country before, a distinctly American kind of casualness.

Sportswear and I appeared on Seventh Avenue at just the same time. We both spelled the arrival of something highly democratic and uniquely American on the fashion scene. I was a kid from New Jersey with Italian immigrant parents who had arrived at *Vogue* at the tail end of the time when its young editors were recruited right out of the Social Register. I was plunging into a Seventh Avenue world where the manufacturers were first-generation Jewish immigrants, Lithuanians and Russians and Poles who spoke with marvelous accents and traded remnants and bolts of cloth over breakfast. These manufacturers welcomed me into their world, and I felt a strong bond with them. As an outsider to a privileged and precious world, I couldn't have found a better fit.

It all seemed of a piece for me: Seventh Avenue, the sportswear men, dressing in separates, growing up at *Vogue*. Making it at *Vogue* as I did in those years for me meant much more than just social and professional arrival. It meant finding a home.

Fashion editors have their moments, just as fashion styles do. Jessica Daves, a staid and prudish woman who was editor of *Vogue* when I came on board in 1952, was *the* editor for her time, just as Diana Vreeland was for the off-the-wall 1960s. My moment came in the 1970s, when women changed and the world changed, and suddenly a career-minded woman like me who liked to talk about movement and freedom wasn't just an odd egg anymore, but was suddenly the one person at *Vogue* who was in touch with what contemporary women were doing and feeling. Diana Vreeland was

a brilliant and inspired fashion editor. She had great regard for
Seventh Avenue, or what she referred to as "the men" on Seventh
Avenue—the entrepreneurs, the people who ran it—but she had
no regard for what she thought of as uninspired, "cookie cutter"
clothes. Instead of trying to better them, she took them to their
extreme—or ignored them. And she lived in the realm of fantasy,
with no idea of—or interest in—the lives of real, earthbound
women. And those women, unacknowledged by her and her colleagues in the 1960s, had turned their backs on fashion. They had
also turned their backs on fashion magazines. And magazines like
Harper's Bazaar and *Vogue* took a real beating on the newsstand
in the late 1960s and early 1970s because women weren't interested in reading about or buying clothes that served no purpose in
their changing lives.

That moment of women turning their backs on the old rules of
fashion was my moment. I was selected as editor in chief to bring
Vogue in step with that change, to make the magazine appeal to
the free, working, "liberated" woman of the seventies. We showed
her clothing that *moved*, that *breathed*, wonderful, handsome
clothes that swaggered from Bill Blass, and dashing Saint Laurent
pants suits and Emanuel Ungaro shawls. We beefed the magazine
up with text, with interviews and arts coverage and serious health
pieces, because we knew we were publishing for a new kind of
woman, and we didn't want her to think that we couldn't keep up
with her. And when that woman fell out of favor in the 1980s, in
a fashion moment captured all too perfectly in the pouf skirts of
Christian Lacroix and his imitators, I fell out of fashion too.

The story of my fall from *Vogue* has been told so many times that
it's become the stuff of legend.

On June 28, 1988, my husband, Dr. William Cahan, was home
from a day of surgery at Memorial Sloan-Kettering hospital when
the telephone rang. It was Marie Fauth, a close friend whom I'd

known for almost three decades. "Bill," she said. "Turn on Channel Four news. Liz Smith is saying something about Grace."

Bill put down the phone and raced over to the TV, tuning in to "Live at Five" just in time to hear a pained and uncomfortable-looking Liz Smith (who, after all, is a dear friend of ours) announce that I was to be replaced as editor in chief of *Vogue* by *HG* editor Anna Wintour.

Her full comments, I later saw, had been this:

"Ever since Anna Wintour, the editor of British *Vogue*, was brought to New York by Condé Nast to take over the remake of their *House and Garden* there have been rumors that Miss Wintour would become the editor of American *Vogue*, replacing the veteran Grace Mirabella. Well, now the hot publishing story is that this probably will happen on September 1. Don't ask me why Condé Nast would want to replace Grace Mirabella. *Vogue* is one of the healthiest, heftiest magazines in the Condé Nast chain. You know, if it ain't broke, don't fix it, but they're going to anyway."

Not broke! *Vogue* had never been stronger. It's circulation, which stood at 400,000 when I took over in 1971, was now holding strong at an unrivaled 1.2 million. Our advertising revenues were $79.5 million dollars; our nearest competitor's, *Elle*'s, were just $39 million. In the course of my seventeen years as editor, we had revolutionized the magazine's tone and contents. What was once a magazine for society women had become a magazine for all women who wanted a little style in their lives. We'd brought *Vogue* into the real world. And *1.2 million women* wanted to keep us there.

There had to have been some mistake.

Bill picked up the phone and called me. My secretary had been drilled to know that the only calls I would always take, unconditionally, were his, my mother's, and my boss, Alex Liberman's, and she put him through immediately.

"Grace, this is ludicrous," he said. He filled me in on the broadcast. "What's it all about?"

"I have no idea," I said. "No idea at all." And I promised to call him back as soon as I had some news.

I sat at my desk thinking for a moment, and then headed upstairs to the office of Alexander Liberman, editorial director for all the Condé Nast publications and Si Newhouse's alter ego. Alex was my direct boss at *Vogue*; he had the final word on content and layouts, hirings and firings and article assignments, and he had a wonderful creative vision that had become indispensable to me over the years. He was also a dear friend. He and his wife, Tatiana, had hosted us at his country house in Warren, Connecticut, more times than I could imagine. Bill and I had visited them during the summer in Ischia, and we had spent time together in Paris during the July couture week for almost two decades. Alex had been a mentor to me in the years before I'd become editor in chief at *Vogue*. He'd groomed me for the job and kept me on my toes once I was in it. He also, I realized, had been issuing veiled warnings about my handling of fashion and Si Newhouse for the past few years. But now that the veil had fallen, could he really be so brutal?

I found Alex seated at his desk. Uncharacteristically, he appeared to be doing next to nothing. He seemed simply to be waiting.

"Grace, I'm afraid it's true," he said in his great, melodious voice that spoke of csarist Russia, England boarding school, and Cole Porter's New York.

"I'm sorry, Grace," he said. "I'm just too old."

It was a line which, in the coming days, he would also use to excuse himself before his old friend, Bill Cahan—and with as much success.

"What's that supposed to mean?" I said.

"Don't talk to *me*. It wasn't *my* idea. I had nothing to do with it. Talk to Si."

Leaving his office, riding numbly down in the elevator to my floor, I was reminded of a line that Diana Vreeland, after her own rather brutal firing from *Vogue*, had passed off to Liz Smith: "I have known White Russians; I have known Red Russians. I have never before known a yellow Russian."

Of all her bon mots, this was undoubtedly the best. Better than "Pink is the navy blue of India," anyway.

Pink is the navy blue of India.

I had a moment of self-doubt. Should I have been more like Vreeland, after all? Should I have let myself think like *Vogue*'s new editor, the British import and reputed ice queen, Anna Wintour? That would have been impossible. Perhaps I, too, was just too old. Perhaps they'd just decided to put me out to pasture, at age fifty-nine. It wouldn't have been the first time that such a thing had happened at *Vogue*. I'd only become editor after Vreeland was summarily fired. She hadn't even seen it coming—one day, the men upstairs had just called her in and told her that "it wasn't working out." I, at least, had known there'd been rumors about Anna Wintour's taking over for the better part of a year. But there are always so many rumors in the magazine industry. I had believed what I wanted to believe.

Before leaving Alex's office, I had told him, "You're going to regret this. Not because you fired me, but because of *how* you did it." And, sure enough, when I got back to my office, the phone was ringing. It kept ringing for months. Newspapers, magazines, television stations. Book offers. Scores and scores of friends and supporters.

Was I shocked? Was I broken? Was I furious? Would I sue?

None of the above.

My story caught the imagination of the press, which ran with it for weeks. In the magazine community it inspired a mass outbreak of *Schadenfreude*. There were hopes of fireworks, of recriminations, of confirmations of the rumor that Anna Wintour had been having an affair with Si Newhouse, and had slept her way to the top, after all.

I allowed for no such thing. Instead, I simply told *The New York Times*, "For a magazine devoted to style, this was not a very stylish way of telling me." The quote caught on like wildfire. It was cited as an example of my "grace under pressure." And I felt like I'd had the last word.

We're all the products of our times, of certain moments that mold us and shape us, intellectually, emotionally, aesthetically. Emotionally, I am a daughter of the Great Depression. I was born in 1929, and got my bearings in the world as a child of parents who lost everything they had had in the crash and worked their way back up into the middle class during the years that followed it. Though I was too young to understand what was happening in any real way, I know that as a young child I breathed in the atmosphere of fear and deprivation that seized the nation in the Depression through the not-inconsequential hard times experienced by my family.

Even if you don't remember them, you are destined to live out the emotions you experienced during your first years of life. The Depression shaped my earliest notions of security and money and value, and to this day, despite all the comforts I've come to have in my life as the head of two successful magazines and the wife of a famous surgeon, I still always think about the lessons of my early childhood. I'm impatient with waste. I can't stand people who take a laissez-faire attitude toward money or a let-them-eat-cake attitude toward things that have an important impact on real people's lives. Fashion is one of those things.

Fashion, after all, is at base not a luxury. Beyond their basic needs for clothing, people *need* fashion, need an access to good style in order to compete successfully in the working world. My take on clothing has always been that it's something that has to *work*, but not *just* to work: to work and look good. These days, women need functionally stylish clothes the same way that they need wonderful date books or answering machines or cellular phones; clothing has become a tool, like so many others, to help them organize their day, work effectively, and compete. And there has to be something in between the excesses of fashion and the simply banal.

The eighties just were not my era. I couldn't stand the frills and the glitz and the 40,000-dollar ball gowns. I still believed that *all* women had the right to decent fashion, to solid design, as they'd begun to have in the 1950s. And I hated the elitist attitude that reigned in the fashion industry and made it such that any woman who wasn't willing to spend more than a thousand dollars for a suit couldn't find anything decently designed anymore. And I hated the fact that fashion editors considered it tacky to pay attention to what things cost.

I have never liked fashion-y games; clothes that sing and dance about themselves and prove purely unwearable. Geoffrey Beene, my closest friend among the fashion designers, always says, "If they're not wearable, they shouldn't be called clothes," and I altogether agree. But that thought had no currency in the 1980s. Fashion became a game. The game had its roots in the late seventies, when designers became kings, and it took off hand in hand with the prosperity of the Reagan years.

It was an emperor-has-no-clothes era, start to finish. Clothes were about labels, designers were about being celebrities, and it was all, on a bigger and bigger scale, about money. Until eventually, as the eighties turned into the nineties, fashion came to be about nothing more than itself. It degenerated, like post-modern art, like post-modern architecture, into a self-referential game full of jokes and pastiches that amused the fashion community enormously and did nothing at all for the woman shopping and trying to find something to wear. At the very same time that women were really emerging as a potent economic and political force in American life, there were no clothes for them at all. Susan Faludi called it a backlash; I called it a travesty. And it continues today.

At *Vogue* the eighties were about keeping up with the new French import, *Elle*, which began publication in 1986 and was perceived by Si Newhouse as a major threat to our magazine. *Elle*'s content and layout were typical of the MTV mode that was taking over everything in that time: it had snappy cover lines, flashy photos, and trendy clothing on teenage models that offered very little for a woman looking for clothes that could carry her through her life. Although *Elle* did not, in fact, cut into *Vogue*'s readership, its success made Alex and Si very nervous.

Throughout the late 1980s I was told, time and again, in vague and not-so-vague and charming and not-so-charming terms, to make *Vogue* more like *Elle*, and I couldn't. Or wouldn't. And that, more than any other reason, I believe, is why I was fired.

The firing turned out to be the best thing that had ever happened in my life. The outpouring of support I received afterward, support not just from friends but from strangers, proved to me that despite all the flak I'd been getting from the big boys at *Vogue*, *women* still stood behind me. *Women* got what it was I was trying to do, as their letters and cards told me, time and again and again. For years, in arguments with Alex, I'd felt like I were toiling in a wilderness, alone in my vision but for the few loyal editors I'd assembled close to me during my years at the top. I'd been told I was out of style, out-of-date, out of touch with not only the youth of America (not that *Vogue*, even in its youth-worshiping days under Vreeland, ever was a magazine for the young), but with the women of America in general. And now I saw, for the first time, how many women truly shared my vision. Their letters and phone calls and comments on the street brought that home to me in a way that our readership numbers had never been able to make real.

I realized something else too: that women *needed* a magazine with the kind of vision that I'd tried to bring to *Vogue*. For as the eighties turned into the nineties, and fashion began the downward spiral into the utter unwearability that we're seeing today, I realized that women who wanted—and needed—something decently stylish to wear were more hopelessly lost than ever. As I've said earlier, I believe passionately that women *need* style the way they need Filofaxes and affordable child care. And in the game of fashion that was being played out in the late eighties, they were, increasingly, the losers. And, more than ever, they had so very much to lose.

The story has a happy ending.

About two days after it was in the press that I had been removed from *Vogue*, Ed Kosner, then the editor of *New York* magazine, called me and said that Rupert Murdoch wanted to have lunch with me.

"Do *I* want to have lunch with Rupert Murdoch?" I thought. In my mind, he was a tabloids man. (That's how much I knew!) I couldn't imagine what he or I could have had to offer each other. But then, I thought, what did I have to lose? I told Ed that I would *love* to meet Mr. Murdoch.

We had lunch at the Côte Basque, a wonderful French restaurant in midtown Manhattan. As we made small talk under the dining room's murals of southern France, Rupert surprised me suddenly with a question: "Do you think there's a woman without a magazine? A woman who's been left out by other magazines?"

And I, warming immediately to the topic, said yes.

Who is she? he asked.

She's a very smart woman, I said, who isn't necessarily twenty-three anymore, and doesn't want to be. She's in her mid thirties, or maybe even older. She's a woman who's too smart to be spoken to the way most women's magazines today do. She's a woman who's sick of being talked down to and has stopped buying women's magazines because of it. And I, I said, am tired of ignoring her.

Rupert listened intently and said that he agreed. Then we passed on to other subjects and finished our lunch. And as we were preparing to say good-bye and leaving the restaurant, he said to me, in what I came to realize later was his typical way of saying a thousand large things in one small sentence, "Let me go over the figures."

A few months later I had a magazine. And hundreds of thousands of like-minded women found they had an advocate in the fashion world. Together, we forged a new vision for what a woman's *style* magazine should be. And, until its recent upheaval, it enjoyed some great success.

Mirabella's readers were highly intelligent, literate, innovative movers and shakers. They were the women who have always been the driving force behind everything that I've done. They are my crowd, and I dedicate this book to them. They are the real style-makers.

CHAPTER 1
FROM NEWARK TO NEW WORLDS

One day in the 1950s, when I was a junior editor at *Vogue*, Babs Simpson, a senior fashion editor, returned to the office from an appointment with a "find." It was a rather odd and beautiful bathing cap, perfectly sculpted and ornamented, whose design Babs had closely worked out with Adolfo, then the newest and biggest name in hats. It was an extraordinary thing—for a bathing cap—

and when Babs showed it to me, I made a great show of my appreciation.

"I'm fascinated," I said excitedly, murmuring words like "wonderful" and "extraordinary" and fingering the cap. "It's absolutely terrific, fabulous. How much does it cost?"

She turned to me, her penciled eyebrows arched to the heavens. Her expression, frozen by shock, was a portrait of affront.

"What does that matter?" she asked. And with a miffed smile and a little shrug, she tossed her head and swept away.

At *Vogue* in the 1950s—as in the 1940s, the 1920s . . . the 1960s—you didn't ask what things cost. What things cost—what one might have to do to *earn* them—were questions that were *dreadfully* middle class, and if they arose (if you were smart), you shrugged them off with a gesture of fatigue and boredom, leaving your questioner to wonder if she might be better off at a place like *Life* magazine or at *Good Housekeeping* or at *Glamour*. Life at *Vogue*, as in its pages, was all delight, fabulousness, wealth, and beauty. Everything was "wonderfully attractive" and "amusing" and "fun"—defining words for a class of editors who had never really known life to be otherwise. It was a place where, as a well-known story holds, when a writer once asked a pregnant secretary what kind of baby—boy or girl—she wanted to have, the young woman is said to have replied, "Oh, a fun baby!"

It was an attitude in which the snobbery was so refined that it eclipsed itself in a kind of unseeing beneficence, an all's-well-with-the-world sort of stance which not only rejected all that was unattractive and un-fun in life, but resolutely refused even to see it.

The let-them-eat-cake attitude is still prevalent among the fashion editors of *Vogue* today. But it's all affectation now, whereas once it was a very natural outgrowth of who the *Vogue* editors were and how they had been brought up. The stereotype of *Vogue* as a final finishing school for the daughters of the very wealthy was not without its basis in truth. Salaries were so low they were called "pin money" by staff, and the story of a washroom bystander overhearing one young *Vogue* editor telling another, "I'll have to get a real job now, Daddy can't afford to send me to *Vogue* any-more," was a standard on the midtown Manhattan joke circuit for decades. "Don't send your daughter to college, send her to *Vogue*," was another swell line. And it wasn't altogether a joke.

No one, in my day, attended journalism school before applying to *Vogue*. Good taste, good breeding, long legs, and a certain *pzazz*—as Diana Vreeland liked to say—were the things that likely *Vogue* prospects were made of. Condé Nast, the legendary founder of the magazine empire that today bears his name, used to hire *Vogue* editors from among the pretty young women he met at Park Avenue dinner parties, and that practice, in a variety of forms, remained standard for decades. In its own way it made good business sense: the point was to staff the magazine with the kind of women who were *Vogue*'s readers—women who had the kind of taste and style that *Vogue* demanded, women who were prominently placed in society, women who could serve as *Vogue*'s emissaries to the highest reaches of the worlds of fashion and high society, which were usually one and the same. And so, while there was always somebody solid running things—even in the age of Diana Vreeland, who was more solid than she liked to let on—there was always a significant presence at the magazine of girls from "good families," as we then called them.

In my early days at *Vogue*, these "girls" included Margaret Ingersoll, the fabrics editor, who was descended from George Washington; Virginia Thaw, of the railroad and coke magnate Thaws, whose sister married the Earl of Yarmouth and whose forebearer, Henry Kendall Thaw, murdered the architect Stanford White; Countess Consuelo Crespi, one of the twin O'Connor girls of New York; Cathy McManus, of the New York and Southampton Murrays, who later became Catherine di Montezemolo; Peggy Talbott, daughter of Harold Talbott, who was Secretary of the Air Force in the Eisenhower Administration; Mab Wilson, who married the Count Von Moltke and whose daughter was Alexandra Isles of Klaus von Bulow fame; and Millicent Fenwick, whose mother drowned in the *Lusitania*, whose father was American ambassador to Spain under Calvin Coolidge, and who went on after *Vogue* to become a congresswoman. Most of the "girls," thanks to their upbringing, had very good taste. Some, like Babs Simpson, turned out to be wonderful fashion editors. Others did not.

I came to *Vogue* when the magazine was at a turning point. Under editor Jessica Daves, a rather frumpy minister's daughter from Georgia, the visions of loveliness from good families were beginning to share masthead space with those from "nowhere," who were hoping to make their own names in the fashion world. The entry of these new "working girls"—we were certainly not hailed as "career women" then—meant that little by little, and by no means overnight, a few daughters of the middle class—and even of *ethnics*—began to make their way into the blue-blooded regions of *Vogue*. Some were ex-models; some had started working straight out of high school. Muriel Maxwell, who was beauty editor when I arrived in 1952, was a key example. She had been a top Ford model in the 1940s, had worked on Seventh Avenue, and, to top it all off, was the daughter of a rabbi. She eventually, after leaving *Vogue*, was left by her husband and ended up an alcoholic and on welfare—or so the story goes, and I think it could be legend, the colorful talk of old *Vogue* editors who still, to this day and in their retirement, have trouble thinking of her as one of *them*. And yet she was. And so was I.

I too was not what you would have called a girl from a "good" family. As I already mentioned, my parents, Anthony Mirabella and Florence Bellofatto, were both Italian immigrants, though my father, through some twist of fate, had actually been born here, and then had spent his early life in Italy. He was an enormously likable but poorly educated and rough-sounding man, who, before the Great Depression, made a good living selling Majestic radios. He also was a gambler, a lifelong, devoted gambler, who bet fearlessly and relentlessly on horses and cards and anything else he could get his hands on and had probably won and lost a thousand fortunes before the stock market crashed and he lost everything.

My father made up for what he lacked in polish with extraordinary charm—an attribute which served him well with his customers, but was less useful in dealing with my mother. She looked down upon his family, which lived in a lower middle-class Italian neighborhood of Newark, two branches of brothers and in-laws doubled up in a single-family house with my grandfather stowed away in a cold-water shack in the rear. It was maybe this last detail—the shack, with its coal-burning stove and my steely grandfather, offering visitors shot glasses of pure alcohol, and serenely terrifying the living daylights out of his sons—that just made the whole scene too much for her.

Her own family was considered a bit more high class. They were from an area near Sorrento, and had been what is called "land poor" in Italy, which means that they had plenty of property but no cash, and had had, over the decades, to sell off more and more of the land just to get by. My mother's father had been a landscape painter in Italy—an ill-paid if gentlemanly profession—and her eldest brother, John, was a wonderfully cultured and educated man who had studied for the priesthood. They all, though, like my father's family, ended up crossing the Atlantic in steerage, and arrived in New York via Ellis Island after a terrible incident in which the person who was supposed to meet them at the dock in Manhattan got the days wrong and never showed up.

Life in the New World didn't get much easier after that. My grandfather took work painting houses and offices and public areas, and he died, just a few years after his family joined him here, when he fell down an elevator shaft trying to paint an elevator. My Uncle John became an engineer. When I came to know him he had exactly the same silhouette as Benito Mussolini: the same line of the face, the same height, the same body shape. He was extremely meticulous, and always dressed with an eye to perfection, in a shirt and a vest and a tie. He also had that peculiarly Italian propensity for waxing philosophical to the point of borderline pomposity and enjoyed seeing others squirm in their ignorance—as I used to do, during my Italian lessons with him, when he'd explain little couplets I didn't understand in Latin, and then feign shock when I'd look at him blankly.

My father was less charmed with my Uncle John than was I, particularly on the subject of Mussolini. Uncle John took the old line that Mussolini made the trains run on time literally. He also put great store by Bellofatto family lore which held that a distant relative of ours—a cousin perhaps, or a great-uncle—had been the man who had introduced Mussolini to the Italian people in a Roman square. During the Second World War my uncle sided with the Italians and my father, who was a flag-waving American, simply couldn't abide it. Our Thanksgiving and Christmas visits to my mother's relatives became constant shouting matches, involving much gesturing, threats of tears, and the regular spectacle, after dessert, of my father inviting my uncle to go back to Italy. Not surprisingly, our visits to that side of the family soon became less and less frequent.

My Newark was like Philip Roth's—a city of strivers pushing forward from immigrant enclaves and grabbing hold, as best they could, of the American dream. That wasn't easy during the Depression, particularly for my parents, who lost everything they had in the crash. Some of the money was lost when stocks they'd bought on margin went bad. And then the last chunk disappeared when the officer of the bank my father had deposited their savings with embezzled the money.

The story of that disaster is woven, like an often-repeated bedtime story, into the fabric of my earliest childhood memories. That's largely thanks to my mother, who seems to have sworn to herself, after the disaster, that the memory of my father's folly would never stray far from our daily imaginings. She kept it alive through the presence of a dented coffeepot, which was always prominently displayed in the kitchen. The coffeepot was a relic of the battle that raged between my parents on the day, after the crash, when my father had come home and told my mother that the last of their money was gone.

As she told it, he had walked into the kitchen and calmly said, "I always knew that man was a crook."

She, just as calmly, then asked him, "If you knew he was a crook, why did you leave our money with him?" And, without waiting for a reply, she lobbed the percolator at my father's head.

The fact was, although the stock market crash was an *unprecedented* disaster, it wasn't the first financial crisis that my family had known. My father's being a gambler was a constant danger, and it left my mother in the unenviable position of sitting at home waiting for disaster to strike, and hoping against hope that she'd be able to find a way to prevent it. The Great Depression, however, was something that even she couldn't have foreseen. And yet, when it hit, she was in a certain sense prepared to deal with it. She was used to picking up and going on, and so when she had to go to work after the crash, she found a job on Seventh Avenue as a sample hand for a children's wear manufacturer.

I was still a very small child when my mother started going off every morning to work. Perhaps these days, when nearly all mothers work, children adjust to it as part of the normal course of life. I, however, took it very hard. I was used to having her around all the time, and then suddenly she was gone, and all I had left at home was an Irish girl—always an Irish girl—who was paid to mind me. I can remember so clearly, as though it had happened just yesterday, how I used to feel, standing at the window and watching my mother walk down the steps as she went off to work in the morning. It was like waving somebody off on a ship. I used to cry and cry and cry, and then recover enough by four o'clock to be able to go and meet her at the train or the bus stop when she came home. I'd run up to meet her and she'd pick me up in her arms and give me a hug. It was a comfort, of sorts.

As Prohibition ended and the war began, and my father's new sales items, wines and liquors, began to be in demand, my family started to make its way onward and upward. I remember my childhood and early teen years as a series of moves to better and better neighborhoods of Newark, which was then a city of mostly

lower middle-class, immigrant communities, each sharply delineated by the fine gradations of race, national origin, and prosperity.
With each move, life became a bit better: apartments became bigger and turned into houses; cars grew newer and no longer had
their doors held shut with rope. The only down side to our upward
mobility, for me, was that it meant I had to leave the Catholic
school, Saint Rosa of Lima, where I'd very happily spent my early
school years. While most people think back to Catholic school in
those years with something akin to horror, I recall having thrived
there. I loved the structure and the order of parochial school life,
the priests and the nuns and the rituals of mass and confession. It
was an age when nuns still rapped students over the knuckles with
a ruler, but I never received such punishment. The nuns knew
about my father's stock in trade, and every November 30 or so
made sure to see that he came into school for a conference on my
progress, during which they delicately coughed and let him suggest
that they might like some brandy for their sore throats. A few bot-
tles kept them flush with health through the winter, and kept my
knuckles clean throughout the year.

Mark Twain once said, "There's something nice about Newark.
I think it's the suburbs." He was undoubtedly right. When I was
about to start junior high school, my family made its greatest
move—to suburban Maplewood, New Jersey. This was another
world altogether, an upper middle-class suburb, where people
stayed put all their lives, where friendships were formed in kinder-
garten, and people knew each other's families and life histories
inside and out. It was a difficult adjustment at first, but I quickly
found my bearings, and high school, at Columbia High, became a
vaguely pleasant time of fervent tennis playing, hanging out at the
ice cream shop with my best friend, Jane Kruger, dating boys in
uniform from the local army base—all boys seemed to be in uniform in those World War II days—and of taking home economics,
a subject at which I failed dismally, though I did for a brief point
in time know how to make a very nice cream sauce.

When the time came to apply to college, I decided I would attend Smith or Wellesley. These were the only schools, I believed, where the kinds of girls that I knew would consider going to college: Smith and Wellesley, Vassar *perhaps*, or maybe, if circumstances demanded it, Holyoke or Barnard. I was promptly rejected by both, and was left in quite a bind. I had already turned down Goucher College and Skidmore, both of which had accepted me early. But the fact that I had skipped two grades in school was held against me; I was sixteen, and had learned no arithmetic, and Smith and Wellesley felt that it was too soon for me to start college. Wellesley suggested I spend a year at Dana Hall (a prep school) and then reapply, but I didn't want to fall behind my friends. I had put all my eggs in the basket of Smith and Wellesley, and now I was left with egg all over my face.

Finally my parents, in a perhaps unconscious show of unified action, took over. We headed up to Saratoga Springs, New York, where my father immediately took me off to the racetrack. My mother then got on the phone and called the Skidmore admissions office. Through some miracle, she found someone there in July and managed to get me an interview. Somebody, by chance, had dropped out of the freshman class, and I got back in. And the next thing I knew, I was at Grand Central Station, waiting for a college-bound train, and saying a terrified good-bye to my father.

It was a heady moment: the first member of our immediate family was going off to college. My father was unnaturally solemn. I assumed he was just sad to see me go. And then I realized, as he cleared his throat to speak, that he'd been chosen by my mother to accompany me to the train station in order to deliver a few last words of fatherly advice. My mother, no doubt, had insisted upon it. It was the kind of thing that she would have thought proper. And it would have saved her from a last good-bye.

My father gave me a hug and looked at me very seriously. "Your mother told me that I should talk to you," he said. I nodded expectantly.

"So," he said, "consider yourself spoken to."

And that was the end of that.

Saratoga Springs was a gambler's town, which meant that it was one of my father's favorite places on earth. It was the kind of place where you always had the feeling that there was a little action going on somewhere down a side street, a little action that maybe wasn't quite obvious or quite above board. In the racing season, there were people coming and going from hotels and heading out to the races, booking bets, winning and losing money. When my father would come up to visit, he'd stay at the Grand Union Hotel, which had a wide, glamorous stairway that my father said always reminded him of Ingrid Bergman in the movie *Saratoga Trunk*, and he'd take me to dinner at some funny, very swell little restaurant out near a lake, which I always thought had gambling going on somewhere in a back room. In the winter, though, the place was totally dead. You could have snowball fights down the center of Main Street. The snows came and stayed and all the action just disappeared.

My first winter was cold and icy. The snow fell early and hung in for months. My future at Skidmore did not look too bright. I declared my economics major and decided that I would transfer after a year to Smith. And then spring came, and the countryside was beautiful, and you couldn't have paid me to leave.

I fell in love with the campus, which was then made up of an area about four blocks wide of wonderful old Victorian houses. I loved the informality of it all, the sweaters and the jeans, the communal duties like KP. It felt like real Americana to me, almost like walking onto a stage set from *Hello, Dolly*.

I had some wonderful teachers: a professor of modern drama who won my heart on the first day of the semester by entering the darkened classroom slowly and solemnly reciting the opening lines of *Hedda Gabler*, and a marvelous economics professor named Mr. Cheney, who kept running for governor of New York on the Socialist ticket. He made his deepest impression upon me, though, not for his political views but for the fact that he once handed back an exam of mine covered in red ink, and marked at the top with the words, "Where the hell did you learn your arithmetic???"—which was a more than valid question to raise to an economics major.

I had a couple of very swell pals, including Jocelyn Lavin, the actress Linda Lavin's sister, who was from Maine and was wonderfully talented, and Yvonne Cameron, a young woman from Shaker Heights, who was very attractive and refined. We wore a perfume called Suivez Moi—"Follow Me"—and we wore the same shade of shiny, very brown lipstick. We also had a rather nasty habit of trying to lose our fur coats—by leaving them in an unlocked car, for example, or draped over an unattended pile of luggage—just to collect the insurance money. Every Friday night we went and drank coffee and ate waffles in the local hamburger place in town, which had the best chocolate cake with white icing I've ever had in my life. Perhaps unsurprisingly, in my four years in college, I gained thirty-seven pounds.

It was a good time to be a college student. The world was less frazzled and hectic, time passed more generously, and the weekends seemed longer and more leisurely than they do today. On the weekends we went on group blind dates and to mixers and teas and tailgate parties at schools like Williams and Dartmouth. Just like all the other young women at Skidmore (who weren't already engaged), I loved to get invitations to the boys' schools. I loved turning them down even more. As is true today, I wasn't particularly social, and tired easily of people, so the idea of spending entire weekends with a group, having fun around the clock on a shared communal schedule, wasn't something I relished, particularly if that schedule included sitting outdoors freezing through a football game.

While Skidmore was widening my sights intellectually, an equally important opening of my horizons was happening on the social scene during my college vacations. You could call it the start—however meager—of my education into society, and it would prove, in later years, every bit as important as my bachelor's degree.

Bunny Hawes is the name I attach to this time. Bunny—the

name sounds like it was made for a debutante, which Bunny was, a New York debutante from a very wealthy family who lived in Brooklyn Heights. She was a tall girl with blondish hair and green eyes whom I'd met toward the end of high school while vacationing with my parents at Spring Lake, which was then a very beautiful resort in New Jersey. My family always stayed there at the Warren Hotel, while Bunny's put up at the Monmouth, which was the swellest of all the swell hotels right on the water. I was a tennis fiend in those days, and every morning would go over to the Monmouth's great courts to take lessons with the pros and to play the hotel's guests in games that the pros set up for me. Bunny Hawes was one of those guests. We became fast friends, and her family drew me into their circle, introduced me to all their friends, and included me in all their activities. And before I knew it, I'd been drawn into Bunny Hawes's New York.

It was a brave new world for me. It was tales of boarding school told in torrents of giggles at the King Cole Bar at the St. Regis, and tea dancing with Groton boys at the Park Lane Hotel, and debutante parties and their after-parties at the Plaza during the so-called season. It was a far cry from the world I'd grown up in. The first society I'd ever known was the Saturday afternoon gamblers' scene at Lindy's, the legendary Broadway restaurant renowned then for its cheesecake, rude waiters, and hint of the underworld. If you wanted a piece of the action in the late 1940s in New York, you went to Lindy's, where "action" was a gamblers' game. My father, who sold his rum at Lindy's during the week, was drawn in like clockwork every Saturday, looking for his weekly card game with "the boys." The "boys," much like him, were polished card-players and dashing wine and liquor salesmen. Some had maybe been bootleggers once and maybe still were; others were the type who knew where you could find a hot craps game, or a hot card game, or who could get one going for you. They were all a little sharp, a crowd that was a bit too sharp and a bit too well tailored, with their Countess Mara ties and white-on-white shirts and little bit of nail.

On the weekends my mother and I used to follow my father around at Lindy's, as we did in other "in" places, from restaurant to restaurant, as he sold his product, Ronrico rum, and sold bartenders and restaurant owners on the daiquiri, a drink he introduced into this country. We were ushered, with him, to the best tables in the most popular restaurants and clubs in the city— places like Gallagher's and Ruby Foos, and El Morocco and the Stork Club, all places where my mother would order her cocktails with Ronrico rum by name, and where I, by example, learned my earliest lessons in marketing and customer relations. I saw that Ronrico rum was a hit at the Stork Club, at the Astor Roof, and at Lindy's not just because it was good, but because Anthony Mirabella was a person that the owners of these places liked to have around. People enjoyed his company. He was engaging. He was a regular guy, and people trusted him.

These were key lessons, which, I think, have served me well to this day. Because I believe that no matter what you're doing— whether it's promoting Ronrico rum or selling suits, or working to bring readers to *Vogue* or *Mirabella* magazines—you're always selling something. And, ultimately, what you're selling is yourself. I was struck very strongly by the truth of this a few years ago, when I went to give a talk to the Washington Advertising Club. John Mack Carter, the editor of *Good Housekeeping*, introduced me, referring to me, at a certain point near the end of his remarks, as "the daughter of Anthony Mirabella and Florence Bellofatto." It was as though he was going out of his way to let the audience know that I was not somebody who was born to a glorious family or a glamorous lifestyle. It was as though he wanted to announce that I was a *different* kind of speaker. And I am sure that I felt the audience lean forward and *listen* differently because of that. It proved out something that I'd learned long before: by being a little more part of the "real world," I can take people by surprise and disarm them. People who are expecting a high society fashion maven are startled by the sound of me. It so happens that I don't *have* any other way of sounding, but they don't know that, and they give me credit for coming across as a straight shooter.

Of course, when I was a teenager, none of this straight shooting was very mysterious. I was who I was, which wasn't someone for whom Bunny Hawes's world of luncheons and the Junior League came naturally. It simply wasn't my world and I knew it, but back then I either wasn't smart enough or foolish enough to care too much about that, and Bunny, from the very start of our friendship, went out of her way to include me in everything she did, and to make it clear to her friends that because I was with her, I was *okay*. Bunny was rich on the old model of New York wealth, which meant that she didn't show it, didn't talk about it, and, in fact, went out of her way to surround herself with the kinds of objects that people with less money would do anything in their power not to own. When I think back on her crowd, I'm always reminded of the old Frank Sinatra song: "When I was thirty-five . . . and the girls went around in limousines, their chauffeurs would drive, when I was thirty-five . . ." except for the fact that Bunny herself drove a terribly beat-up old car, the reason being, as she said, that she wasn't willing to be bullied by taxi drivers, and with her dents and her rust and her pearls, she was quite a sight on the road.

If I had had, in those days, to describe to anyone who Bunny Hawes was, it would have sufficed to say that she was the type of girl you would see dancing all night at the Stork Club. And anyone even remotely in the know would have known exactly what I meant. *The New Yorker*, in the days when it was funny and clever, at one time referred to the Stork Club as "a noncharitable institution for seemingly homeless but undeniably well-turned-out waifs . . . an unofficial annex of the Junior League, with a rather late curfew and a larger visitors' gallery." It was the prime watering ground for the wealthy, worldly social set that came to be known, in the 1930s, as Café Society, and flourished in the glory days following the Second World War. It was also the unofficial office of the legendary society columnist Walter Winchell, who, from his table in the ultra insider Cub Room, watched the comings and

goings of such celebrated clients as J. Edgar Hoover, Joan Craw-
ford, Rocky Marciano, Orson Welles, Helen Hayes, Mary Martin,
Tallulah Bankhead, Jack Kennedy, and, of course, the ubiquitous
Duke and Duchess of Windsor. Grace Kelly and Prince Rainier
first revealed their engagement at the Stork Club; Ernest Heming-
way and Louis Untermeyer had a fistfight in the Cub Bar, and
General Douglas MacArthur was feted there after his ticker tape
return from Korea.

I'd learned something about the club world from going around
with my parents, who always used to take me to El Morocco for
special occasions. With its zebra-striped interior, palm trees, and
soft pink lighting, El Morocco was once described in *The New
Yorker* as "a fashionable photographer's studio, open evenings for
the convenience of those who have to sleep during the day." Morocco was, throughout the 1940s and 1950s, the undisputed center
of gravity for the most glamorous people in town—the celebrities,
international smart set, and generally high profile characters who,
through talent or money or birth or sheer outrageousness, made it
into gossip writers Leonard Lyons's and Cholly Knickerbocker's
columns on a regular basis. Erich Remarque, Salvador Dali, John
Huston, the Duke and Duchess of Windsor, and Joe DiMaggio were
regulars at Morocco, where they danced to Chauncey Gray's orchestra and Chiquito's rumba band, received their mail, and
sipped cocktails, "staring in rapture at people they haven't seen
since lunch," as it was said in those days.

It was at El Morocco that I first became aware of great style. I
remember that there was a couple, from Buffalo no less, who used
to go to Morocco every Friday and Saturday night. My family got
to know them a bit because we were always shown to a banquette
right next to theirs. The man was a very successful lawyer and the
woman had wonderful hair and wonderful bones and an incredibly
great body, and all she ever ate was steak and spinach or steak
and a salad. That was the way she stayed in shape. And that was
my first stylish image.

It was also at El Morocco that I learned my first object lessons in social desirability. Morocco's seating was strictly stratified: banquettes were the best spots, followed by tables close to the dance floor, and the strata were forever shifting, according to the relative status of newcomers who came in later and later into the night. You might, for example, come into Morocco for dinner at nine, and be thrilled to find you had a table just a few steps from the dance floor. Then you might, an hour later, see a new table suddenly set up in front of you. Then another. And another. And before you knew it, you were seated in the middle of nowhere.

Nowheresville, at El Morocco, was called "Siberia." It was embarrassing to be seated there. And it was wonderful, on the other hand, to be greeted like a long-lost friend and led, with a great show of style, to a banquette, with nods and smiles greeting you every step of the way. To be known and welcomed by John Perona, the club's lean and perpetually tan owner, was for some the height of social acceptance, and to be invited to his own table was a dream almost beyond imagining. To be banned by him was an absolute nightmare. It didn't matter to New York's smart set that the Italian-born Perona had started out as a busboy, and had had a less-than-genteel early career as a sparring partner for the Argentinian prizefighter, Luis Angel Firpo, "the wild bull of the pampas." He was the king of East Fifty-fourth Street. He set the rules. "He made black tie and formal attire the uniform of the night" as his obituary summed it up in 1961. He was on to something.

New York society was changing, moving away from bloodlines to talent, money, and notoriety. These were shifting categories, often of dubious value, and they cried out for social arbiters to decide who was "in" and who was "out." John Perona was one of the first to know how to make money out of it. Sherman Billingsley was another.

Billingsley was a former small-time bootlegger from Oklahoma, whose past included three months at Leavenworth. Called the "unacknowledged dictator of café society," by contemporaries, he had a genius for cultivating his own "in" crowd that was almost as pure as a science. He communicated with his staff through a complicated system of coded hand signals. When he pulled his ear, it meant a waiter should call him to the phone. If he pulled his nose, it meant not to cash checks for a certain set of clients. The discreet hand signals, of course, only worked on outsiders; initiates watching him operate had the added pleasure of knowing that they, too, were in on the game. Billingsley treated his favored guests to special presents, ranging from an orchid to a car. Admission to his Cub Room, a long, narrow room away from the orchestra and rumba band, was the definition of being established. Being banished by him was intolerable. One never knew where, among the boorish, the ax might strike. Once it was Jackie Gleason, whom Billingsley called "a drunken bum." Another time it was Humphrey Bogart, who, at the height of his fame, lamely rejoined, "You stink."

I never made it into the Cub Room. But my family and I always enjoyed special treatment at El Morocco because of my father's business contacts. That meant that we were always seated on one of the banquettes, and on my birthday, we would receive a beautiful basket of fruit with a candle on it. But it was at the Stork Club, with Bunny's crowd, where I really learned the pleasures of being "in." Bunny's was precisely the kind of crowd that restaurants like the Stork Club wanted to attract, and that brought us some delightful perks. One was exceptional service. Another was the fact that we never had to pay. We'd lunch, and sit and smoke, and occupy a table for hours, and when at last we rose to go, we each would leave one dollar on the table for the waiter, which we considered the proper thing to do.

It was the same thing if we'd go to El Morocco, where we'd sip cocktails all night, night after night, and hardly ever see a bill. That was the way Perona did things. As time went on, he would monitor the careers of the young men who took us out, and would send them bills, by the by, after college, as they made their way up the corporate ladder. When he'd deemed that they'd made sufficient progress, he'd send them a little bill. Then another little bill. Then another. And if their career paths derailed, he sent the bills home to their fathers—career counseling, Morocco style. And it was the same thing at the Blue Angel, the same at the Champagne Gallery, and in all the fashionable clubs around town.

By the end of my freshman year in college, I was, thanks to Bunny, an *insider*. I too was dancing all night at the Stork Club, lounging on the banquettes at El Morocco, going tea dancing at the Park Lane, and dancing to the wee hours of the morning to the big band tunes on the roof of the Astor Hotel. And, in the middle of the night, I was still catching buses home to New Jersey from the Port Authority bus terminal. My new world wasn't, in reality, so very far apart from my father's. It was just another table over.

Two plays came out in New York while I was in college that have always profoundly reminded me of my father. The first was Damon Runyon's *Guys and Dolls*, which for me lifted scenes of life right out of a Saturday afternoon at Lindy's—with the "boys" and their "chicks" and the men just like my father, who perhaps lived a bit too fast and pushed their luck a bit too hard. The second was *Death of a Salesman*.

My father died in August of 1947. Too many years of overeating, cigars and cigarettes, late nights and debt caught up with him one evening while he was away on business, and he suffered a fatal heart attack in his room at the Palmer House Hotel in Chicago. He was fifty years old. My mother and I were at the Monmouth Hotel in Spring Lake, New Jersey, when the call came. We packed up and headed home in a state of shock. My father's luggage arrived and, like zombies, we unpacked it. We mechanically went through the motions of preparing for his funeral.

After my father died, my mother and I did what we had to do. And when we came up for air, after the fog of the shock of death had cleared, we found in the harsh reality of daylight that my father had left behind a mountain of debt and virtually no money to pay for it.

There is something liberating about having your worst fears come true; you realize that you have no choice left but to survive, and that striving for survival is the best antidote to fear. With her worst fears confirmed, my mother, in the weeks and months after my father's death, showed a strength that I think neither she nor I had ever thought possible. She gave up her apartment and moved in with her sister. She found another job, this time in a South Orange clothing store. She swallowed her pride and accepted help from my father's friends. Thanks to the aid of one wonderful friend, Mack Kufferman, she was able to keep paying my tuition. I finished out my four years at Skidmore without a break, without loans, without a scholarship. My mother scrimped and saved, and I went to formals. I wore fur coats. I had a car.

It's not an atypical story, I think, for immigrant parents and children of that generation. They gave us everything, and we repaid them with our success. It was a bargain, of sorts.

CHAPTER 2
LOOKING FOR *LUXE* IN THE WORLD'S LARGEST STORE

A few years ago I gave a talk to a group of teenage girls at a very competitive private school in suburban New Jersey, not far from where I lived when I was in high school. I'd been invited there as part of a guest speaker program on young women and work that had been established by a pair of the school's parents after their grown daughter committed suicide because she felt she wasn't successful enough in the working world. I told the girls the story of my life, and gave whatever well-intentioned advice I could offer, always suggesting that a career was the best route. Afterward, one of them raised her hand and, groping for the courage to speak, asked me, "Ms. Mirabella, would it be okay if, when I get out of college, I don't get a job at all? Would it, do you think, be okay if I just got married?"

I assured her that I thought it would indeed be quite okay.

And then I said a quick prayer to my mother, and asked for her forgiveness.

My mother, guardian of the dented coffeepot, was a master of instruction by example. While she never once sat me down and told me that she intended for me to have a career, her entire life was an object lesson in the dangers of financial dependency, and she made very sure that from the earliest age I understood that. What my mother taught me—and what she showed me—was that being married wasn't any way for a woman to secure a good life for herself. Her experience had shown her that a woman couldn't count on her husband to give her a sense of security, that she had to build that for herself and work to create her own life. The end result was that I always assumed that I would have a career. Going to work was for me an intrinsic part of growing up, more intrinsic a part, in fact, than was getting married. This was an odd belief to have in the late 1940s, when "Rosie the Riveter" was being driven out of the factories and all American women were being encouraged to go back into their homes and leave working to men. Nice middle-class girls in my day were brought up to dream of wedding bells and diamond rings, not of being made head buyer for Saks Fifth Avenue. Employers wouldn't hire a woman if she was married or soon-to-be. They figured that she didn't need the money and would leave to have a baby as soon as she was trained. And in many cases they were right. Many of the girls I went to college with never even tried to have careers. They found fiancés or husbands or they took jobs as secretaries and bided their time until Mr. Right came along and brought their working days to an end. The concept of a dual-career marriage really did not exist.

There were exceptions, of course, and they tended to come from strongly academic women's colleges, which had come into their own during the Second World War as important training grounds for future female professionals. I intended to be one of those exceptions.

I majored in economics because I had wanted to have a businesslike way of looking at things. I didn't want to major in English or French and hope that something would just "happen" to me after graduation, as many girls then did, because letting things just "happen" always seemed to me to be a rather dangerous proposition. I wanted more control of my life than that.

I started working in high school, when a family friend who had a wonderful sportswear shop in South Orange offered me a job a couple of afternoons a week plus Saturdays. Feller's sold high-quality separates, the kind of clothing that well-dressed people then wore when they weren't dressing up, and which now is the most dressed up that anyone *ever* gets. There were Scottish cashmere sweaters with labels like Bryn Mawr or Pringle or Ballantine, marvelous names for wonderfully soft, richly textured and colored sweaters, whose folding and unfolding and folding again took up the greater part of my day. Once at Skidmore, I started working every summer in the college shop of a department store called Hahne & Company, which was the Lord & Taylor of Newark. The college shop was the department that all the better stores used to open in August for girls going back to school or going away for the first time. There were sweaters and slacks and blazers and skirts, which I assume one really could have worn for any occasion, but which were sold here as being uniquely appropriate for campus life. The stores used to try to get a student from each of the more prestigious women's colleges to come and work in their college shops before going back to school, and being selected was something of an honor. I loved the contact with customers and was thrilled to be working with sportswear, which was precisely the kind of clothing that I wore the most. I also wore the most wonderful suits—MonteSano and Pruzan and Carmel suits—and they gave me a certain basic knowledge of quality and fabric and cut which I put to real advantage, years later, when I went to work in the emerging area of American sportswear. In those years, though, a career in "fashion" was the furthest thing from my mind. It was too abstract, too otherworldly, too unreal. The fact of working in a store was real; the idea of owning a shop seemed a likely goal. I decided that I wanted to be a clothing retailer.

When I graduated from college, I went to look for work in the retail world. Retailing was one of the few places then for women with real ambitions. While few made it to the very top of the corporate ladder in the 1950s (Lord & Taylor's president, Dorothy Shaver, being the notable exception), women were nonetheless starting to establish a very real presence. I rounded up all the contacts I had, having been told that connections are everything, and quickly found that that was true, as was something else: getting your foot in the door through a contact was all well and good, but once it was in, you had to do all the rest of the legwork on your own. And that was the hard part.

The first person I turned to for advice about getting a job was Sumner Sternberg, a friend of my father's who was well known in the retailing world. Sumner knew me quite well, and more importantly, he knew Edwin Goodman, the founder and then president of Bergdorf Goodman, the terrific specialty department store on Fifth Avenue and Fifty-eighth Street. Via Sumner, via Edwin Goodman, I got an interview with the Bergdorf Goodman personnel director. Or rather, I had an interview with the personnel director's assistant, who sat and spoke with me while the director himself sat at the other end of the room with his back to us. All of which left me in the awkward position of trying to maintain eye contact with my interviewer while attempting to project my voice over her head to the shadow figure in the corner.

With all the blessed self-assurance of a twenty-one-year-old, I spoke about my experiences at Feller's and at Hahne & Company. I told of my degree in economics, my interest in retailing, and of having been the editor of my college newspaper—all of which the personnel director's assistant undoubtedly found riveting. She ticked off my credentials one by one with her fingernails, repeating each one out loud, then she smiled at me viperishly and said, "Well, we don't really *have* that much here."

"Make a place!" a voice then shouted from the other end of the room, and the man it was attached to called to my interlocutor. She went over to him, and they mumbled together for a while. She then came back and said, "My boss told me I should make a place for you in the store."

And as I sat thinking about what it would be like to be the youngest vice president ever, she went on, "We would like to offer you the job of assistant salesperson."

"Assistant what?" I sputtered.

"Assistant salesperson. In the handbag department. We will pay you twenty-eight dollars a week. No, wait," she said, checking her notes, "you commute. Make it thirty-two."

I thanked her and said I'd have to think about it. I bit my lip all the way downstairs in the elevator. And then I laughed myself down Fifth Avenue, thinking about the fact that I'd seen myself as the youngest store vice president.

My next call was to a wonderful family friend in South Orange, a Mr. Landisi, who was a vice president at Bamberger's, a Macy's store in Newark. He sent my résumé along to Virginia Carlin, a former lieutenant commander in the WAVES who was the Macy's director of executive placement, and asked that she consider me for the Macy's executive training program. The training program was a long shot, and I knew it. Virginia Carlin interviewed about a thousand applicants each year for the twenty-five-odd slots on the training squad, and I, with my economics BA and college shop sales, was small change compared to the seasoned retailers, MBAs from Harvard and Wharton, and scions of great store owners from around the world who were my competition.

That I was a woman didn't help, either. Although department stores were some of the few places at which women could hope to build real careers in the business world of the 1950s (stores were considered natural places for women because they dealt in things—like clothes and shopping—that women were assumed to be familiar with), the Macy's executive training program was the most serious business and was held in very high regard by the whole retailing community. The training program was intended to take smart and talented entry-level recruits and turn them into buyers, in the hope that they would eventually become an important part of the Macy's organization. The entire process, if all things went smoothly, took nine months to a year. First, recruits worked through the different departments of the store, from selling or assisting department managers to working in display or comparative shopping, before receiving their first assignment, or being "placed" in a job.

Macy's didn't expect everyone to stick it out for the long haul. But they did hope to get a significant percentage of executives out of the training program. Women were considered a bad bet, as far as staying power was concerned. As always back then, the thinking was that if the women were going to get married—as all were assumed to be planning to do—they wouldn't wait five whole years to do so for the sake of a job, and certainly wouldn't keep working once they were married.

I had a double handicap: being a woman and not having a master's degree. But I also had Mr. Landisi's letter—and I was young. And persistent. And I made a pretty convincing argument to the effect that I wasn't about to go off to marry and have children. Lots of interviews followed, with merchandise managers and vice presidents and the head of personnel, and then there was a very anxious period of waiting. Finally the good news came: I was an executive trainee. I would wear a white flower on my blouse, ride in the executive elevator, and be called "Miss Mirabella" by salesclerks decades older than I was. I would be paid fifty-seven dollars a week. I was golden.

The post-war period was a wonderful time to be starting work in retailing. The stores were flooded with goods after the deprivations of the war years, and customers had money and were eager to spend it. You saw the joy, the desire to consume lavishly in the big-skirted "New Look" of the post-war years, and you saw it filtered down in the day-to-day life of New York's department stores, where "price wars" raged between such competitors as Macy's and Gimbel's, and where expensive coats and suits flew off the racks of luxury stores like Saks. Material had been scarce during the war; so too had leather, and I remember so clearly how after the war the shoe department at Saks was *packed* with customers, most notably with South American women who bought shoes by the carload—stacks and stacks of boxes—which were carted off, most unceremoniously, by the uniquely surly men who worked in the shoe department then.

In those days department stores were important in a way that they are not today. In that era, before malls and discount outlets and chain stores took up so much of the market, they were *the* great halls of merchandise, and they provided an enormous variety of goods at much more varied prices than they do today. Which isn't to say that they all aimed at having something for everybody; on the contrary, each store aimed for a certain style, a certain specialty market, and a certain clientele, and you knew the minute that you walked into any one store, and smelled the perfume and saw the flowers and doormen or bargain tables, precisely where you were.

The stores were owned then by individual families: the Gimbels, the Marcuses, the Goodmans, and they hadn't yet been spun off into chains. Each store had its own aura and decor and quirky details—the Charleston Gardens restaurant at B. Altman's, where the false front of a plantation house loomed over lunchers, or the special scent of the ground floor at Saks, and the windows at Lord & Taylor, so filled with the sensibility of Dorothy Shaver and of American style. There was an attitude, a sensibility that accompanied these details, and they were important clues for customers, who knew, for example, that Lord & Taylor was the place you just *had* to go to get your clothes before you went to college, and where you *had* to buy your first Claire McCardell dress; that you bought your really good suits—MonteSano and Pruzan, Carmel suits—at Saks, and you went to Best & Company for its children's department. Unlike today, when the stores all carry the same product and have essentially all become carbon copies of one another, the stores used to fight with manufacturers and designers for exclusivity rights. They prided themselves on having different merchandise and on having unique contracts with manufacturers. Lord & Taylor, for example, was *the* store for American design. But all that changed in the 1970s, when designers became all-powerful and began making deals to promote their names everywhere until eventually all the stores started carrying the same thing. The stores were bought up then by large conglomerates and started to take on the feel of the real estate ventures that they had become. They lost their sense of purpose, of *conviction*.

In the 1950s, though, all that was still a bad dream away. The department stores in those days actually prided themselves upon playing a civic role in the life of the city. The concept of a man like Bernard Gimbel, founder of the parent company that owned Gimbel's and Saks, or of Edwin Goodman at Bergdorf Goodman was that a department store wasn't just there to buy and sell fragrances or cosmetics or clothes; it was to be a meeting place, a kind of common ground to entertain and amuse and shelter and feed community members who would gravitate in and out of its doors with the ease and naturalness they'd feel in visiting a neighborhood pal. And people responded to this vision. They came for lunch or tea and to browse, and they shopped because it was a pleasure to do so.

Macy's, the world's largest store, was all of this exponentially. It was a massive institution, a 45-acre, 2.1 million-square-foot store that spanned an entire city block, and whose construction had caused the demolition of 33 city buildings. It had 168 sales departments, 18 miles of pneumatic tubes for shuttling cash through the building, 30 elevators, 6 miles of floor space and corridors. It was a *world*. The world of Macy's, from an employee's point of view, was about power. Macy's buyers could buy anything, anywhere—and made it their business to do so. The food halls alone were stupendous, stocking foie gras from France and cheeses from Italy, Spanish sausages and wonderful breads and pastries—this in an age before the Concorde brought *pain* Poilâne in from Paris daily and "specialty food" stores had opened on every corner of the Upper East Side. The food halls were exotic and special, and if you played your cards right, you could go down for an hour and sample everything at noon and call it lunch.

Customers came to Macy's just to have a place to spend an afternoon. Mothers would tell their children to "get lost," then shop and lunch in peace and retrieve them, when they were done, in the lost children's department just before the store closed. New employees got lost in the store all the time, because in addition to the selling floors there were the basements and office corridors and stockrooms, miles and miles of hallways, which were rumored, some said, to have trapped certain employees for days and days at a time.

The Macy's training squad was like many highly competitive training programs for talented young hotshots in that it was an equal mixture of prestige and grunt work. The prestige came from the fact of knowing, within Macy's and in the retailing world at large, that if you were part of the training squad you were among the best and the brightest emergent retailers around. We trainees got special attention from Jack Straus, then chairman of the board at Macy's, whom we usually only saw walking through the store screaming about how messy everything was, but who did take a few hours each year to address us at meetings, as did senior buyers and merchandise managers, who regularly lectured us on the ins and outs of department store retailing. People deferred to us, on the sales floor, when they saw our executive carnations. On Thanksgiving we were asked to march in costume in the Macy's parade. Those were the high points of the job. Grunt work was how we spent the vast majority of our days.

Macy's was known then for its pledge of selling at six percent less than its nearest competitor. This meant that the store had constantly to check its prices against those of the other stores. This was rather dreary and thankless work and it fell to us young titans to do it. We ran around the city, checking the price of pillowcases at McCreery's, of advertised sweaters at Best & Company, or of coats at Wanamaker's. Comparative shopping, it was called. We counted the number of candies with soft centers in the boxes at Altman's noting how many had soft or hard centers and how many were caramels, because if their box of candies had more hard centers and ours more soft centers, then they weren't the same value, since soft centers were better than hard centers. That was about as interesting, intellectually, as things got. Our comparison shopping assignments alternated with sales assignments on the store's selling floors; my first and most memorable assignment was in the sheet and towel department, where I folded up towels eight hours a day after people unfolded them, looked at them, and decided that they didn't want them.

When Macy's wanted to inject some real competition into the brew, they let loose the man who was head of the tables department, a no-holds-barred merchant who was a vice president of merchandising and whom I was never really sure whether to despise or admire. To teach us entrepreneurial skill this man would set down a table—rather like El Morocco waiters would do, at a moment's notice—in the middle of the aisle of whatever department you were working in and leave it, while you filled it with wallets or towels or scarves, and then return, an indeterminate number of hours later, check your receipts, and if you hadn't sold as much as you should have, he would whisk that table away and award it to a more deserving colleague of yours in another department. He was like a cop, fast and furious, and he harbored no excuses. You didn't sell, you lost your table, and that was that.

It was a very stressful situation. For although the table business

was an ordeal, it was also how you proved your stuff as a would-
be merchant to your bosses. It gave you a way of showing that
you knew how to draw customers in, to present your merchandise
attractively, and to move what had to be moved. So the competition to get one of the tables was fierce, as was the pressure to watch
your merchandise closely and be sure that it was looking good.
And if it wasn't looking good, you had to be resourceful in figuring
out how to improve your display without stepping on anyone else's
toes. You couldn't just shift the position of your table, or beef up
the lighting over your display, for example. The floor space—or
lightbulbs—might just be the property of your friend over in handbags. So you used a bit of ingenuity, you showcased your wares
creatively, and then you crossed your fingers and prayed. When
things went poorly, you called it bad luck. When they went well,
you called it talent.

One might think that this race for floor space would have bred
cutthroat competition among the trainees. But it didn't. Instead, it
inspired in us an intense feeling of embattled camaraderie, a kind
of siege mentality which made us all feel like co-conspirators
rather than competitors. Our greatest joy, as Macy's trainees, was
to outwit the designs of our boss, John McGrath, a kind of field
commander with a very dry sense of humor who, in the spirit of
good enterprise, used to make it his business to try to set us off
against one another as much as possible.

But we foiled him at every turn: when he sent us out on comparison shopping assignments, we'd pool our work so that we
wouldn't have to run from department to department in six different stores. I would check the towels, for example, and a friend
would check the sheets, and then we'd move on together from
Gimbel's to Altman's or Bergdorf's. When a group of us were sent
up to White Plains one evening to do an inventory check on the
branch store, we stopped for a delicious dinner in a charming
roadside restaurant along the way, and arrived at the White Plains
store hours late, then had the nerve to question the entire inventory, which left those employees (who hadn't yet, I'm sure, had

their dinner) working all night redoing their inventory. It didn't, I'll wager, make us the most popular kids on the block, but did give us an experience to laugh about for months to come.

As often happens, I think, when young people work together under intense conditions, we trainees became inseparable. We worked together, wasted time together, smoked cigarettes together, and drank chocolate milk together in a crummy little cafeteria on Thirty-fifth Street. We used to take the meal tickets that Macy's gave us over to Child's Restaurant on Seventh Avenue and Thirty-fourth Street, and buy our dinners together for a dollar each. And if we felt rich enough to pay more than a dollar, we went out to restaurants or to clubs. As one of five women in a crowd of about twenty-five, I received plenty of invitations and had my pick of dates.

It was a wonderfully collegial crowd, full of big talents, who all were passionately interested in merchandising. There was a man named Irving Cole, who went on to become a vice president at Montgomery Ward, and a set of dashing Australians—Bayles Meyers, whose family had founded Meyers' Department Store in Melbourne, then the largest store in the Southern Hemisphere, and David Lloyd Jones and Dale Turnbull, who soon became my close friends. David Lloyd Jones was a marvelous, very attractive, lean, and blond young man whose father had started David Jones Ltd., the big department store in Sydney. He was a swashbuckling businessman who loved to find a way to turn an extra dime, and always seemed to top everyone's performance when it came time to compete for tables. He loved selling, loved beating us all at it even more, and made it all seem like a kind of marvelous game.

It was a wonderful time to be young in New York. New York was a fun, vibrant city, fully alive in a time that I always think of as the most truly glamorous that we've ever known. The glamour of the 1950s wasn't the celebrity stardom—the tell-all, mud-wrestling, Lear jet-flying vulgarity that it's become today. And it wasn't even the glamour of talent that we came to know and appreciate in the 1960s, glamour that Richard Avedon, who documented it in that time, called "the appearance of the possibility of achievement."

Glamour in the 1950s was, rather, pure *style*—style as a concrete reflection of a certain specialness in a man or a woman, more talent than celebrity, and certainly something more than sheer appearance. Mike Nichols, who is enough of a contemporary of mine to know what I mean, once called it, quite aptly, "the glorious moment continued and absorbed into personality." Which is why, I think, when we remember the glamour of that moment, we attach it to people—Audrey Hepburn so very notably, and Grace Kelly. I, personally, always think of Kay Kendall, striding across a room in a film called *The Reluctant Debutante*, floating as she walked, tall and graceful, in a long dress with a sweeping feather boa drifting back behind her. It wasn't her clothes that made her glamorous; it was her energy, her movement, her élan. As Billy Wilder once described glamour, hers was a "means of transportation."

Audrey Hepburn, Grace Kelly—like Jackie Kennedy Onassis, who would eventually emerge as the (last, perhaps) reigning queen of American glamour—presented a perfect fusion of their personalities (or what we believed them to be, at least) and their style. You could see Grace Kelly or Audrey Hepburn around town in those days in places like the Stork Club and El Morocco. You could also hear Fred Astaire perform on the roof of the Astor Hotel, or see any number of remarkable plays on Broadway, which was a veritable hit parade in those years. *Guys and Dolls*, *The King and I*, *Pal Joey*, and *South Pacific* were at one time, I recall, playing all at once. You might see Douglas Fairbanks, Jr., at the theater. Simple things guaranteed your access to glamour. You could feel glamorous in your *clothes*, when cocktail dresses were cut with something called an "over-the-table neckline," incorporating the dream of having drinks at El Morocco right into their design. And you could stay out all night without fearing for your life, or take the bus home to New Jersey at 3 A.M. from Port Authority as I always did, and you could get by in an evening with just a few

dollars, because New York was a livable, largely affordable place
in those days.

I was still going to the Stork Club and El Morocco then, taking
in the wonderful-looking women in their marvelously cut dresses
dancing with their handsome, dashing men—all, unfortunately, I
now realize, luxuriously chain-smoking cigarettes—and I was also
discovering other New York nightspots with my new Australian
friends, who always seemed to have a sister or a cousin or an uncle
in tow, always lovely people from Australia set on enjoying themselves out on the town. We went dancing in the sunken garden or
in the Trianon Room at the Ambassador Hotel on Park Avenue, to
the Blue Angel, and to a wonderful place on MacDougal Street in
the Village called the Champagne Gallery, which was set up like a
living room with comfortable sofas and armchairs. Though I found
the Macy's crowd a wonderful group generally for sitting around
and talking, I have to admit that I was particularly taken with
Dale Turnbull. Dale was about six feet tall, very slim and blondish,
with that typically Australian fair but ruddy look and plenty of
energy. His family owned a string of movie theaters in Australia,
and his father headed up Twentieth Century Fox's distribution
there. Dale loved to tell the story of how once, when he'd gone to
meet an American associate of his father's from Twentieth Century
Fox at the Sydney airport one Sunday and found him fuming, because his luggage had been lost, he'd made a quick phone call to
David Jones (his brother-in-law in later years), then had taken the
man to downtown Sydney, thrown open the gates of the David
Jones Emporium—a store whose size rivaled Macy's—and humbly
said, "I hope you can find what you need."

Dale lived at the Yale Club, and was always in the peculiar spot
of never having any cash, because for some reason possibly having
to do with the war's just being over, he couldn't take money out of
Australia. So everything that he did had to be put on his Yale Club
tab: he ate all his meals at the club, and purchased theater tickets
through its concierge, which meant that on dates with Dale, one

ate chicken à la king (or another dish typically served at university clubs) and went to the theater a great deal.

We went so much, in fact, that I'm afraid I began to take it all a bit for granted—which was why, one now-memorable evening, when Dale called me at the last minute to see if I wanted to go to the theater, I didn't think twice about saying no. After all, I'd been to the theater the night before, and I knew that we'd very likely go the night after. And after that. So I said, "Gee, I feel rotten," and begged off with a sore throat, though the truth was that I just didn't feel like making the effort to get dressed up and go out.

"But I have some friends I want you to meet," Dale said.

I, envisioning another cabload of delightful and unnaturally tall Australians, hemmed and hawed and suggested that I might be coming down with a fever.

"Who are your friends?" I asked, signing off, just to keep the conversation going a bit longer.

"Well," he said, "Cary Grant and his wife, Betsy Drake. They want to go to the theater and then to dinner. It's too bad that you're not feeling well."

"I feel *fine*," I thought. "Miraculous recovery."

But I said nothing. It just would have been too obvious.

I stayed in and washed my hair. And to make matters worse, Dale called me the next day and told me that after the play they'd all run into Deborah Kerr, who was in New York performing on Broadway. And I just died, all over again.

Of course, the glorious New York I was discovering wasn't *everybody*'s New York. It was Dale Turnbull's New York—a fashionable smart set, which extended from the Upper East Side to the kind of crowd that lived out in the swell precincts of Locust Valley, Peacock Point, and Glen Cove. With Dale, I started going out to Long Island for Sunday lunches and black tie dinners in places where there were horses and indoor tennis and outdoor tennis and giant, sloping lawns, and while I'd like to say that I moved in this world with all the naturalness and self-assurance that I often didn't feel with Bunny Hawes's crowd, the fact is that I didn't. I didn't quite feel like Audrey Hepburn playing Sabrina, not like the daughter of the butler or anything that drastic, but I didn't feel entirely at ease, either. For while I *was* Dale Turnbull's date, and not some young interloper from the tennis courts of Spring Lake, I was still at times acutely aware that Oyster Bay was a far cry away from my home.

I suppose my sharpest sense of this came when Gates Davison, a good friend of Dale's, whose family had an extraordinary estate in Oyster Bay, invited us out one weekend for lunch. With careful planning and much forethought, I dressed in what I thought was my chicest casual wear—a wool jersey dress and beads and a good deal of lipstick—and when we arrived, I realized, to my utter despair, that I was dressed completely inappropriately. This was the world of Brooks Brothers' hand-me-downs and good quality dowdy sweaters. For a fashion aspirant it was a complete and utter humiliation. The kind of thing you can obsess over in your early twenties, and make it your point in life never to repeat.

It can't have been an accident that my key friendships, in my early years before *Vogue*, consistently brought me in contact with smart, socially prominent young New Yorkers. Yet, I honestly don't believe that this had to do with my having aspirations toward "society." Rather, I think that my eye has always led me to whatever is most attractive, in clothing as, on a profounder level, in people, and to worlds that these people inhabit. And that, I think, accounts for the trajectory that led me, consistently, almost inevitably, forward toward the world of *Vogue*.

Macy's was more of a pit stop along the way. For the glamour of New York that I loved so in those years seemed to stop outside of its doors. Inside was brazen commerce—wonderful commerce, brilliant commerce—the kinds of things that made the great merchants of America into legends, but didn't exactly endear them to the Locust Valley or Newport crowds. Though I appreciated the real-world lessons in merchandising that Macy's offered, my heart wasn't really in the learning. My aspirations were elsewhere.

And so, I began to grow disenchanted with The World's Largest

Store. I mastered sheets and towels and was moved on to main floor candy—putting my knowledge of hard and soft centers to the test—and then to ladies' lingerie. There, I began seriously to doubt for my future. It was Christmastime; the men all had been given assignments in the toy department, which was considered real, challenging labor, and it was clear that given the paucity of women in my program, I was bound to end up permanently assigned to one of the lower-status, purely "ladies'" departments like lingerie. I can't honestly say that at the time I had my stirrings of feminist outrage at this discrepancy. I just assumed that the men were put in toys because the work was physically harder and accepted it as a fact of life. Instead, I fumed about the fact that lingerie really and truly did not interest me. And as I looked around at the halls of merchandise at Macy's, I realized that the problem ran much deeper than that of nightgowns and girdles. It was that, in general, I found myself yearning for something more—not just toys or home appliances—but something more akin to the sense of quality, of *luxury* even, that I'd loved in the days when I'd worked among the fine cashmere sweaters at Feller's.

Macy's wasn't known as a place to buy really good clothes. The Little Shop, where the better clothes were sold, was universally acknowledged to be the weakest part of the store. That, to customers, didn't matter that much. After all, Macy's was on Herald Square, not on Fifth Avenue; it was the place of the six percent discount and the great food halls and the parade, and it wasn't necessary, most shoppers thought—nor even desirable, Macy's retailers wagered—to buy the best cheese and the best suit all in the same store.

But the lack of *luxe* mattered to me. And as the months went by at Macy's I realized that I didn't want to participate in merchandising on that basic level. I didn't want to be just any kind of a retailer. I didn't have the drive to be a big-time retailer that fueled the ambitions of buccaneers like David Lloyd Jones, who knew that his goal in life was to go back to Sydney and become chairman of David Jones Ltd. I didn't have the passion he showed, the love of selling that enabled him to sit and talk about it all for hours over devil's food cake in Hamburger Heaven after work, or at the Champagne Gallery in the Village on the weekends. David Lloyd Jones was made for department store retailing; it ran in his blood and he thrived upon the game of it, with the sheer pleasure and joy another man might just put into football. The tragedy of it was that he died just ten years later, of cancer, before he'd had the time to really put any of his grand ideas to the test.

The training program was one of those experiences that clarify perfectly for you what you don't want, paving the way for you to find what you do. I didn't want, I realized, to be encased in a big emporium of *stuff*. I loved clothes and I wanted to be surrounded by them, but only if they were the very best. Indeed, I realized, it wasn't clothing that I was after at all; it was—that word at last— fashion.

In order words, I wanted something better. That side of me had emerged that would carry me through the rest of my career—my feeling that if it wasn't the best, I just wasn't interested. That may seem a kind of precious attitude, an odd conceit for a kid whose family had narrowly escaped financial ruin twice and who was still, in those years, living at home in a modest garden apartment in Maplewood and using her salary to help her mother out with the rent, but in the context of my family it wasn't.

My parents were unusual, I think, in the fact that having lived through a hard time in the Depression didn't give them a permanent "Depression mentality," or make them perpetually fearful so far as my own future was concerned. On the contrary, from a very young age, I was made to feel that the world was mine to conquer and that there was nothing I couldn't do if I set my mind to it. I was never in my life told to make choices for safety's sake or to take the first thing that came along in my life if it offered some money. Rather, it was as though, having lived through such a difficult moment, my parents knew that it was possible to have ups and downs in life and to survive. They always brought me up to believe that if I didn't like what I was doing I should change it and move on to the next thing. So I felt very at ease in doing so, and in making sure that I did things in precisely the way I wanted to do them. I never felt that I had to stick with something just for the sake of sticking with it.

After about six months, which was just around the time that Mr. McGrath was starting to think of placing us in departments as junior buyers, I decided I wanted to get out. I had the feeling that I was going to be placed in lingerie, which was absolutely not where I wanted to be. So I called up an old friend of my father's who had always been very kind to me and had from time to time invited me out for drinks while I was at Macy's, and asked him if he could help introduce me to different people in the department stores. He got me an interview at Saks.

Saks Fifth Avenue was the antithesis of Macy's. It was considered a snob store. Things were what was called "gracious"—right down to the large and couch-filled ladies "lounge" on the fourth floor. It was a place where I'd spent wonderful moments with my mother as a teenager, shopping for great tailored suits on Saturday afternoons, lunching then at Hamburger Heaven next door—and returning, more often than not, the next week, to return the suits and compensate with another hamburger. Saks was the store you could count on for finding the best coats and suits, a store where, unlike at Macy's, shopping was less a utilitarian act than a pleasure, a kind of thrilling voyage to sweet-smelling, silk-laden terrains.

When you walked into Saks in those days, you found yourself awash in a wave of perfumes—Bal de Versailles, Chanel No. 5, Joy de Patou—smells that lulled you into a feeling of otherworldliness as you made your way past enchanting displays of silk flowers and Sea Island cotton shirts and the finest, most beautiful kidskin gloves from Europe. A uniformed elevator operator in white cotton gloves took you upstairs to departments like the enormous millinery shop on the fifth floor, presided over by the imperious Tatiana du Plessix, a Russian emigrée née Iacovleff who was distantly related to the nineteenth-century radical Alexander Herzen, and who, after having married and divorced the French nobleman Bertrand du Plessix, had kept the *particule* professionally, though in her personal life she was known as Tatiana Liberman, wife of my future boss, Alex. Also on the fifth floor was the Salon Moderne, a custom-order dress shop which held weekly fashion shows and attracted the likes of Mrs. E. F. Hutton and Mrs. Pierre Du Pont.

You sensed a smallness and a singularity of vision at Saks in those days—much as you do, uniquely, at Tiffany's today—which showed itself in the great attention to detail and the meticulous care given to maintaining quality standards in every department of the store by Saks's president, Adam Gimbel. Gimbel ran Saks with the pride and particularity that you can generally only find in a family store. A former Yale architecture student, he had himself designed the store's art deco lobby, with its mahogany and marble detail. His tastes and inclinations were reflected throughout the store, as he essentially tried to reach a clientele whose desires matched his own. His friends smoked Havana cigars, so there was a humidor on the main floor; they owned second homes in Southampton and Palm Beach, so he opened branch stores there. He installed his wife, Sophie, a Southern woman of famously good taste, and whom he'd first hired at Saks, to counsel buyers on what was "chic," as the Salon Moderne's designer. She decorated her salon to have all the elegance and élan of a Parisian couturier's showroom: she mixed the paint for its pale, pale blue walls herself, and studded them with sconces and moldings, scattered black-lacquered coffee tables, sofas, and settees around in an arrangement that suggested the most uncasual kind of comfort, which was basically what Sophie Gimbel was all about. She also, like the couturiers, shrouded her designs in secrecy. So fearful was she, like the French, of manufacturers seeking to copy her designs and sell them to stores like Ohrbach's, which would then mass-produce them and sell them to *le peuple*, that she let no one into her salon unless he or she had been "introduced" and given high-security clearance.

Though it was never clear if her salon actually made any money for Saks (her grand visions, which were often inspired by costumes borrowed from the Brooklyn Museum, required tens of thousands of dollars in often-unused fabric stock), Sophie Gimbel's taste was indisputable, and her renown as a woman designer in the late 1940s and early 1950s was virtually unchallenged. She made the cover of *Time* magazine—no small feat for a businesswoman. She entertained Christian Dior, wealthy New York families like the Loebs and the Gregorys, and also had ties to Hollywood, and was said to have been the first person in New York to entertain Ronald and Nancy Reagan.

My job at Saks was a good deal less glamorous. I was hired to be the assistant to the sales promotion director, Colleen Utter, who was in charge of advertising, windows, and the presentation of all merchandise in the store. She was also the highest-placed female executive at Saks, and her office, which was adjacent to the eighth-floor executive suite, allowed me a view of Adam Gimbel—a rather short, refined man with a powerful presence—in his daily comings and goings. Watching Mr. Gimbel was about as close to power as I got. For it was my job to take care of things like scheduling Miss Utter's luncheons, taking care of her correspondence, and generally acting as her secretary, which was a problem for me on several counts: first, that I didn't have any secretarial skills, and second, that I didn't care to learn any, coming out of Skidmore and the Macy's training program.

This was perhaps not the ideal attitude for a new employee; but then, I had that Mirabella if-you-don't-like-it-leave-it attitude in my veins, and I had yet to see any reason to stem it. So, after a few months of laboriously typing letters, I told my boss that sales promotion wasn't really my thing, and that what I really wanted was to be where I belonged in the fashion department. "I would love it if I could be there," I said, "and if I can't, well, maybe I should just do something else."

Miss Utter looked at me and smiled. "Well then," she said, "maybe you should do something else."

Then she stayed silent, just long enough to let it sink in that I had just lost my job. And when she saw that I had descended into a state of inner torment, she addressed me again.

"There's somebody at *Vogue* that I want you to see," she said.

And she called up a woman named Mildred Morton and sent me over to the Graybar Building.

Did I think when I stepped out of the elevator onto the black and gold star-embossed floor leading to the *Vogue* reception room and asked the Chanel-suited receptionist to please announce "Grace Mirabella for Mrs. Morton" that, one day, all of it would be mine?

I did not. I'd learned a few lessons at Bergdorf Goodman's, in the towel department at Macy's, and from Colleen Utter. Delusions of grandeur were the furthest things from my mind.

CHAPTER 3
WHEN GLAMOUR WAS THE NAME OF THE GAME

What was on my mind, as I walked out the black and gold elevator doors on the nineteenth floor and headed down toward *Vogue*'s offices, was a bit akin to Dorothy's message to Toto: *I don't think we're at Macy's anymore*.

Not at Macy's, not at Saks, not anywhere where the vulgar business of buying and selling was taking place—not in theory, at least. I was in *Vogue*land. Marvelous-looking young women milled around in the corridors. They looked down their noses at me as I waited patiently in the all-white reception room, raised their eyebrows, then went about their business, like ballet dancers scurrying off a stage. When they spoke to one another, they tossed their words over their shoulders, their voices rich with the horsey echoes of boarding school and Southampton, and I could hear chirps of foreign languages peppering the echoes of phone conversations in the background. Great plumed birds of women in hats and scarves and wild-colored sweaters swept in and out of a line of small offices all stretching down one side of a hallway. On the other side came and went dashing men—I. S. V. Patcévitch, president of Condé Nast, his shock of white hair blending in with the office's snow-white walls; Alexander Liberman, then art director for *Vogue*, in his very perfect, English tailored suits and little Russian mustache. Alex, who had been hired by Condé Nast himself to work at *Vogue* in 1941, was already a famous figure in the New York publishing world. He was famous for his talent, his vision—it was he who worked with Irving Penn on the black and white cover photographs that defined *Vogue* in the early 1950s—and for his charm, which was evident from the smiles and little blushes that greeted him as he made his way down the hallway.

One man, oddly dressed, I thought, like an undertaker, had his office on the woman's side of things. He was, I was soon to learn, the Baron Nicholas de Gunzburg, a nobleman of indeterminate lineage and nationality. Some said he was German, others said he hailed from Russia or Brazil. Some said he was from a rich Russian banking family and had been ennobled by the czar; others sniped that he had bought his title in Europe. Still others maintained that he had purchased it in Cole Porter's apartment. Little was really known about him apart from the fact that he at one time had reportedly had something to do with a Russian ballet company and once had acted in a German film called *The Vampire* where he played a poet who spent two weeks in a casket. He'd been a great skier in his youth and a terrific dancer, and had won prize cups for the Charleston. He was said to have come from Paris after his father had died and the family fortune had disappeared, leaving him with no more money than was sitting in his checking account. He'd come to America and, after paying for his travel expenses, had used all the money he had left to throw a grand ball. He had impeccable taste (hence his position as a senior fashion editor) and a terribly dry wit and was known in and around *Vogue* as much for his uniform: white shirt, black suit, black knitted tie, black hair slicked back, black socks and shoes, and black Hermes notebook, as for his deadpan ability to make the most staid *Vogue* editors collapse into giggles at dull moments at fashion shows.

The receptionist, a girl with great big eyes, wearing a Chanel suit and earrings, smiled at me sweetly. She was Louise Liberman, and from the label of the black coat that she had draped over a chair I could see that she was wearing Norell as well as Chanel. Had I followed her downstairs to her car I would also have seen a late-model Lincoln Continental, and had I looked even further I would have found that her mother owned three of the biggest buildings on Seventh Avenue. But I didn't know any of that yet. All I saw was a nice, attractive kid doing her summer job.

I had had a brief interview with the head of personnel, Mary Campbell, who had once been Condé Nast's secretary. Miss Campbell, I'd learn, was a kind of Mother Superior for the *Vogue* flock; she dispensed advice and Kleenex and made sure everyone had a rose when she started work as well as her own personal coffee cup. Now, I followed the stars down the hallway to the office of *Vogue*'s executive editor, Mildred Morton. Mrs. Morton was a poem of paleness: blondish, with pale pale skin, small and very slim and cool as an iceberg. She was sitting behind the palest blond-colored wood desk I had ever seen, and had had the walls of her office painted the palest, most perfect beige. She was dressed as she always was in a Ben Zuckerman suit or a Norman Norell knitted dress of the faintest gray and whitest white, and with her vaguish beigeish hair, she literally faded into the woodwork. Personality-wise, however, there was nothing faded about her.

Diana Vreeland always used to say that Mildred Morton (or Mildred Gilbert, as she'd become by that time) had a black heart: the coldest, cruelest heart imaginable. I never saw her in quite that bad a light; I merely thought that she had ice in her veins, which was a tad less dramatic. It wasn't so much that Mildred was *evil*; it was just that she was fiercely competitive, obsessive about her work, and stuck to her goals with a ferocity that always reminded me of a dog wagging a stick and refusing to let go until he got his way. Competitiveness was like a vital force coursing through her body. It came through in her every move, her every gesture, every word, always cloaked in a thick layer of charm so that its force shook you, softly, like a gloved iron hand.

I imagine that it's hardly a flattering thing to say about myself that Mildred Morton seemed to take an instinctive liking to me— but she did. She looked me up and down appreciatively, as if sizing up whether or not I had what it took to survive in the runwaylike hallways of *Vogue*. This was a typical tactic; it was said that Miss Campbell could judge if a woman was right for *Vogue* by the length of her legs, her cheekbones, and the way she tied her scarf. (The rumor was that being flat-chested helped too.) And if she came up short or fat in any of those areas, Miss Campbell would send her to *Glamour* or, if she wore glasses, to *Mademoiselle*.

"Why do you want to work at *Vogue*?" Mildred Morton asked, fixing me with her icy stare.

"I want to work at *Vogue*," I said, "because I want to be around the best of everything."

"Well then," she said, "you've come to the right place."

Ever since its founding by Arthur B. Turnure and Harry W. McVickar in 1892, as the "dignified, authentic journal of society, fashion and the ceremonial side of life," *Vogue* had always been about the best of everything—the best clothes, the best parties, the "best people." Turnure was the founder of the Grolier Club, and McVickar was Stephen Whitney's great-grandson, and their friends, who provided early financial backing for the magazine, including Cornelius Vanderbilt, William Jay, Peter Cooper Hewitt, and other members of Mrs. Astor's "Four Hundred"—the richest and most socially prominent members of New York society. These American aristocrats brought plenty of prestige to the new magazine, but, unfortunately, imparted little of their own money-making ability to it. *Vogue* floundered financially until 1909, when Condé Nast, an ambitious Midwesterner who had previously been advertising manager of Collier's magazine, purchased it, with the determination to make it turn a profit. He made *Vogue* the standard-bearer for his new breed of "class publications," a revolutionary idea in magazine publishing which rested upon the belief that the best way to attract advertising was not to push endlessly to boost circulation, which was costly, but to guarantee advertisers a readership eager for their products by narrowing the target circulation and tailoring the magazine in such a way that its readers would correspond demographically and exclusively to the profile of that advertiser's customers.

Though Nast, in his early years at *Vogue*, changed the magazine's focus from society to fashion coverage, he fully realized that its fortunes were intimately linked to its maintaining a loyal following among America's most moneyed and "well-born" circles. If *Vogue* were to strengthen itself, he believed, it had to resist being democratized. In a 1913 essay on class publications he magnanimously put it thus: "Even if we grant for the sake of argument that 'all men are *created* equal,' . . . we must admit in the same breath that they overcome this equality with astonishing rapidity . . . The publisher, the editor, the advertising manager and the circulation man must conspire not only to get *all* their readers from the one particular class to which the magazine is dedicated, *but rigorously to exclude all others.*"

The prime way that Condé Nast made sure that his magazine upheld the standards of its desired class of readers was by gathering in and around *Vogue* precisely the kind of people he wanted to be reading it. In the 1920s the cocktail parties in his thirty-room penthouse at 1040 Park Avenue drew everybody who was anybody in the New York world of theater, society, arts, and letters: Lynn

Fontanne, Edna St. Vincent Millay, Arthur Hammerstein, George Gershwin, Fred Astaire, and Tallulah Bankhead. His editors, whom he often hand-picked himself at cocktail parties, became legends. In the 1940s, when I was growing up reading *Vogue*, there was Babs Willaumez Rawlings, a terribly elegant British woman who shocked prevailing tastes by wearing *pants* to work with white silk shirts open down to her navel, and open-toed sandals with bare, beautifully pedicured feet, and Barbara Cushing Mortimer, the "working girl" among the three Cushing sisters of New York high society (the other two, Minnie and Betsey, kept busy with their marriages, respectively, to Vincent Astor and James Roosevelt, followed by John Hay Whitney). While at *Vogue*, Babe was married to Standard Oil heir Stanley Mortimer. Before that marriage, she had lived occasionally at the St. Regis with Russian prince Serge Obolensky, prompting a member of the Burden family to quip, "Morality is for the middle classes." She eventually became Mrs. Bill Paley.

Mary Jean Kempner, daughter of a rich Texas family, was there too, as were Sally Kirkland, Bridget Tichenor, Eleanor Scully Montgomery, and Allene Talmey, the legendary feature editor who had to her credit the fact that she had reduced to tears at least once nearly every writer that she had ever worked with.

These women defined *Vogue* at a very special time in the magazine's history. Paris fashion production had been stalled by the war, Coco Chanel was in disgrace for collaboration, and the magazine had had to begin, for the first time, to give serious attention to American fashion. It had also begun to pay attention to the world beyond Park Avenue: Lee Miller's photos of London during the blitz and of the Dachau and Treblinka concentration camps had made the magazine take an uncharacteristically serious tone, as had Mary Jean Kempner's and Sally Kirkland's coverage of the war in Europe and the Pacific. Meanwhile, luminaries like Cecil Beaton, Yul Brynner, Cole Porter, Salvador Dali, Norman Parkinson, Blumenfeld, and Noel Coward roamed the halls, making the working days at *Vogue* charming and amusing and not too taxing.

Before the war, if Condé Nast happened to be around at 5:30 or so, he'd often pack up whoever was around and whisk them uptown in his limousine for martinis on his terrace.

Now, there *was* a magazine to put out—twice a month at that time too—and Condé Nast wasn't foolish enough to think that you could entrust such big business to somebody's nice cousin from Oyster Bay. That cousin—who could, perhaps, be counted upon to put *Vogue* in touch with six generations of Rockefellers but was likely not to have *any* idea of how to type letters to them—was a good candidate for a position of consulting editor, a job which then, as is the case now, was often unpaid, but conferred upon both the magazine and the editor the prestige of the association. The rule was: you let the women with the marvelous taste and wonderful contacts run around farther down on the masthead, but for an editor in chief you needed someone solid.

Edna Woolman Chase, *Vogue*'s first editor in chief, was a case in point: she was a little old-fashioned woman with purple hair, jabots, and lace, who had begun working in the circulation department at *Vogue* in 1895, at the age of eighteen. Though at times she must have seemed like a boarding school marm overseeing a class of debutantes, she commanded enormous respect. She was a well-known figure in Paris, and upheld everything about *Vogue* that was exclusive, aristocratic, and grand. One story I've heard repeatedly claims that when an editor at *Vogue* tried without success to commit suicide by throwing herself under a subway train, Mrs. Chase said, when she came back to work, "My dear, we at *Vogue* don't throw ourselves under subway trains. If we must, we take sleeping pills."

I came to *Vogue* the same year that the venerable Mrs. Chase stepped down. But her successor, Jessica Daves, had her feet just as firmly rooted on the ground. One might even have said that she had feet of clay—wide feet and short, heavy legs—in sum, she was about as *un*glamorous and unfashionable as her editors were divine.

And they *were* divine then, those women of *Vogue*. They were glorious peacocks, all grandly gesturing. They didn't walk then, they swept; and they didn't speak, they intoned. And the sound of them was that of a charming, protected world of summers in Newport sailing yachts and a life made up of all that was the best of the best.

The image that has always stuck particularly strong in my mind was of a glimpse I caught once of Bridget Tichenor, the accessories editor, walking arm in arm down Lexington Avenue with the British photographer Norman Parkinson. She was five feet nine and very lean; she wore bracelets all the way up to her elbows, and a very slick head of hair, long eyelashes, and a wonderful Italian sweater, orange and black, with opaque stockings and a flat shoe and an orange beret. Norman Parkinson, a slim, tall, tall man with a great mustache, wore a wonderfully cut jacket and custom-made shirt—and together they were two of the tallest, most colorful people you'd ever see—like two birds of paradise. People stopped dead on the street and stared at them. And the looks on their faces were something between amusement and admiration. They were more than outrageous. They were some kind of remarkable.

The fashion editors were like creatures from another planet to me. They were deities, revered and untouchable. And even if their aloof stylishness hadn't made them that way, there was a wall of formality in the office that insured they'd never get too close to mere mortals like me. That kind of formality doesn't exist anymore, nor that rigid sense of hierarchy. These days, you get on the masthead of a magazine like *Vogue* just for occupying space in an office. But then, it was different. You had to work your way on, and entry-level staffers, like secretaries, had a long way to go. A secretary, for that matter, was then called a secretary, not an "assistant," and if you were one, you would never call your boss by her first name. If one of her friends called, you'd never speak to her as though she were *your* own nearest and dearest friend—and then forget to give your boss the message for a week or two. You'd never call up Rosemary Bravo, the president of Saks, for example, as my assistants have done in recent years, and say, "Rosemary,

Grace Mirabella is here for you." That would have been unthinkable. The divide between editors and the young women who were just starting out was sacred. And everyone, I think, liked it that way. It added to the mystique.

The editors were worldly, unhindered by the kinds of worries about what the neighbors would think that made my mother cast a watchful eye over me in my blue jeans. Many of them had married and divorced a multitude of times, which was interesting, because even though divorce wasn't accepted generally the way it is today, at a place like *Vogue* it lent a certain *mondaine* air to the editors, and made their lives appear all the more Noel Coward-esque. Divorce, taking multiple husbands, wasn't so much an embarrassment as a way of building a pedigree. Take Catherine Murray McManus di Montezemolo, for example. Her family was prestigious enough to start off with—the Murrays of Southampton and New York were one of the city's "best" families, and Mr. McManus was a good catch for his time, but Alessandro di Montezemolo was a marchese. Or my eventual assistant: Louise Savitt. She began life as Louise Liberman, became Louise Savitt when she married tennis champion Dick Savitt, then did a stint as Louise Melhado, wife of investment banker Frederick A. Melhado, and finally, in 1987, married Henry A. Grunwald, the former editor in chief of Time, Inc.

For a kid from New Jersey, someone who didn't grow up riding horses on a family estate, this world was a revelation. It was ladies' day at the finishing school, only I felt like I'd come in a quarter of a lifetime too late, and I had an insurmountable quantity of catching up to do. I figured I'd always be an outsider. For I, at twenty-three, didn't yet realize that fashion editors are a separate breed of women, *apart* from their breeding—that a large part of their whole purpose in life is to make you feel like they're "in" and you are hopelessly "out." They wouldn't be doing their jobs properly otherwise.

I wasn't so cynical in my thinking then. I was swept up in the enormous pageantry of it all. It was great theater, opera really—or musical comedy—all gestures and grandiosity and drama, like scenes lifted right out of Gertrude Lawrence's performance in *Lady in the Dark*. The performance of the role of fashion editor was terribly important; if you had a fur coat, for example, you couldn't just take it off and hang it up, you absolutely had to fling it—literally, negligently fling it, over a chair, then walk away and ignore it, which absolutely nobody else in the world was doing then. You were hired, after all, for gestures like those—a way of being and acting and looking that could catch an editor's eye while you were out dancing and cause her to come into the office the next day and say, "I met the most wonderfully attractive young woman last night at Morocco, and she was simply adorable . . ." and then follow up, "You know, _____ is *such* an interesting woman and has great taste, and she would probably be *amused* to do something for you . . ."

That's the way fashion editors often were found then; you "picked up" someone who was in the right group who had style and taste and knew the right people. You didn't have to know the market. You just had to be able to *present*. Because if you were the right kind of person and you had a certain style and enough pizzazz and were known in certain circles, then the Seventh Avenue crowd was delighted to know you. It was your style that counted to them. You came in and looked like something and *presented*— and they thought they were dealing with *somebody*.

Vogue's readership was only about 250,000 then, which gave us a certain sense of community with our readers. Everything was much, much smaller. The world was smaller, in a sense. A young editor like Denise Lawson-Johnson, if she had a grand party to attend, would walk right over to Harry Winston or Van Cleef and borrow some jewels, then return them the next day. Twenty-five years later, if she'd done this, she would have had a bodyguard following her wherever she went—and you often did, in later decades, see guards from different jewelers lined up outside an apartment where a dinner was being held, or outside the ballroom of the Pierre or the Plaza. But times were different in Denise's day.

Once, after she borrowed a lot of jewels from Harry Winston for a Friday night party and woke up on a rainy Saturday morning afterward, not wanting to take the jewels back but also knowing she couldn't hand them over to someone else because they were so valuable, she put herself in an old raincoat, tied a scarf over her head, and took the bus up Fifth Avenue in the rain, then walked into Winston pretending that she was her own maid. She handed over the jewels, which she was carrying in a paper bag so that no one would know they were anything valuable, and said, "Miss Lawson-Johnson borrowed these and asked that I return them."

Vogue didn't have a terribly *professional* atmosphere. It was genteel. You made virtually no money at all, and never discussed it—just as you didn't discuss whether the magazine did, either. It didn't feel like a commercial enterprise. The fashion offices were all arranged around one big room decorated with models' photos on the walls, and they were so small that they were often compared to horse stalls. None of the editors ever closed their doors (those who *had* doors). The studio was right up the street, so that when the people who were going to be photographed for the magazine— the great painters and writers and actresses of the day—came in, you'd meet them and talk to them, while all the arrangements were made for their shoot.

There was less work too, even though *Vogue* was bimonthly in those years, and it was quite simply because the magazine only had—as Alex Liberman always put it—four digits of information per issue. You could do an issue with forty pictures and a couple of written words wrapped around them very easily. The pages were big and empty; if you showed a suit, you didn't push yourself to think of four ways that a girl might wear it. And you never ran a series of pictures to cover the story of ten women marching on Washington. You never had the ten pictures. Or the women marching. The World War II era was over. *Vogue* in the 1950s, in the McCarthy era, was notably silent on all that was political, or problematic, or complicated, or unpleasant. It was a picture book.

In those days, if *Vogue* ran features on women it wasn't because they were congresswomen, it was because they had great style or taste. That, quite simply, was what the *Vogue* woman was all about. Marella Agnelli, wife of Fiat chairman Giovanni Agnelli, was one such woman, and we photographed her all the time. Luciana Pignatelli was another. They were great beauties, and not in a plastic and perfect, soap opera actress sort of way. They were something else entirely.

Women like this were really *Vogue*'s reason for being, and it was incredibly important for us to be able to seek them out and have them in the magazine. That was why it was so important for *Vogue* to have editors who were well connected. A large part of many editors' jobs was to be out and about spotting women like this, talking to them a bit, and then reporting back to *Vogue*'s society editor, Margaret Case, and the fashion editors. And when a woman was "discovered," the benefit worked both ways, both for the magazine and for her. Lauren Bacall, for example, was spotted by Slim Keith, who ran back to Diana Vreeland at *Harper's Bazaar* and said, "You've got to meet this marvelous girl." Vreeland had her photographed, and basically launched Betty Bacall's career, before she went out West to act in Hollywood.

It was essential that the magazine have people around the world who knew people who were in the right spot so that if some drop-dead young woman walked in the door they'd be able to call up and tell us about her. You also needed the daughters of powerful people who could pick up the phone and tap into whatever world you wanted access to, for a shoot, a trip, or a story. And I'm not talking about knowing the police chief. It was about knowing the Secretary of State. The ambassador to France, to Egypt, to Turkey.

The assistants at *Vogue* often were the kinds of girls who had these connections. They came to the magazine out of an interest in fashion and in search of a social place to be. It was a refuge from the grubby work world, and it welcomed them. *Vogue* was a playground for them, and allowed them to be exactly as they were: attractive and frivolous and fun. They zipped around town in their

Lincolns and Ford Thunderbirds and did things like eating their peanut butter sandwiches at the great table in the fashion department all dressed up in a selection of Sally Victor's most marvelous, magnificently flowered hats.

Things weren't that much fun for Jessica Daves. In addition to her big legs and wide feet, she had bad hair, and a short, round body, and in her early sixties she looked the way somebody in her late seventies might today. There were frequent humiliations—the couturiers in Paris consistently failed to recognize her and treated her with some disdain. Alex Liberman and his wife, Tatiana, always used to tell the rather evil tale that she had once, at one of their cocktail parties, attempted to bite into a deviled egg without first removing her veil. The ignominy lasted even after her death; in her obituary, *The New York Times* quoted an erstwhile friend who said, "She was a portly woman with a face that resembled a baked apple, and if she wore custom dresses, they looked like ready-to-wear." I'm sure that the insult rattled her in her grave.

I personally always thought that except for her carriage and her sound, Jessica Daves looked like a matron of a girls' school. Everything about her was unappealing. Every gesture looked like she'd picked it up from someone else and hadn't gotten it quite right. She must have been terribly insecure. Despina Messinesi, who was in Paris working as an editor for her in the war years, used to tell me that Mrs. Daves had had such a complex about her legs and her hair and her treatment by the Paris couturiers that she would change her clothes about fifty times before venturing out of the hotel to view the collections. She put on her voice, I always thought, much in the same way that she fussed over her clothes, and spoke with all the airs of her editors, but since she *wasn't* one of them she got it all wrong. When she spoke, you got a very precious-sounding delivery that rankled, and when she attempted a few words of French, her voice became very small and high like a child's and was particularly annoying.

She was considered prudish in her tastes—not unusual for a prudish time when an editor like Nancy White (niece of the legendary Carmel Snow), who succeeded her as the editor in chief of *Harper's Bazaar*, always thought it a little suspect if a girl had her hands too close to herself when she posed in a trench coat. Jessica Daves didn't have much of an eye for fashion (her idea of a great fashion story was to do something with the fact that cars were getting smaller, causing women's clothing to shrink—something which could have been very interesting, sociologically, in the hands of a more able editor, but, under Mrs. Daves's feet, was not), and she didn't have much of a feel for photography either—which probably served Alex Liberman quite well, as it allowed him to mastermind the great photography that was going into *Vogue* at that time: Irving Penn's great black-and-white covers and Cecil Beaton's portraits.

But Jessica Daves had other strengths. She was an excellent text editor and had a wide grip of culture, and she worked hard to make *Vogue* more serious, to prove that a woman's world wasn't just made up of "frills and clothes" as she put it. What clothes there were (for *Vogue* was still almost exclusively a fashion magazine), she wanted to be more accessible to middle-class women, and she made an effort—a heresy, some at *Vogue* believed—to include some moderately priced fashions in the magazine's pages. She also had a very sharp business sense and a strong understanding of merchandising. Her background had been as an advertising copywriter at department stores like Best & Company and Saks, and she had joined *Vogue* originally as fashion merchandising editor in 1933. Under her leadership, *Vogue*'s merchandising department became very active and the magazine for the first time became truly service oriented. Designers' names and store credits began to appear on the same page with the fashion so readers knew where to purchase the clothes.

Mrs. Daves also oversaw a lot of creative promotional work, which included the creation of store guides, on "How to Use This Issue" printed on a different paper in a special front section of issues of the magazine that were to be sent to selected retailers. Stores were very important to the magazine in those days. They had a great deal of power, and a great deal of money, much more than they do today. And there were more big, fashionable stores then than there are today. The store guides were designed to help them plan sales by summing up the main fashion themes of the issues, highlighting what the trends and hot colors were. It was a highly successful venture, if not, in fact, at times overdone, to the point that *Vogue*—like other fashion magazines at that time— almost seemed to operate from the point of view of the stores, and chose to make its fashion points with the numbers we knew the stores had bought.

By working for Mildred Morton, who as executive editor was responsible for walking the thin line between advertising—the magazine's "business side"—and editorial, making sure that the two were working in synch, I became part of Jessica Daves's modernizing revolution. It was humble work at first: I was responsible, along with two other young women in a windowless office called the editorial credit department, for finding out which stores carried the clothes we featured on our fashion pages, and for making sure that the stores would in fact still stock those clothes by the time our readers had seen them in *Vogue*.

I suppose that Mrs. Morton liked the job I was doing, because eventually she moved me out of that department and made me her assistant, by which she meant for me to be her surrogate—a kind of spy, really, in the editorial department. I was given a desk in fashion editor Bettina Ballard's office, and it was my lot to sit there, facing the wall in my corner, with my back turned to her and to the room, day in and day out, and essentially keep my eyes and ears open to collect information to report back to Mildred Morton about what clothes were being selected and whether or not the choices filled her credit needs.

Bettina Ballard was a legend. She was a striking-looking if not beautiful woman of epic grandeur, with a long, sharpish nose. She was a grande dame on such a grand scale that once when she was doing a photo shoot in the Bois de Boulogne in Paris and had bent down to insert some more newspaper to fluff up a skirt, a passerby, frozen by the mere sight of Bettina on her knees, stopped and sputtered, *"Qu'est-ce qu'il y a, madame? Qu'est-ce qui se passe?"* thinking that something horrible had happened.

Bettina had been in Paris during the war working for the Red Cross, and had become friends with designers like Balenciaga and Jacques Fath. She developed magical abilities to have clothes made for her at record speed—and when the war ended, had swept back into New York wearing a new Chanel suit, navy blue with a white collar and a Chanel beret—which had been miraculously made for her just days after the disgraced Chanel had presented her first post-war couture show. Each time Bettina returned from Paris, she was filled with wonderful stories and wearing the latest creations from the couture. She was almost unbearably chic, and could daily be heard dictating letters to some countess or another, saying she was terribly sorry that she and her husband couldn't be in Monte Carlo that year, but they'd so much rather be in Tangiers. . . . She was constantly writing to people like Mona Bismark or on the phone with someone named Suki or Missy. Through her stories, you saw the whole Fred Astaire crowd dancing by in the night. You heard Cole Porter music playing in her voice. I was terrified of her.

As might be surmised, Bettina Ballard and Mildred Morton were not the best of friends. Each pretty much believed that the other was doing all that she could to run the magazine into the ground. Neither had any solid grounds for this charge; it was, rather, that Mildred's military efficiency clashed horribly with Bettina's flamboyant creativity, and since they were such carefully constructed creatures, each found her entire reason for being negated by the other.

It was Mildred Morton's job to make sure that *Vogue* developed and maintained good relations with major stores, and to develop projects like fashion shows that the magazine and the stores could work on together to their mutual public relations benefit. Her concern always was that the editors weren't minding the business side of the magazine, both in the sense of public relations and in the ways they treated people who might advertise in the magazine. Editors stood manufacturers up for appointments, they didn't return telephone calls; they misplaced clothes, they underestimated the time they needed to photograph them and didn't call to explain (as they still don't today) . . . all this was cause for a dressing-down by Mildred Morton. She believed very strongly that the relationship of a fashion magazine to a store was very important, because it was through the store that the magazine and the merchandise had a real impact on the reader/consumer. She also made no bones about the fact that the magazine's lifeblood was its advertisers and cultivated them—the manufacturers, stores, and designers—so that they felt that they had a stake in *Vogue*, and, with their ad dollars, put their faith in the magazine, which, they trusted, would provide them with a positive editorial climate. She was also the person whom advertisers called to register their complaints—often at the tops of their lungs, and with threats of canceled contracts hanging in the air—about the editorial treatment that their clothes had received in *Vogue*.

Making good on the implicit promise of preferential editorial treatment that *Vogue* offered its best advertisers was perhaps the most challenging aspect of Mildred Morton's job. For it was one thing to intend for an advertiser to find his clothes displayed advantageously in *Vogue*; it was another to get the fashion editors to make it happen. One way that Mildred Morton did so was by circulating a "Must" list for each issue—a list of manufacturing houses that the editors had to remember in print. Unlike today, when some of the Seventh Avenue fashion houses are veritable empires, with so much advertising money that they don't *need* a mention in *Vogue* to catch women's eyes, in those days, maybe even more than today, a designer or manufacturer could be *made* by *Vogue*, and a "free" plug was a prized possession indeed. We'd also balance our credits to make sure that department stores were mentioned in proportion to their advertising and assure that if Saks Fifth Avenue, for example, didn't want to share a credit with a Brooklyn store, that it didn't. The "must list" was a scandalous practice journalistically, of course, but was standard at fashion magazines in those days, where no one was above saying, "thank you" to particularly strong and faithful advertisers. The sportswear manufacturer David Crystal, for example, always cut a deal where he took six pages of advertising in an issue, which he used like a brochure to send to the department stores. In return, we'd give him a cover. Deals for covers were rare, even in those days. But it would be dishonest to say that it didn't happen, or that nothing like it goes on anymore.

Another thing Mildred Morton's staff had to do was to make sure that *Vogue*'s little "thank you"s were keeping pace with its competition, *Harper's Bazaar*. Someone in the merchandising department always had the job of keeping a list of how many credits *Harper's* gave to, say, Seymour Fox or Ben Zuckerman in any given month, and it was incumbent upon us to match this so that we could then go to them for advertising and prove what a supportive editorial climate we were providing. We always said then that *Harper's Bazaar* was much more craven than we were in these sorts of editorial practices—that they would always make a deal.

Mildred Morton was really quite brilliant when it came to dealing with advertisers and did a great job of improving *Vogue*'s connections to retailers. She had a way of making advertisers feel that it was a privilege, almost a gift, really, to advertise in *Vogue*, which only made the stores and manufacturers more avid to do so. She had a keen understanding of her market, a breadth of knowledge about her product and the people she was dealing with that was truly remarkable. I've never seen anyone else like her, particularly not in the crop of know-nothing editors of today. I'm sure I learned more from her than I'd care to admit. Her lessons were cogent, if not always absolutely kind: Never make small talk. Never talk to anyone but the person at the absolute top. If you want the right answer, get it from the person who can make it stick.

Though I always had a grudging admiration for Mildred Morton, as might be expected, editors like Bettina Ballard were far from keen on her. They felt Morton was trying to take away the editorial freedom of the magazine, to steer its creative juices just in the direction of making money. Her presence in the hallway always seemed to spell trouble—as, in fact, Mildred was not above marching into the fashion or beauty department at *Vogue*, and, after practically lifting an editor up by the hair, taking her over to Seventh Avenue and having her explain why an advertiser had been stood up for an appointment or in any other way been slighted.

Needless to say, Bettina Ballard, who regularly turned up her nose at the mere thought that something practical might be going on at *Vogue*, did not welcome my presence in her office too warmly. The whole idea that I might want to know what was going on in editorial so that merchandising could do something with it seemed to her not quite up to the standards of her department. She allowed me to sit in my little hovel in a corner of her office, which was really more like a big salon, with a huge French table in the middle and no desk, but she did not speak to me. She never said good morning or good-bye—never acknowledged my existence at all. I sat in on run-throughs and on her meetings with editors, and then I'd quietly relay the information to Mildred Morton. I was invisible; and had not Bettina's assistant, Barbara Sage, made an effort to be nice to me, it might have been forgotten that I existed at all.

Which was why when a chance encounter at the *Vogue* elevator banks one evening taught me that she had, in fact, been thinking about me for some time, I could not have been more shocked.

It was the end of a very long and frustrating day and I was punchy and cranky and exhausted. I closed my eyes briefly and leaned upon a wall, and the next thing I knew, when I opened them, I saw the unwelcome apparition of Mrs. Ballard. We stood for a moment in silence, it painfully clear that neither of us had the slightest idea of what to say to the other. Bettina looked at me steadily, in the haughty, down-her-nose way she always looked at

everyone, until eventually I began to get anxious, and in my panicked state I began to speak.

"You know, I'm supposed to be going to Europe in a month,"
said I, "and I wouldn't mind working there. In fact, I wouldn't
mind not coming back."

And she said, "Would you really like to work there, say, in
Italy?"

And I said yes. And that was that.

We made it downstairs and she left. As was usual, she did not
offer me a ride home. And the next morning she breezed into her
office—*our* office—and over her shoulder, still not looking at me,
she floated out, "Grace, the Italian designers Simonetta and Fabi-
anni are at the St. Regis. I told them about you last night. Go over
and see them. They may have a job for you."

I called them. They invited me for dinner. We met in the King
Cole Bar and they offered me a job. And all of a sudden, Bettina
Ballard, who had never even spoken to me in the fashion department, invited *my mother* to come in and have dinner with her and
her husband in their renovated carriage house on East Seventy-
first Street. And Bettina, charming as charming could be, convinced my mother and convinced me that going to Rome for fifty
dollars a month was the best thing I could possibly hope to do to
learn and to broaden my sense of good taste and develop into the
kind of delightful young woman that *Vogue* was all about.

My mother was sold, even though it meant that she'd have to
contribute part of her salary to supplement mine and that she'd
have to be, once more, truly alone. I was nearly sold too—but I
wanted to run the idea past Jessica Daves. It's hard to leave a place
like *Vogue*, hard to leave being near the top, especially when you're
young and have the sense of hanging in on a shoestring and suspect that you may not ever be quite so lucky again. My friends at
the magazine warned me that the antagonism between Jessica
Daves and Bettina Ballard was so great that if I wanted to exit
Vogue gracefully and with some hope of coming back, I should
never let Mrs. Daves know that it was indeed Bettina who had

gotten me the job. Bettina Ballard, it seemed, had always thought that she herself should have been given Jessica Daves's job, and had tortured her for years. So I went to Jessica Daves's grand office, and I told her that I had organized the whole thing myself. Deferentially, I asked her, "What do you think I should do?"

She said, "If I were your age, I'd do it." Then she added, "I'm not going to tell you that I'm going to promise you the job that you have when you return. But do it. And when you come back, talk to me."

A blessing but no guarantees. That was enough for me.

One weekend soon afterward, I told my friend Gates Davison that I was going to Rome to live and work. He said that he happened to have a wonderful friend who was living there and who, he was sure, I would find just delightful. Her name was Tish Baldrige, and she was working at the American Embassy for Clare Booth Luce, the ambassador to Italy.

Letitia Baldrige is now best known for the fact that she worked as White House social secretary in the Kennedy administration and has written a number of books on manners, most notably her *Complete Guide to Executive Manners*, which she published in 1985. But then, she was just Tish, which was no small matter: she was six feet one, twenty-something, daughter of a prominent Washington family (her father had been a congressman), fluent in French and jovially conversant in Italian, and already something of the towering presence she would become as the reigning critic of American boorishness. She was a product of Miss Porter's School and Vassar, had studied for a year in Geneva, and, before the ripe old age of twenty-one, had been presented at court in England. She had also before coming to Europe worked as a psychological warfare officer for the CIA. She wasn't someone to take lightly.

After I arrived in Rome and had settled into the Hotel Inglaterra and spent a few days walking around getting oriented, I began to make my way down the long phone list I'd compiled from well-wishers back in New York. One of my first calls was to Letitia

Baldrige. I introduced myself, mentioned the Gates Davison connection, and basically let her know that I was alone in a strange
city, knew no one, and would really be quite thrilled to meet her.
She gave me the coldest reception possible, took my phone number, and hung up. A few days later I answered the phone to hear a
loud, very grand voice booming in my ear, "Do you speak any
Italian?" And I, immediately knowing it was Tish (how many people did I know in Rome anyway?), crossed my fingers and said, "A
little."

"Good," said Tish (for it was She), "I've thrown together a
group of eight people, five of whom are Italians, and we're going
to have dinner. Why don't you join us?"

I was out the door in seconds flat. Tish and I hit it off immediately. And a few weeks later she invited me to become her room-
mate.

The gods couldn't have smiled any more generously upon me.
Tish's apartment was a bright and sunny two-bedroom with a few
pieces of furniture and a kind of recessed lighting in the living
room that we thought was very glamorous. It was in a modern
building next to the zoo in Parioli, the residential section of Rome,
right across the street from the house of Ingrid Bergman and Ro-
berto Rossellini. Rossellini allowed Tish to park her car in his
driveway, and often, when he was cutting out on his wife at 3
A.M. and Tish was returning from a night of revelry, insisted upon
walking her home across the street, a safety precaution which he
claimed was absolutely necessary.

From her work at the embassy, Tish knew everyone who was
anyone passing in and out of Rome, and our apartment, where the
good Scotch Tish purchased for two dollars a bottle always flowed
freely, became a kind of unofficial checking-in point for visiting
Americans. I found that the people I'd been told to look up in
Rome by friends and colleagues in New York showed up in my
living room before I even had the chance to call them. I would
come home in the evenings to find Mary Martin or the young
Henry Luce or Vincent Price or Marcia Davenport or a senator or

various and sundry European nobles sitting on the sofa—all friends of Tish's. I had learned, with a very skilled language teacher provided by Mrs. Luce, that Italian is quite an easy language to learn to speak not well, and as my fluency increased, I made my own Italian friends too, people I met in the fashion world who were often, like my boss, Simonetta, from Rome's oldest and most distinguished families. Nearly every evening there were cocktails in our apartment, followed by dinner and dancing and long evenings of talking and laughing. We flirted; we fell in and out of love with various Italians and Americans, and Tish and I schemed together like old school friends, working out intricate hand signals to indicate when to ditch a man or give an interfering female the brush-off.

Tish was a wonderful friend, deeply funny and very, very smart. She was also rather studiedly grand, so much so that Mrs. Luce one evening actually took it upon herself to bring her down a peg at one of the embassy's parties. It was a cocktail party for all the people who had participated in the signing of the Trieste Agreement, the decoders, translators, and aides, right down the line—"little people," as far as Tish was concerned. Tish assented to come, then stood around in the Villa Taverna looking rather aloof and above it all until Mrs. Luce came along and said she wanted her to meet an absolutely fascinating young woman *telefonista* who happened to be studying the guitar. Tish too, at that time, was studying guitar and prided herself upon the progress she'd made, particularly in learning Italian songs. So when she met the young woman, she looked down her nose at her and said, "Can you play any Neapolitan songs?" which she considered some of the more difficult pieces that she was trying to master for her own repertoire.

And the young woman replied, "I'm afraid that I can't." Tish smiled. The woman continued, "I've only been studying for one year with Mr. Segovia."

At that moment Mrs. Luce turned and walked away, but not before I saw the twitch of a giggle flash over her face. I knew that she had set Tish up on purpose. And the charming thing about Tish was, she immediately saw the humor too and repeated this story about herself over and over again for years.

As two young, blond, and attractive Americans, Tish and I hardly lacked for dinner dates. And we didn't have to worry about the kind of overbearing harassment that often troubled other American women in Italy, then as now. Our housekeeper—or perhaps I should say our "duenna," Brandina, who was missing a few teeth—had an instinctive dislike of the male gender. She made sure, whenever we brought men into the house, to put her size fifty-two bust directly into our line of vision, and then started vacuuming the living room or disinfecting the kitchen, or found any other similarly noisy or foul-smelling work she could do, just to be sure that whatever romantic mood that might have been preparing itself was quickly quashed.

Her presence couldn't dampen the fact, though, that Rome in 1954 was an enchantingly romantic place. Every Christmas, the shepherds would come from the Abruzzi and serenade us under our windows. The clubs and restaurants we loved—great chic spots like La Cabala and the dark, intimate Osteria dell'orso, with its violin players and medieval setting—were candlelit and filled with sound and movement; people danced closely together and whispered and went off for long walks in the moonlight. Italian love songs, like "Volare," were all the rage. The Romans were happy and willing to risk their hearts on love. They were coming alive, reveling, for the first time since before Mussolini, in money and plenty and beauty and a general sense of well-being. Post-war Italy was booming: Italian design—in cars, in fabrics, in costume jewelry, in shoes and leather handbags—was number one in the world. Emilio Pucci was designing extraordinary patterned silk dresses and terrific T-shirts. Italian sweaters were enjoying a heyday. People who weren't already rich worked twelve hours a day, six days a week, and got rich. They buzzed around town on tiny motor scooters which made a terrible noise that no one minded.

There was a sensuality to that time that was intensely stylish, aestheticized—like the moment in *La Dolce Vita* when Anouk Aimée comes out of the house, rather wonderfully adjusting her belt, and in a moment you know that she's spent the night with Marcello Mastroianni. You register that fact, but at the same time you take in that she's in the best goddamn belt and little black outfit and you know that she's done whatever she's done in the best possible style. That was Rome for me: snapshot moments of incredible style and sensuality: perfect legs in wonderful shoes, lovely manicured hands holding marvelous handbags. Where did the feet and the hands go with such accessories? Dancing, splendidly, off into the night.

We, as Americans, felt like we were part of that boom. We were honored and revered and—even better—our dollars were worth a comparable fortune. We could dine handsomely on three dollars per person (not that we ever paid) and could happily, on meager "working girls'" salaries, afford to load up on Gucci shoes and bags and marvelous, bright-colored sweaters and costume jewelry, and custom order shoes purchased at D'Alco, which was then all the rage in Rome. We ate foods that we'd never even seen before: tiny artichokes that grow only in the sandy soil around Rome, incredibly sweet, small melons. We drank wine by the case.

The glamour of Rome at that time surpassed anything known in New York. Women ran around in superb shantung pajamas and shocking pink raw silk palazzo pajamas and tunic tops, linen skirts and suits during the day, and bolero jackets, and lots of wonderful sports separates, by designers like Laura Aponti. It was the time when Audrey Hepburn was filming *Roman Holiday*, and there was always some kind of filming going on, actors and actresses always combing Rome by foot, and extraordinary parties after the shoots. "Old Audrey," as Vreeland always called her, and as I've always referred to her in my mind, though I never met her, was always out and around on the streets and in the clubs and restaurants that we loved.

Rome was so much smaller then, so much more personal that if there was a star around you saw her and felt as though you knew her, even if you didn't, because somebody you knew undoubtedly did and the proximity of everyone and everything was so great. I did meet Fellini then, and his wife, Giulietta Masina, and Marcello Mastroianni, and saw Sophia Loren and Gregory Peck and Gina Lollobrigida around too. There were no paparazzi yet, and stars hadn't the walls of defensiveness and of real defense—bodyguards, publicists, agents—that we associate with the "beautiful people" of today. They strolled up and down the via Veneto and you could stare at them just as brazenly as you liked. You could easily meet Sophia Loren, and if you wanted to work with her and she liked you, she might just hand you her phone number and say, "If you need me, just give me a call," as I did, for *Vogue*, just a few years later.

Rome then, in many ways, was like a small town, or rather it had the feel of a city that's on the rise, but hasn't quite yet *arrived* as a hot spot. The streets weren't cluttered. Cars were still at a premium and there were no traffic jams. If you wanted to have a coffee on the via Veneto you could give a man fifty lira, and he would quadruple-park your car in the street and then watch it while you spent a few hours in the café watching the parade of amazing-looking people go by. And you could see everyone that you knew in Rome in the space of an afternoon, and if you missed someone, then you could be sure that he or she saw you and that by the time that the evening's cocktail hour rolled around, the news of your spotting had been circulated and been formulated into some absolutely astounding form of gossip.

There were so many people to gossip about. Besides the stars, there were the beautiful people of Rome like the jet-setting couple Count and Contessa Rudy Crespi. Even more fascinating then were the hangers-on, the somewhat questionable, slightly mysterious, oddball sorts of people who collect in fashionable circles without anyone ever quite figuring out why they were there. One man, who went simply by the name of George, was someone whom everyone knew and didn't know. He was forever showing up in restaurants and sitting down at your table and being introduced only to write down all the names of your friends in a little note-book. We all said he was a spy, which was undoubtedly what he wanted us to believe. The CIA would probably not have approved of his style, though: he drove around Rome in a little car that was permanently stuck in first gear, which meant that to drive with him guaranteed that you'd be carsick in minutes. He was undoubt-edly a friend of Tish's.

My job with Simonetta and Fabiani was a classic glamour posi-tion in that it paid practically nothing but gave me access to every important person in Italian clothing design as well as every promi-nent American manufacturer who happened to pass through Rome. It gave me an in-depth exposure to the workings of a great couture house, *and* it allowed some of that house's splendor to rub off on me. I learned about fabric and cutting and skills like how to judge a hemline with your eye rather than a tape measure—the *ne plus ultra* of fashion authority in those days. In a sense, Rome was my own sort of finishing school—a high-caliber education in European style and top quality that would teach me how to have a more demanding, more discerning eye for clothes and let me come back to New York precisely the kind of polished *Vogue* woman I saw around me every day in the office.

Simonetta and Fabiani were themselves an education.

Simonetta, one of the most highly respected post-war Italian designers, was a marvelously good-looking woman and a duchess, whose first marriage had been to the nobleman Count Galeazzo Visconte di Modrone. What Simonetta's noble blood had be-queathed her was an absolute disdain for the lower classes and a sense that she had every right to show it. If you were unfortunate enough to be one of the young kids working for her at pinning or cutting in her workshop on the via Gregoriana, what your status entitled you to was a thorough and nerve-racking chewing-out nearly every day of your working life. Simonetta had the kind of voice that could echo through the lobby of the Hotel des Baines in Venice like an air-raid siren, and if its full volume was turned against you, it was a near deadly weapon. I'd never seen one class of person trample so blatantly on another in America before. I used to think that the only difference between me and those young girls was a passport. But there I was wrong. The fact that I'd come to Rome from *Vogue*, via Bettina Ballard, made Simonetta see me as something of an equal. I was never treated to a lashing from her brutal tongue—except once, very controlledly, in Venice, when we were staying at the Lido and I made the error of getting us a bath-house on the "wrong" section of the beach. On that occasion Simonetta very quickly let me know that I'd effectively put us in Siberia and, containing her rage, turned her back and refused to speak with me for the rest of the day.

Simonetta, whose collections had a great appeal to Americans like Andrew Goodman (Goodman was such a supporter that Simonetta named her second child, Bardo Andrew Fabiani after him), specialized in designing elegant sportswear and very feminine, full-skirted cocktail dresses. Alberto Fabiani, her husband and, so it happened, top competitor, was also one of Rome's most success-ful couturiers and made wonderfully tailored suits and coats which sold extremely well both in Italy and abroad. Fabiani, known as "the surgeon of suits and coats," was, despite his fine tailoring skills, more of a practitioner of the great Italian art of *la dolce fa niente* than he was a diligent businessman, which meant that he generally spent the late morning on the job, then broke for a long lunch, then a siesta and often an afternoon at the beach—all of which he was forever inviting me to do with him, among other amusements that he promised back at his apartment. I resisted; Fabiani was notorious in Rome for coming on to every girl who crossed his path, and I was not particularly flattered or impressed. Nor did I feel harassed. For me, it was all part of la dolce vita of Rome: an invitation to lunch, a siesta, a trip to the beach . . . and when it was innocent, as one could always manage to make it be in the end, it was absolutely delightful. Simonetta was, I imagine, less charmed by Alberto's winning ways. She tolerated his infidel-ities, however glumly, as so many other Italian wives did then and perhaps now.

Aside from trailing women, Alberto Fabiani's greatest pleasure in life was hanging out with his friends—"the boys"—those ubiquitous Italian men with cigarettes and big laughs that I knew so well from my growing-up years. Outside of their company, and aside from flirtatious come-ons, he was a man of few words—though I did hear him once deliver an absolutely delicious one-liner to Irene Brin, who at that moment was the Rome editor for *Harper's Bazaar*. Irene Brin, a very grand woman, always turned up her nose at Italian designers and dressed exclusively in Balenciaga, claiming all the while that she did so because to wear Italian designs would have been to show favoritism. This pretense drove Fabiani up the wall. So one day, when she pranced into his salon to see his collection, wearing her Balenciaga suit, Fabiani, uttering the most words I think he'd ever put together, said, "That's a wonderful suit, my dear. Balenciaga has done more for you than your husband has ever done." Which was his way of saying that the suit made her look pregnant, as all of Balenciaga's suits did a bit at that point. It's doubtful whether that comment endeared his collection to *Harper's Bazaar*, but Fabiani wouldn't have cared about that kind of thing. And in that splendidly lighthearted post-war time, he was able to get away with it. Most of the time.

Sometimes, Fabiani's games became hard work for me. I found that it was a lot easier to play with him at avoiding his amorous advances than it was to keep his business dalliances in line. Fabiani was a great tailor, but he wasn't much of a businessman, and he wasn't too smart about recognizing his limitations in that area either. So that, in the 1950s, when he decided to join the march of the times and get into ready-to-wear—a step that Simonetta, who was the better businessperson, avoided, deciding to let Fabiani ruin himself first and learn from his mistakes—he found himself in a bit over his head. It was part of my job to try to help him stay afloat. This wasn't easy, especially since it was Fabiani's habit to take off to the beach or on vacation whenever things heated up too much. This habit proved especially problematic one season during my stay in Rome, when Fabiani, having received his first-ever large ready-to-wear order—from Macy's, no less—decided to deal with the stress by taking a few weeks' vacation in Venice.

Now, from having worked at Macy's I knew that it wasn't the kind of store that gave you a second chance. You had one shot with their buyers, and that was it. You weren't late and you didn't make mistakes. So I was, understandably, a bit nervous about the whole thing, and relaxed only when I saw at last that a shipment of coats had arrived in the salon ready for Macy's. My peace of mind was short-lived, though. A few days after the delivery, Franco, a small man who ran the salon for Fabiani as his accountant, came to my office and told me that all the coats had been lined with the wrong fabric.

"What are we going to do?" he asked me.

"Tell Fabiani," I answered.

Later that day, after he'd had his daily phone call with the boss, I asked him what Fabiani had said.

"He didn't say," Franco told me.

"Why not?" I asked. "Didn't you tell him?"

"No," he said. "He didn't ask. And I never trouble him with problems when he's away on holiday."

I stepped in at that point, reordered the coats with the right lining in them, and worked it all out. But that exchange has never left my mind. It was pure Fabiani. Pure Italy.

My work for Simonetta and Fabiani consisted of a lot of this kind of troubleshooting. I also did what they, rather uniquely, labeled public relations: basically, I did whatever Simonetta wanted me to. I helped her with her accessorizing, helped have hats made for a show, booked models, and made connections for her and Fabiani. I wined and dined store presidents from the states when they visited Rome, and took out American manufacturers, who regularly came over to Europe in those days to buy patterns or dresses from the custom order houses to copy and mass-produce them back home. When Simonetta and Fabiani joined the other Italian designers in showing their collections in Florence (the precursor to today's Italian couture shows in Rome and Italian ready-to-wear showings in Milan), I worked in the showroom selling the clothes, working particularly with private American clients.

Some of my encounters with Americans really put my diplomatic skills to the test. My first meeting with a well-known American coat and suit man is one example: I was in my office one day when a vendeuse came running in for help. Something was up, she said. There was a prosperous-looking American couple in the showroom and the wife had tried on many coats without choosing any, while the husband, instead of falling asleep as most did, had watched her with rapt attention.

"I asked if I could help," she said, "and the woman told me that she didn't even *like* coats. Then, a few minutes later she wanted to order a coat with the lapels of one model and the buttons of another and the shape of still a third. That's when I said that I had to consult with you."

It was clear to me that this difficult couple was, no doubt, a manufacturer and his wife looking for designs to steal. So, as politely as I could, I talked them out of the showroom and into the street. Green as I was, though, I didn't recognize the would-be pirate until, a few nights later, I was invited out for a drink at the Excelsior Hotel with Nat Bader, founder of Originala, another very big American coat and suit manufacturer. At the bar he introduced me to an American couple who he felt sure I'd want to know. If they recognized me, they didn't let on. And I didn't either.

Other encounters were more pleasant, as when I met the film producer Sam Spiegel, who came into Fabiani's salon with a young woman. With a bit of a smirk, he introduced us, "Grace, this is Mr. Sam Spiegel. Mr. Spiegel makes pictures." After which, Sam Spiegel, who happened by then to have made pictures that included *The African Queen* and *On the Waterfront*, absolutely charmed me by defiantly gesturing with his hand to make a frame and then saying, "Not this kind of picture."

By then, I was in demand myself, the kid from *Vogue* who, thanks to Tish, knew everyone on the diplomatic circuit and, thanks to Simonetta and Fabiani, knew the whole fashion world

too. I became a kind of magnet for visiting Americans in the fashion world who wanted to get plugged in and find out where the
best parties or the best collections were. I was introduced all
around, and it was wonderful for me both socially and professionally, because the manufacturers who back in New York would still
have been out of my reach now became people I socialized with,
and who depended on me, even, to help them get their bearings in
Rome. The contacts were invaluable, and they started paying off
right away in Rome when Sally Kirkland, the former *Vogue* editor
and war correspondent, who was by then the fashion editor for
Life magazine, began hiring me to do freelance fashion sittings in
Italy. For my first shoot ever, I traveled to Portofino, a resort fish-
ing village on the Italian Riviera, where we stayed in a lovely
mountain villa right across the port from the Hotel Splendido, and
I put together a wonderfully funny, bright, and charming story
about Italian "play clothes"—lots of striped T-shirts and short
slacks and bathing suits and pretty girls in sandals, all shot up in
the hills. Down in the port there were wonderful shops including
an ice cream parlor that had a special sundae made from strawber-
ries and ice cream which one of the models absolutely loved to eat.
She would start at 11:30 in the morning and, to our horror, would
continue all day. Which proved to be quite a problem because, as
the days went on, you could see the weight building on her body,
forcing the photographer, with each strawberry sundae, to keep
having to crop the picture, higher and higher up from her hips.
She piled away such an incredible number of the things that finally
we gave up and included a picture of her eating as part of the
shoot. And the sundaes became a fashion accessory.

Doing that shoot elevated me, for the first time, fully into the
ranks of a working fashion editor. It was a great leap forward from
editorial credit checking. I was thrilled, and Sally Kirkland must
have liked my work too, because after I'd spent about a year in
Rome, she asked me if I'd be willing to come back to New York
and be an associate fashion editor for *Life*. Her offer couldn't have
come at a better time. Much as I loved Rome, sometimes la dolce

vita had become a bit too much—like during couture week, when Simonetta and Fabiani joined all the Italian designers in showing their collections to the stores of the world and the press, and then followed up on their shows with marvelous parties that lasted well into the morning. The parties, which were often held in enormous palaces flowing with champagne and filled with music and dancing, were enchanting, and often deadly affairs—as I learned, one morning, when I nearly overslept on the very first morning of selling in Florence and woke up, at 9 A.M., only because Bergdorf Goodman's president, Andrew Goodman, called me to ask if I wanted him to bring back anything to my mother in New York. The episode scared me enough that I've never again overslept a day in my life, and it also set me to wondering if I was perhaps getting a bit soft in the brain. I was having so much fun that, in my anxious way, I was starting to feel that I had to be doing something wrong. It was clear to me that much as I loved Roman life, it was indeed a holiday and that if I wanted to get on with my career, there was serious work to be done back in New York.

Divided within myself as to what to do, I sent a cable to Bettina Ballard. I kept it brief: "Thinking of coming back. What think?" Her response, which I received in just a few hours, was even briefer. "Come back."

You didn't second-guess Bettina. I packed my bags and kissed la dolce vita good-bye.

CHAPTER 4
UP THE
LADDER AT
VOGUE

I came back from Rome full of Italy and vaguely dreading living again in what I now considered the charmless United States. On the plane, as the skyscrapers of New York loomed menacingly closer, I plotted out all the ways I would keep my new *dolce fa niente* lifestyle going once I was back at home. I decided to take long lunches, to see my friends for an *aperitivo* every evening, and to tool around town in my new little Fiat, which was currently crossing the Atlantic by boat. That happy resolution lasted about as long as it took me to get from Kennedy Airport to Maplewood, where the moment I stepped out of the car, I could hear the telephone ringing. I swept up the stairs and into the house—Gucci shoes flying, burgundy Simonetta coat trailing behind me in a way I hoped was simply fabulous—and ran into the entry foyer.

"*Pronto*," I said as I lifted the receiver, having returned to the states, as so many young travelers to Europe do, having forgotten how to speak proper English.

"Grace?" It was Sheila Kilgore, a good friend from *Vogue* and a loyal source of gossip. "You won't believe what's happened."

"What?" I said, English restored. "Tell me."

"Bettina's quit. Everyone's in an uproar. Jessica Daves is changing things, and no one here knows if she'll have a job tomorrow. How was your flight?"

I felt my anxiety level returning to normal. *Buon giorno* New York.

I called up Sally Kirkland and told her that I'd be glad to accept her generous job offer. The next day I entered the Time-Life Building for the first time. I told myself that at *Life* I'd have twice the stature I could hope for at *Vogue*, even *if* Jessica Daves were to offer me a job, which, in the current state of things, seemed less and less likely. I did such a good job of cheerleading myself that after I finished filling out forms in personnel and submitting to the usual physical exams, I really did feel enthusiastic, and decided to pop in on Sally Kirkland.

Sally was curt, but I knew how temperamental fashion editors could be and didn't worry about it. I went home, and was busy working on savoring my last bit of Roman mellowness when the phone rang with a call from a cool and abrupt Sally. She said she'd called to say that upon reflection she'd decided that I wasn't right for the job.

"I'm sorry, Grace," she said, not sounding sorry at all. "But we just can't have anyone here looking the way you did when you came into the office yesterday."

"What do you mean?" I asked.

"That *sweater*," she said. "Let's just forget it."

I was dumbfounded. The *sweater* wasn't some ratty old thing I'd pulled off the back of a chair on my way out the door. It was one of a group of absolutely super knit pieces that I'd brought back with me from Rome. It was fuchsia and black, with a boat neck, long sleeves, and truly incredible striping, and had been designed by Laura Aponte, who happened to be one of the best Italian sportswear designers of that decade.

Could Sally Kirkland possibly not have known a Laura Aponte sweater when she saw one? I doubted it. Something else was going on. I began to suspect that Sally hadn't had the right to hire me in the first place, and was now casting about for reasons to cover up her mistake. After all, in the magazine world, covering up a mistake by blaming an underling is standard procedure. But that suspicion didn't keep me from spending a few agonizing days pondering the fact that I was not only jobless but clearly *style-less* too. Before I had time to get into a serious funk, though, my problems were solved. Jessica Daves came through with a job.

It wasn't exactly glamorous. I was to be the *Vogue* "Shop Hound"—the person responsible for finding out what special and charming new things were being sold in the little shops in places like Madison Avenue and Bucks County, Pennsylvania, and on the North Shore of Chicago and telling readers how to send away to buy them. I was so excited to be back at *Vogue*, and so eager to stop shop hounding and impress Mrs. Daves enough that she'd let me do some fashion editing, that I took to my job like a virtuoso, tramping up and down Madison Avenue, befriending store owners, cultivating phone contacts, and generally proclaiming my love for *Vogue* through a devotion to shopping that was truly remarkable— especially as I'm not a good shopper. And, after about seven months on the job, it paid off. Jessica Daves promoted me to the rank of junior fashion editor. At twenty-five, I was *Vogue*'s youngest fashion editor ever. Never mind that it was only in the bathing suit market. I had *arrived*.

People on the outside of the fashion world—we on the inside always call them "civilians"—often have trouble understanding what it is that a fashion editor does. Part of that lack of understanding is snobbism. I found that out shortly after I became a fashion editor at *Vogue* and *The New York Times* ran a story about me, which they titled "Editors Who Never Write Staff Fashion Magazines." Their take on me—"Though she's called an editor and listed as such on the masthead, she never lifts her manicured fingers to a typewriter"—stands out in my mind to this day for all it says about the way "real" journalists look at fashion journalists and how far down their noses that look goes.

The truth is, there isn't that big a difference between what general interest journalists and fashion journalists do. Which isn't to say that fashion journalists aren't an odd breed. Who else can talk of the "hand" of a fabric (the way a fabric feels against the hand), or the "tonalities" of a stocking, or the "glory" of a dress, or the "texture" of a look? Who else could become terribly interested in things that are "matte," and spend meeting after meeting discussing what it means for an item of jewelry to have "natural dullness" and how to photograph it? Fashion editors can see how a twisted suede belt with a gold edge tied around the waist of a tweed jacket "lifts" the tweed, "creates" the texture . . . or they can see how the tonality of a leg blends with the hem of a coat, how the opacity of a stocking draws out the shine of a shoe. They can see things that other people don't even have the words to describe. And they can find fashion logic, indeed, they can find fashion history, in just about anything. They're not beyond crying, or sighing, or clapping, or fainting over that history-in-the-making, either.

But beyond all the trappings of atmosphere, the slight sense of fevered hysteria that pervades every fashion department I've ever worked in or seen, what fashion magazine editors do is report and write stories, just like any other journalist. In our case, however, the reporting consists in going out and seeing manufacturers and

designers, checking out what's going on in lingerie or shoes or accessories or separates, then "editing" that "text" of reported material not just by choosing words, but by sorting through racks of
clothes, and then picking the clothes that fit together to make a
coherent story in pictures. In a successful fashion feature, the pictures, rather than the verbal captions, tell the story: through their
setting, or their style, or their lighting, or their mood, they make
the clothing speak—not just about a way of looking, but about a
way of feeling, or of being.

You have to be a truly marvelous stylist to be able to make
clothing speak. Babs Simpson was that kind of stylist; I never was.
While I could put together a decent shoot—assemble the clothes,
work with the model and the photographer, and while I could always judge well what was or wasn't a good picture, I just didn't
have the creative flair it takes to be a great sittings editor. What I
was particularly good at was thinking things through and seeing
things through, working "just a little harder and longer than anyone else," as someone not-so-flatteringly once put it—something
that Jessica Daves, lonely at the top with her flighty staff of peacocks—clearly appreciated. She kept promoting me and promoting me, from the bathing suit market to knitwear, and then to
sportswear and better sportswear—which was where the action
really was in the late 1950s.

That action started every weekday morning in the coffee shop
in the sportswear building at 498 Seventh Avenue. There, from
eight o'clock on, you could sit at the counter with a cup of coffee
and watch as all the best names in American fashion drifted in and
out, eating, smoking, making deals, and checking the pulse of their
friends and competitors before beginning their workdays. There
was Ben Reig ordering coffee for takeout; Ben Klein, Anne Klein's
husband, reading the trades. There were the knitwear men: Mike
Geist and Bob Goldworm.

It was like being in the center of the marketplace in an old
Jewish village in Eastern Europe—only here, the Jews were victori-
ous, prosperous, jocular, beaming, and glowing with tans that

grew deeper each winter as the trips to Miami Beach increased and the white-on-white shirts they all wore to offset their tans grew whiter. There was arguing, buying and selling, and eyeballing and trading. Maybe someone had five bolts of lace he didn't need and wanted to trade it for some gabardine. Maybe someone else wanted to get rid of some coat lining. Maybe the factory workers were on strike across the street. There'd be grumbling in the coffee shop and then, quietly, coffees would be hand-delivered to the striking workers; bosses would stand in the cold by the picket lines asking questions about workers' wives and families, swapping stories.

The fact that there weren't yet any star designers, that the manufacturers, prominent and rich though they were growing, were first-generation immigrants still a bit rough around the edges and eager to please, meant that doing business with the men of Seventh Avenue wasn't a matter of seeking an audience through an army of publicists and assistants, but rather came down to knowing when to pull up a chair in the coffee shop and join in the conversation. It meant knowing how to joke and talk business all at once—and, above all, how not to take the lofty business of being *of Vogue* all too seriously. All I had to do was close my eyes and pretend I was with my father and his *Guys and Dolls* friends. It came naturally.

After breakfast, if I had calls to make and no change, I would drop into Bill Blass's office at Maurice Rentner and use his phone, then leave him teasing notes like: "It's 8:45. I'm here, where are you?"—virtually guaranteeing that if he had something new to show that day, his first thoughts would be of me. I'd drop in on my good friend Bob Goldworm over at the knitwear building at 1410 Broadway, admire his marvelous fabrics, knitted in Italy, and his new, revolutionary knitwear designs, and then would beg him to cash a five- or ten-dollar check for me so that I could have some money for lunch. In full sight of whoever happened to be in his showroom—models, buyers, competing editors—he'd slowly peel one dollar after the other off his billfold, then dangle them over my head, saying: "The proof! The proof! I want everyone to know, she's on the take." Or he'd hold on to the checks and not cash them, bring them down to the coffee shop and flash them around, asking, "Anyone want Grace's check? I'll sell you a ten-dollar check for nine bucks, because at *least* I'll know I'll get the nine bucks."

The joke stuck—and it played—because there *were* a good number of fashion editors then who were "on the take." They took clothes, they took cash, and in exchange they gave favorable mention to a manufacturer's collection. I'm sure that this still goes on today; and, in a sense, the fact that the whole industry runs on the mutual dependence of designers and magazine editors means that the line between building a good business relationship and inappropriate largesse is, and has always been, a very easy one to cross. In the 1950s we market editors worked so closely with manufacturers that it was particularly easy to blur the line between professionalism and personal advancement. Some fashion editors began to take themselves for designers, with what could be disastrous results. Some manufacturers took the fact of a close working relationship with *Vogue* as an excuse to demand special treatment editorially.

It had everything to do with the smallness, the informality, of Seventh Avenue then. In the 1950s fashion editors were intimately involved with how manufacturers developed collections, the directions they took with design, the colors they chose, and how they were going to make what they were working on work for their magazine. The idea was to find five or six designers and really stick with them, from season to season and from line to line, giving them thoughts, filling them with optimism, stirring them to do the kind of work you wanted to see. If you were covering a certain manufacturer, you'd drop in on his designer—who was, after all, an employee and not a media star—and you'd check out fabric swatches and drawings and sketches; you'd debate and argue and admire and suggest, never push but always suggest, ways that a line could be improved. You didn't do this, of course, with the up-market dress and suit makers like Ben Zuckerman, or with the Clare Potters of the business. You did it with the newcomers, who were hungry and coming up. And even so, you had to be very careful not to give offense. The key, I found, to doing this was to borrow a Condé Nast habit and offer up opinions in the form of questions, things like: "Do you really want to do skirts that are that long/that short?" or "Do you really want to do colors that look like the mold under a rock?"

How to tell the owners of Kimberly, a very successful and wonderful knitwear company, that their new line was less than wonderful that season? I agonized and came up with: "Listen, last year you wrote *My Fair Lady*. This year you didn't." And they thanked me for it. Even Ralph Lauren, at the dawn of the designer era, was someone you could sit down and just talk to: I remember once letting drop that I'd just walked by a billboard in the theater district that showed Margaret Sullavan leaning on the headboard of a bed looking absolutely marvelous in a pair of white men's pajamas, and a few months later I saw a line of men's pajamas for women on sale in Bloomingdale's.

Sometimes you'd get shouted out of a showroom. And then, later in the day, you'd get a phone call: "Come back tomorrow. I'm going to show you something else." Or: "Listen, I've just found a fabric. I've found my colorings. Come down and look." And like that, you'd start building relationships and building up trust, and the fact was that working together was good both for the manufacturers and for *Vogue*, because *Vogue* needed good clothes to show and the manufacturers needed *Vogue*'s power to sell their collections. Mike Geist, for example, a good knitwear manufacturer, was always willing, no matter what his production schedule, to drop what he was doing and make up whatever it was that we needed—turtlenecks or halters or cropped knitted tops—because he knew that, once they were featured in *Vogue*, they would sell.

Vogue's power couldn't be underestimated in those days. If we said it was the year of sweater dressing, everyone was in knits. If we said hemlines were falling, they fell. It was a sign of the times; clothing wasn't about personal expression, about the freedom to be—as it became, ostensibly, in the early 1970s. Clothing was about looking stylish and *appropriate* according to the very set demands of different settings and different times of day. You could use phrases then like "coffee table shoes"—shoes I always said belonged in coffee table books—or "over-the-table necklines"— necklines that looked particularly good when viewed at El Morocco from the tabletop up—without sounding ridiculous. Because women really did want to be told what to wear when, and when *Vogue* was doing the talking, they listened. Before the 1940s and 1950s, all fashionable women dressed in Chanel and Balenciaga, or in Courrèges dresses or in Ben Zuckerman suits—because that's what the women were wearing in *Vogue*. And the women with less money and as much desire for style bought high-fashion knockoffs at Ohrbach's and the look was the same. That's why, when *Vogue* began promoting sportswear, it was an event. The terms of appropriateness changed; you weren't going to start dining at The '21' Club in the same clothing you'd wear to the Automat, but you *could* go in a tweed jacket and a plaid skirt. Clothing became *sportive*, and women followed.

Jessica Daves was often mocked for saying that what brought about the moment of sportswear in American fashion was the fact that cars had gotten smaller and that women needed more comfortable clothing so that they could get in and out of them. It was a rather pedestrian way of putting things but, in reality, it wasn't far off the mark. One fashion invention of the late 1950s—the culotte—really did come about to enable women to move in and out of cars with greater ease. And sportswear *was* about movement. It wasn't clothing for women who languished, or who lounged on their settees—the favorite pose of *Vogue* fashion models in the 1940s. In the 1950s the women of *Vogue* were shown modeling separates alongside shiny red Cadillacs. The inference was that America was on the move, and so were they. (We didn't realize just *how* "on the move" they were.) And they needed clothing that could get them places. Which isn't to say that the women of *Vogue* were hopping off the page into boardrooms; they weren't.

But they were at least branching out beyond their living rooms. What sportswear, and its presence in *Vogue*, acknowledged was that even the debutantes, society matrons, and women of leisure who were *Vogue*'s stock readers *did* thing sometimes, and needed clothing for living in the world. And this acknowledgment, partial as it was, marked a profound shift in *Vogue*'s thinking about women. It was an awareness that women needed to live in the world—a conviction that I would try to bring into force and up-to-date two decades later.

However unfashionable, however old-fashioned she might herself have been, Jessica Daves brought *Vogue* into the post-war era and positioned it so it could survive in an increasingly democratic America. A career woman, with no particularly great social aspirations or standing, she was perfectly suited to the "real world" message of sportswear. But, as I would learn time and again through the decades, what makes an editor great in one era can be her downfall in the next. And as the 1960s dawned and the Beatles invaded and a tidal wave named Diana Vreeland was unleashed upon *Vogue*, *Vogue*'s women of the 1950s—Jessica Daves, Mildred Morton—fell out of favor. Jessica Daves was shuffled upstairs with the title of "editorial adviser," which was a polite way of saying she'd retired, which was a polite way of saying that she'd been let go.

With Vreeland in as editor and Daves out, I kept waiting for the other shoe to drop. And, for a while, it looked like the next casualty might well be me.

According to legend, Diana Vreeland's career in fashion began when *Harper's Bazaar* editor Carmel Snow saw her dancing one evening on the St. Regis Roof and was so taken with her white lace dress, bolero jacket, and crown of red roses that she knew she just *had* to make her an editor. That story may or may not be true, but it probably is. Other things that are true are that Vreeland was born Diana Dalziel to the Scotsman Frederick Young Dalziel, a stockbroker, and Emily Hoffman, somewhere around the turn of the century. ("Age is terribly boring and . . . so American I can't get on with it," she liked to say.) And it's probably true that she spent her early childhood in Paris and came to the United States just before the First World War. Whether or not she really grew up, as she claimed, with such companions as Diaghilev, Nijinsky, and Isadora Duncan and, in lieu of a formal education, studied ballet with the Russian choreographer Michel Fokine and horseback riding with Buffalo Bill Cody is a matter of faith. As was much having to do with Diana Vreeland.

When Diana Vreeland began working at *Vogue*, the whole air, the entire sound of the place, changed. Diana Vreeland didn't just sweep down the hallways, she loped. A stream of orders, barks of laughter, and bits of commentary announced her arrival at each doorway she passed. Her voice was low and throaty. It projected, hornlike, into every office. She moved in a murmur of cashmere, long skirts and cowl necks and shawls, always the best fabrics, the deepest colors, always smartly draped around her long, lean form. Her hair was jet-black, her lips and cheeks scarlet.

The walls of her office were a deep red too, with black-lacquered furniture and leopard rugs and upholstery. When she was in, she burned Rigaud scented candles and incense. When she worked, she kept her desk bare, save for a single stack of lined notepads, which never were filled beyond the first page. Every day, Vreeland ate a peanut butter sandwich for lunch with a half-melted bowl of ice cream. Then, a nurse came and gave her a vitamin B-12 shot. It was said that her maid ironed her newspapers and her dollar bills, blackened the soles of her shoes to make them look like new, and washed and ironed her bed sheets every morning while she took her bath. That kind of order, it was said, was how Vreeland kept her mind clear. Clear of the messy workings of everyday life; filled with the ephemera of her imagination. Whether or not all of this was true, we ate it up.

It didn't take long before half the office was moving, and standing and dressing and speaking, like Diana Vreeland. Sittings became a day at English riding school or a night at the Paris Opera Ballet. The office became a sort of *Lady in the Dark* stage set, all grand opera and movie glamour and make-believe, breathtaking beauty and mind-numbing pronouncements and heart-wrenching exclamations on whatever subject had seized Vreeland's imagination on any particular day. Everything was "duhvine" and "moving" and "extraordinary." New colors—"deep clay pink," "a deep shrimp," "the lapis lazuli of Catherine the Great," were added to our mental palettes. Clothes had to be "adventurous and amusing."

"We are in show business," Vreeland declared, "and exaltation must preside."

Nothing Vreeland said was subject to question. If she said, "The world is black," *Vogue* showed black and we didn't discuss it. If she said, "Pearls are large," they were large and that was that. Her personality expanded into a kind of web that caught us all up and became the personality of the magazine. For some, being spun out in the magic thread of Vreeland's thought was sheer enchantment. For others it was pure torture.

At first I could not stand Diana Vreeland. I knew her face from the rounds of fashion shows and showrooms we both passed through in the late 1950s and early 1960s. She'd never acknowledged my nod; it wasn't her style. I knew her work from the pages of *Harper's Bazaar*, where she'd been a contributor since the 1930s. She was someone who, while my family and millions of others were struggling through the Great Depression, had written a column called "Why Don't You?" in which she'd made such timely suggestions as: "In your drawing room, have a mirror table like Miss Constance Collier's, with a diamond pencil so that your guests can sign their names in the glass . . . have your bed made in China . . . wash your blond child's hair in dead champagne, as they do in France. . . ." She'd risen to prominence as a fashion editor during the war years, when leather was rationed and she made fashion history (and Capezio's fortune) by putting the women of *Harper's Bazaar* in ballet slippers. She'd discovered

Lauren Bacall and Halston, and had popularized the turtleneck sweater. By 1962, when she first came to *Vogue*, she was already a legend, immortalized by Kay Thompson's "Think Pink"-singing portrayal of a flighty fashion editor in the movie *Funny Face*. And yet, the rumor was that when Carmel Snow had retired as editor in chief at *Harper's Bazaar*, she urged the men running Hearst Magazines to pass Vreeland over for the job, arguing that she lacked the discipline and judgment to head a magazine.

When I first heard that Diana Vreeland was coming to *Vogue* as associate editor, I resolved to get as far away from her as possible. I'd been promoted by then to the dress market, a coveted assignment usually saved for more senior fashion editors. The dress market was made up of houses like Harvey Berin and Ben Reig and Patullo, solid, well-respected manufacturers of expensive women's dresses. It was the world of Norman Norell, where the shows were dirgelike black tie events, where one sat on a little golden chair and piously and solemnly considered the greatness of the designer's work. I always felt like I'd died and was attending my own funeral. I had asked for the dress market because it had seemed like the grown-up place to be, a stepping stone on the celestial passageway that would lead, one day, to covering the godlike Ben Zuckerman. The dress market, I thought, was mature. Once I got there I realized it was moribund. Norell was doing chemise dresses, dresses under jackets, and homages to Chanel, and despite his great tailoring, his dresses made women look old.

As an editor, you couldn't collaborate, you couldn't suggest a bit of modernity to the likes of Norman Norell. Norell harbored no discussion. He allowed no contradictions. He permitted *Vogue* to photograph his clothing on the sole condition that he first choose the shoes and accessories, and he sent a fussy woman along as a chaperone every time his clothes left his showroom.

There was no joking around, no gossiping, no sending out for coffee with the dressmakers. There was hushed silence, broken only by the sound of gloved hands clapping after collection showings. I was bored beyond all belief. And the dress crowd found the idea of having a thirty-year-old "kid," hot out of the sportswear market, combing through their illustrious showrooms for *Vogue* downright insulting. Perhaps, as they saw sportswear eating up more and more of their market share, they thought *Vogue* was trying to send them a message. And perhaps they were right.

The specter of Diana Vreeland's arrival was the last little push I needed to beg that Jessica Daves take me out of the dress market. "Marketing" was the hot new word in town, and though I didn't quite know what it meant, I figured it had something to do with merchandising, and that had always interested me. So I asked Jessica Daves if I could be named fashion marketing editor, a new position that she had just created.

"If that's what you want to do," she said warily, "we'd be glad to have you. But I warn you, once you leave the fashion department for the business side, you may never get back in again."

I said I didn't care. Vreeland was in, and I wanted out. So I spent a year in marketing, dodging Mildred Morton, who was once again my boss, being absolutely miserable and pining so for the fashion markets that when Vreeland was promoted from associate editor to editor in chief of *Vogue*, in January 1963, and shortly afterward asked that I return to her stable of fashion editors, I came flying without a backward glance.

Mildred Morton was less happy with the decision. She had by then added to her arsenal of weapons the power of the transatlantic phone call, and after I made my announcement and went on vacation to Italy, she called me at every stop along my itinerary, on every single evening of my trip, and tried to talk me out of it.

It was torture. I was on a wonderful trip with my mother, driving from Milan down to Florence. We stayed at a magical mountaintop inn at the same time as Elizabeth Taylor and Richard Burton, and were deeply flattered by the fact that when they saw my name in the register and somehow found out that I was from *Vogue*, they read "press," and dodged us at every turn in the dining room, lounges, and pool until finally, in desperation, they left the hotel in such a hurry that their car ran off the road and landed in a ditch. It was the first time anyone ever accused me of being a journalist and I found it very exciting.

Less exciting was waiting hours and hours by the phone for Mildred's calls to be put through. Mildred being Mildred this one last time convinced me that no matter how bad Vreeland might be, she couldn't be any worse. But part of me did, nonetheless, sympathize with Mildred's plight. She was seeing the end of the merchandising oriented age of magazines, an era she had worked so hard and so successfully to bring about. She believed that *Vogue*'s lifeblood was Seventh Avenue, and had trained me to succeed her in that belief. Vreeland treated Seventh Avenue as if its lifeblood were *Vogue*. And now I was defecting to her side.

What I hadn't realized was that being a fashion editor for Diana Vreeland would prove to be like no fashion editing I'd ever done in my life. In the past, my job had been to comb my market, find the best picks of the season, bring the clothes into the office, wheel them into Jessica Daves's office, and then, in a meeting called a "run-through," present them, making my pitch for why I needed six or eight pages of the magazine. At my first run-through with Vreeland, I selected three racks of dresses and presented them, making a case for a story about how the look of dresses that season was wool jersey. Vreeland listened, not saying a word. At the end I asked her if there was a problem.

"Well," she said, "I wasn't looking for a market report. I thought you were going to *give* me a little something."

"Like what?" I asked. I thought I had given a good deal.

"A *little something*," she said. "A *dream*."

I went back to my office and hung my head in my hands. How was I supposed to turn a Harvey Berin cocktail dress into a dream? Vreeland had made some suggestions: "Go back into the market and think about *what might be*. Think about putting women in bias black. Or in things with hoods. Or in chemises and long skirts over pants. Think about what might be wonderful."

"What the women who shop in my market want is quite simple," I said. "They want us to tell them what Norman Norell wants them to wear and where to find it."

"If that's the case," Vreeland said, "I have a solution for you. *Give 'em what they never knew they wanted.*"

What Vreeland wanted didn't exist in my market. Often, it didn't exist at all. She wanted a fantasy, made real in fabric. If the look didn't exist, she'd invent it, and she'd leave it up to us, her fashion staff, to find a way to produce it.

I tried. I combed the markets. I forced myself to think about fashions that didn't yet exist. When I looked to the dress men for ideas, they looked at me as though I were crazy. I gave up. And a few run-throughs later, Vreeland threw in the towel too.

"It isn't that you're not doing a highly *professional* job, Grace," she said as she took my market away. "It's just that . . . I think you're a sportswear person at heart."

If I'd been more of a fan of Vreeland, I might have found her delicate way of demoting me to be rather charming. But I wasn't, and I didn't. And I wasn't so foolish that I couldn't read between the lines. Vreeland was a pure product of the Parisian couture. She'd been brought up on it. Her tastes were as aristocratic and European as mine were democratic and American. Her disdain for the middle class was as strong as her distaste for the concerns of everyday life. Daily life, she always said, was one of the most boring things one ever could conceive of; why would *Vogue* want to have anything to do with it? Ready-to-wear barely qualified as fashion in her book. She called sportswear "boiled wool," said ready-to-wear fabric was "like the covering of an old tennis ball." In labeling me a "sportswear person," she was hardly paying me a compliment. She was sending me a signal. As a fashion editor, my star was on the decline. As, soon, was my ability to occupy the same breathing space as Diana Vreeland.

Vreeland liked to do retakes—two, four, ten—the cost was immaterial. "I'm looking for the *suggestion* of something I've never seen," she'd say, poring over photo retakes in the photographer's studio late at night. She was willing to hold up an issue, rack up thousands and thousands of dollars in models' overtime, photographers' fees, and film processing costs, just to get a look she thought was "duhvine." On the job, this meant twelve-hour days, shortened tempers, snappish models, enormous waste, and, for me, a deep conviction that Vreeland was making life at *Vogue* virtually unlivable.

In her quest for perfection, Vreeland ran me ragged. My taste was never good enough for her. My sittings always had to be reshot. Once, she sent me to Old Westbury, Long Island, kept me out there for a day, and then demanded a retake. So I reassembled the clothes—turtlenecks and trench coats—and I pulled together the photographer and my model, and I prevailed upon Vreeland to allow us to do the retake under the George Washington Bridge, because it was faster than going all the way out to Long Island. We set up again under the bridge, on a kind of island of land between the road and the river, and we worked, and I sent messengers downtown to Vreeland with Polaroids of our shoot, and every hour I had to cross the goddamned highway to go find a telephone to call in to see if she'd seen the pictures and was satisfied. She never was. First, the coat was too long. Then, we'd tied a scarf too tight. A turtleneck was sagging. The sun was too high. Then too low. After the sixth take, on the third day, as the sun began setting, I ran across the West Side Highway once more to a pay phone under the George Washington Bridge and told Vreeland that we were done.

"Oh, no, you're not," Vreeland said. "Have you see these pictures? You've ruined the texture of the coat by showing it with that jersey glove. Reshoot it with leather gloves."

"They *are* leather gloves," I said, shouting above the traffic noise. "You just can't see them in the Polaroid."

"I *can* see them," she snapped. "And they're wrong. If they're leather, give me jersey gloves."

"Get someone else," I said. "I can't take this anymore."

She laughed. "You most certainly can. And you *must*."

That evening I slogged into the office, my shoes covered with mud, and confronted Vreeland in her office as she was preparing to go home.

"Why didn't you just give the sitting to someone else? Someone else who could have done it better than I?" I asked. There were by then editors, newcomers to *Vogue* who had trained under Vreeland at *Harper's Bazaar*, who could do her bidding and loved to.

"I could have given it to someone else, Grace," she said, "but I didn't. I knew that you never would have forgotten the fact that you hadn't finished this sitting properly. You really would have regretted it."

I decided to let the word out that I was looking for another job. I went up to the Drake Hotel and met with Bill Fein, the publisher of *Harper's Bazaar*, and Nancy White, its editor, and they made me a very enticing promise: that if I came over to *Harper's* as a fashion editor, I'd be named the next editor in chief of the magazine. The offer was impossible to ignore, but hard to accept too. For one thing, I knew the magazine world well enough by then to have learned that promises made by higher-ups counted for very little, since no one ever knows if they'll still be around when the time comes to make good on them. I also balked a bit at the idea of leaving Condé Nast to work for Hearst. When you work at the Smith College of magazines, which *Vogue* most certainly was, it's very hard to take any other publication seriously. There's something habit-forming about introducing yourself as being from *Vogue* and seeing strangers bow slightly in deference, something indisputably wonderful about having your calls taken automatically, all the time.

So I said no to Hearst, and then regretted it, and snapped up a job I was offered by the bathing suit manufacturer Catalina. It was a job that demanded no creativity and paid a great deal of money (by *Vogue* standards, at least) and it seemed the perfect antidote, like a drying-out period, to the delirium of Vreeland. I said nothing to anyone at *Vogue*, and was about to formally accept when Vreeland stopped me one day in the hall and said, "It's not the job for you."

I was taken aback. What could Vreeland possibly know about me? It turned out that she knew a great deal.

"You wouldn't be happy working in the marketplace," she said. "It's too grubby for you. You need style, intelligence, a little *pizzazz*. I know that." She also knew that I'd turned down a job at *Harper's* out of allegiance to *Vogue*.

"You belong at *Vogue*," she said. "We will just have to find the right place for you."

The encounter had taken all of two minutes. Vreeland had been so straightforward, so honest and direct, that I wondered if it had all been a figment of my imagination. I got my answer a few months later when Vreeland stopped me in the hallway and asked me to lunch. As lunch, for Vreeland, was normally that crustless peanut butter sandwich prepared by a secretary and eaten at her desk, I suspected that something was up.

She took me to the restaurant in the Graybar Building. She put her watch on the table next to the ketchup and ordered her sandwich. Reassuring herself about the time, she looked up at me and asked if I would be her assistant.

I didn't know what to say. I didn't know whether to be insulted or to laugh. What did Vreeland mean by "assistant"? Did she mean for me to be her secretary? That was unimaginable. It would have been an unthinkable demotion. In the past two years I had become a kind of spokeswoman for *Vogue* on Seventh Avenue. I had traveled around the country, speaking at fashion shows and *Vogue* promotional events at department stores about the new revolution in sportswear. When *Vogue* held an unprecedented fashion show at the Ambassador Hotel on Park Avenue, where we exclusively focused on dressing in separates, I was the one chosen to commentate to an astonished room of store buyers. And when an envoy was needed for a trip to Australia, to give two weeks of fashion interviews at David Jones Ltd. and work with Bernie Leser, then publisher of Australian *Vogue*, on breathing some life into that magazine, I was the one who was chosen.

In Australia I'd been treated like a local celebrity, my photo affixed like a banner to the newspaper's "ladies' page," my evenings in Sydney filled with social events orchestrated by Dale Turnbull and David Jones and his wife, Rosemary. I'd worked on a series of sittings with an important new photographer, a German-Jewish refugee from Berlin who was desperately trying to make ends meet taking pictures for fashion magazines. His name was Helmut Newton, and meeting him was an entire education in the recent history of Europe's Jews. When we met, his eyes still had the haunted look of a displaced person. His mentor, the photographer Yva, had been killed at Auschwitz. He had fled Germany in 1938 and had ended up in Australia via Singapore. Helmut told me about how, just after his release from an Australian displaced persons camp after the war, he had wandered the streets of Melbourne, frightened and alone, and had cried, because there were no cathedrals, there were no grand old houses or monuments or boulevards. It all looked so unnaturally *empty* to him. And that sense of emptiness still dogged him, fifteen years later.

While I was working with Helmut, I was approached by Bernie Leser and his boss, Reggie Williams, and was asked if I would like to accept the post of editor in chief of *Vogue* in Sydney. The offer was thrilling, but impossible: I was expected to turn around Australian *Vogue*, expand it and update it and reenergize it, all the while cutting costs and reporting every expenditure, whether for pencils or phone calls or staff, back to the home office in London. I'd said "no thank you." But the fact that there could be more to *Vogue* than Seventh Avenue and the Graybar Building had stuck with me.

Now I wondered at Vreeland's offer. What, exactly, did she want with me? She didn't like my sittings. She didn't have much interest in my take on style. Could she really mean for me to answer phones and take messages? Would she address me, as she did her secretaries, as "Miss! Miss!"? I was thirty-three years old, and I wasn't about to start making peanut butter sandwiches for *anyone*. It seemed like she was trying to force me out.

"If you're looking for another secretary or another assistant, then you've got the wrong girl," I told Vreeland.

She answered, "If I wanted that, I wouldn't have asked you."

She said she was looking for an associate, someone to help her with the day-to-day running of the magazine. And as she talked, it dawned on me that this "assistant" job was Vreeland's back-handed way of giving me a promotion. There was something about me that Vreeland clearly wanted to have around. She didn't neces-sarily want to have it around in a studio or at a sitting, but she wanted to have it around to help her get a magazine out. And buried in there was some sort of a compliment.

"I admire your honesty," she said simply. "I know that I can give it to you straight, and that you'll do the same with me. And that's what I'm looking for. That is precisely what I need."

Could there be another Diana Vreeland—a thinking, rational Vreeland—behind the gossamer veneer? I'd thought so once be-fore. But I was reluctant to put my trust in that woman. I hated the idea of hitching my professional future to a wish, a hope for a person who, up until now, hadn't seemed to exist. And could I bear being holed up in the *Vogue* offices all day with Vreeland? Then again, did I really have a choice?

I couldn't imagine how to turn a legend down. And after a day and a half of agonizing, I told Vreeland that I would take the job.

She smiled her bewitching smile.

"It's going to be a grand adventure," she said.

CHAPTER 5
LIVING
THE LEGEND

*"Her outline is splendid. Her proportion unique
with the small round head, long throat and legs
but she can look as if she was walking toward a
strange destiny which I am sure most Swedes
are."*

DIANA VREELAND
Memo to staff on "the walkers,"
October 3, 1969

I t was the 1960s at *Vogue*.

It was: lunches at the Colony Club
with Jackie Kennedy and her sister, Lee,
and Truman Capote lurking in the background, collecting gossip.

It was: Andy Warhol with Candy Dar-
ling, Viva and the whole Factory crew
smelling like unwashed underwear and
pot, milling around the *Vogue* offices with
a camera.

It was: Mona Bismark and Wallis Simpson calling for Vreeland on the telephone. And Twiggy dropping into the office with her bodyguard "Teddy the Monk" and her manager, Justin de Villeneuve, who just a few years earlier had been a London hairdresser called Nigel Davies.

It was: go-go boots, miniskirts, psychedelia. Face painting, Veruschka, "space age" fashion. The Beautiful People and the New Talent—*princesses* and *principessas* and Mick Jagger and Cher.

It was: stories coming back from the studio of models too stoned to stand up. Or of models who came back from the bathroom with their makeup all smudged around their noses. Models throwing temper tantrums, stealing fur coats. And no one knowing quite what to do. Or where to go. Or whom to talk to. And everyone eventually bringing everything to me.

"Grace." It was Alex in the art department. "We've got to kill all the pages of Gia's swimwear shoot. She has track marks all over her arms!"

"My God, Grace!" It was Vera in the studio. "A great dane took a bite out of Geoffrey Beene's dress!"

"Miss Mirabella." It was Jade Hobson, a new accessories editor. "There's a designer here refusing to show his stuff until he reads everyone's palm. Please help me get rid of him."

An accessories assistant, her palm read, was crying. The lingerie editor was crying. Another assistant had flown out of the office, shouting, "I can't take it anymore!"

Did I have any Kleenex?

And then, there was Vreeland, 7:30 A.M.:

"Gracie, dear, are you up? It's Dee-Anne. I went to a Donovan concert last night. Yes, *Donovan*. It was one of the most moving, extraordinary things I have ever seen: an entire audience of young girls with the most marvelous hair. Marvelous orange, marvelous red, marvelous black, marvelous chestnut. What do these girls eat? How often do they shampoo their hair? Have they ever cut their hair? How many years' growth is on those heads? Send someone to the public schools of New York to find out."

And so it went.

Every morning, before she left home for the office, Vreeland dictated a series of memos over the telephone to her secretaries. *How come all hats now are beige? How come shoes have no proper heels anymore?* By the time I arrived at the office, the memos had been typed up and circulated, and the editors were up and running, furiously uncomprehending.

What was this stuff about the shoes and the hats? What did she want? What did she mean? Where *was she*?

"Grace, I don't know what I'm supposed to be doing this afternoon."

"Miss Mirabella, what is 'Matisse blue'?"

"Grace, Alex is confused."

Diana Vreeland had inherited an office from Jessica Daves that ran like clockwork. Miss Daves not only was highly organized, she also believed in letting her staff know what she was doing and what to expect next. Vreeland didn't feel that everyone in the office needed to be in on her train of thought. So whereas the entire chain of editorial decision—view of fashion, choice of cover, choice of content and presentation—used to flow easily from the editor in chief to the fashion editor to the art department to the merchandising department, no one knew what was going on, from one hour to the next, with Vreeland but Vreeland. And me.

"Grace, Mildred would like to see you."

"The art department is annoyed."

The art department was always annoyed. Nothing could be sent off to press without Vreeland's signature, and that signature, since she almost never came into the office before noon, could be rather hard to come by. Merchandising, where Mildred Morton labored away in a perpetual state of rage at Vreeland's lack of interest in maintaining the store contacts she had worked so hard to establish, was hostile territory too, and sent barbs my way whenever possible. She too did the features department: Allene Talmey, a powerful wordsmith who had terrified generations of *Vogue* writers into maintaining a standard of excellence, found working with

Vreeland just too taxing and eventually quit. Even Alex Liberman, now the powerful editorial director of all the Condé Nast magazines and who had hired Vreeland, often found he couldn't work with her.

Many of his contemporaries—managing editor Carol Phillips, the old-time fashion editors like Babs Simpson, Cathy di Montezemolo, and Nicky de Gunzburg—were put off by Vreeland too. I saw the Baron once feign a heart attack when Vreeland asked him to cut a train she didn't like off a Bill Blass dress. "Madam," he said, "I'd rather die." It was hard for these editors, who had spent decades working in tandem with the manufacturers on Seventh Avenue, to accept Vreeland's reality-bending creative style. The Baron, for one, didn't hide his feelings. "Oh, Nicky, what *is* the name of that designer who hates me so?" Vreeland once asked him. "Legion," he answered.

The Baron was right.

The manufacturers of Seventh Avenue, who, working in tandem with *Vogue*, had grown rich and powerful in the boom years of the 1950s, didn't take kindly to the way that Vreeland did business. For Vreeland completely revolutionized the way fashion magazines worked. In the past the top couture designers dictated looks and fashion magazines executed them. You never embellished the look. Your job was to make sure that the coiffure was right, the shoes were shined, and the dress looked good. You did not reinvent anything.

Vreeland made fashion out of her dreams. If her dream for the fall was Veruschka as Queen Christina, the Greta Garbo character in the movie by the same name, and no appropriately Garbo-esque costume was available on the market, then a Queen Christina wardrobe had to be made. If her dream for the winter was "Arctic White," and no adequately Snow Queen-like costume could be found, she'd commission one, and the end result in this case was a medieval-looking white evening cape with a hood edged in white mink, a sort of helmet and gloves of silver sequins and long *"prin-*

cesse dress" which, unfortunately for the reader, happened to have been shown on the page under the cape and wasn't at all visible.

It didn't really matter: none of the clothes Vreeland commissioned for these shoots were actually destined to end up in any stores. And if they did—if Vreeland managed to prevail upon a manufacturer and a store buyer to reproduce some of the numbers featured in *Vogue*—they never sold. They were clothes for striding heroically across the Arctic Circle—not for hailing a cab in the snow on Park Avenue. They were sheer entertainment, marvelously perfected looks that raised the craft of fashion sittings to the level of filmmaking, but gave the reader little beyond the page. And for Seventh Avenue, and for the stores that depended upon *Vogue* to inspire their customers, they were the kiss of death.

It enraged designers to see their new creations passed over for coverage in *Vogue* in favor of figments of Vreeland's imagination. But sometimes they were even more upset when Vreeland *did* use their clothes. James Galanos, for one, used to call complaining bitterly that he was losing clients because of the way his clothes were shown by Vreeland's *Vogue*. Norman Norell became very angry when Vreeland had a model wear a beautiful evening dress of his with boots. These incidents, plus the frequent letters from readers who complained that they couldn't find anything from *Vogue* in the stores and couldn't recognize the clothes in the magazine, didn't make my life any easier. For I received the phone calls. I read through and answered many of the letters. It fell to me to explain to the stores and the manufacturers—and to management—why we were showing, say, a girl with no eyebrows and purple hair wearing sportswear, to make a crooked story idea seem straight.

I was Vreeland's shadow, her alter ego. I was the morning check-in point for her fashion editors, the ambassador to Alex Liberman. I was the one who translated Vreeland's thoughts into practice. This meant, in a sense, being able to read Vreeland's mind. If Vreeland cabled to me from Paris, "Personally adore word shawl as suggests the crack of flamenco, long evenings on the grand canal, the embroideries of china and a very positive legend of feminine allure . . . Whistler's mother never spent the nights of which I speak throwing her shawl on and off," I had to tell the fashion editors: "We're going to do a romantic, sensual feature on the new, marvelously colored shawls." And sometimes the editors got it, and sometimes they didn't. And if they didn't, and if they came out of Vreeland's office after a run-through bloodied and beaten and nursing their wounds, as I had so many times at the start, I was the one who handed them coffee and Kleenex and told them to fight on.

Vreeland's run-throughs often were like feeding lambs to a lion. They might as well have taken place in the Roman Coliseum. Models were brought into Vreeland's office, racks of clothing wheeled in; Vreeland sat in the middle of a kind of semicircle surrounded by her most senior fashion editors, her assistants, and me, all of us frowning and taking notes and looking menacingly harsh as we bit our tongues out of sympathy for our hapless colleagues. You'd see a young Jade Hobson who had worked for weeks on trying to find the most perfectly exquisite belt for Vreeland being told that it was terrible, then going out and custom ordering a belt to Vreeland's specifications, only to be told when she presented it at the next week's fashion meeting, "This is trash. Find me something like that *duhvine* belt you showed me last week!"

There were many tears, many casualties. More than one editor threatened to throw herself out a window after a run-through with Vreeland. Secretaries quit left and right. The office atmosphere was somewhat less than congenial. Editors jostled for favor with Vreeland and tried to bury each other in the process. I'd hear screams all the time from the closets where the fashion editors kept the clothes they were putting together for run-throughs: "Who took my black knitted dress? My green platform shoes? My amazing purple bodysuit?"

Editors pilfered each other's clothes for stories; they battled over who had what turf. Normally, each editor had a clearly delineated portion of differently priced clothing markets, with certain designers and manufacturers who were hers alone. But if a certain style was "hot" in one season, it was fair game for anyone who could make a case for it in her story. If this meant theft, or duplicity (older editors would go through the closets of younger ones, offering to "edit" the clothes the novices had gathered), so it was. The laws of the jungle ruled, and only the fittest prevailed.

This, in itself, was nothing new. I'd learned, early on in my career at *Vogue*, how competition for page space could turn the most well-bred young ladies into the cagiest sharks. One "good friend," when we were both growing up through the sportswear markets, had showed no shame about protecting her own turf like a mob boss and raiding mine at will. When I had covered the knitwear market—a "hot" area in the late 1950s—I'd often found, after weeks of work, that nearly half of the clothes I'd assembled for, say, a story on little black dresses would have disappeared, only to reappear in a run-through of "my friend's" own little black ideas.

Vogue was high drama, amateur theater. Everyone was trying to be "adventurous" and "amusing" and "Up . . . up . . . up!" to please Vreeland. Everyone was a star. It was a sign of the times. Vreeland was the first fashion editor as celebrity. Twiggy and Jean Shrimpton were the first celebrity models. "The Twig" and "The Shrimp," plus Penelope Tree, Marisa Berenson, and "Baby Jane" Holzer, with their untraditionally beautiful faces and angular, waiflike bodies, were the look of Youth, the look of the go-go 1960s. Veruschka, the German countess, whom *Vogue* liked to show photographed in body paint and little else, was the look of sexual liberation.

Photographers were becoming big stars too. Bert Stern could only work with ten assistants in his studio. If one of them fell sick, he canceled. Richard Avedon, a protégé from Vreeland's days at *Harper's Bazaar*, soared into absolute prominence through his collaboration with Vreeland at *Vogue*. And he developed an ego to match.

Managing Avedon's ego was one of the most distasteful aspects of my job. It was a constant hassle, a continual fight. Dick liked to control a shoot. He liked to keep his contact sheets and send us only the two or three pictures that *he* thought should run. Grace Kelly used to do something like this too: she always demanded the right to see her pictures after a sitting and would either slash the ones she didn't like with a pair of scissors or simply make off with them in her purse. This was rather annoying. But then, she was a princess. Avedon was just a royal pain. He liked to take our ideas and spin them, "give 'em a little something," as Vreeland would say, only the little something he gave was often enough not what we were looking for at all. For Dick, a sheerly beautiful picture of a girl was too banal. His pictures had to be arch, fresh, blatantly sexual, sometimes so arch, fresh, and sexual that they were ugly and distasteful, and if that was the case, it always fell to me to tell him. He achieved some of his best effects with girls who were utterly strung out on dope, and this sometimes made even Alex uncomfortable. But I was the one who had to come off as the "square." If we needed a retake, *I* had to cajole him. Or if he wanted to get out of a sitting that would have taken him to, say, the center of Jordan, I'd have to remind him of the pages he owed us, of the terms of his contract, of his responsibilities toward *Vogue*.

All of which meant that Avedon considered me Vreeland's pencil-pusher and treated me with all the disdain due to someone in that position. Irving Penn, on the other hand, was a dream. He was someone who talked straight about assignments. If he didn't understand an assignment, he didn't try to reinvent it like Dick Avedon, who was always sure he had a divine insight into the supremely marvelous. He didn't have a demanding ego. He was a minimalist, tough and demanding of his work, and his pictures were stylish and extraordinarily beautiful.

I always considered Penn a seeker of truths, whether it was in taking photographs of working men in American cities or of mountain people in Peru or in taking fashion photographs. He wasn't interested in razzle-dazzle; he wanted pure, exquisite form.

Though this meant he was much more pleasant to work with than Avedon, it didn't mean he was an easygoing sort of guy. I remember one torturous session when I spent an entire day at Penn's studio with a famous French hairdresser who had flown in from Paris. It was a time when if a French hairdresser came into town, you booked him to spend the day showing you what was the wonderful hair of the moment. We were supposed to be doing a sitting of his styling ideas for that year's hair. But Penn hated everything the man did, and each time our model, her hair styled, was put in front of the camera, he would look through the lens and shake his head. Which would mean that the girl would have to go back into the makeup room and the hairdresser had to keep redoing her hair. All day long.

And of course, the more the hair was redone, the worse it looked. In the entire day Penn did not take one picture. He could have shot some film just to make it look as though something were going on. But he didn't see anything to shoot, and he wasn't one to stand on ceremony. And so this poor man, who was spending just a few days in New York, had his whole day wasted. I was absolutely mortified.

After preparing a sitting with Penn, I had to worry about things like whether Avedon was going to protest that his pictures couldn't face Penn's or whether Avedon was going to claim that Penn was trampling on his turf. This kind of behavior would have been unthinkable in photographers working for *Vogue* in the past. But Avedon was the first of a new breed, the photographer as star, and his emergence as a power broker on the scene marked a moment where everyone in fashion—models, photographers, designers— was becoming stars, and a new celebrity culture was taking root that would later change the whole way that magazines like *Vogue* did business.

I didn't like the drugs and the starstruck attitude of the new celebrity age. But I *loved* the glamour. It was a new kind of glamour, the glamour of the inside crowd, the crowd that knew everyone and everything. Society was starting to change; talent and money and success were taking the place of blue blood and debutante balls as tickets to desirability. The look of things was changing. There was a special kind of electricity in the air in those days. You felt it when you went to get your hair done by Kenneth, or went to Bendel's on a Saturday. Everywhere you looked was a parade of marvelous-looking, wonderfully dressed people. *Vogue* was their nerve center.

Being at *Vogue* as an editor also meant being *of Vogue*. And that did great things for you socially. It meant that you were received wonderfully everywhere. Your good looks, your wit, your sense of style—the things that had gotten you to *Vogue* in the first place—kept you afloat in the closed world that *Vogue* lived off of. Even I, who would not, I believe, have been considered a "delightful young woman" in *Vogue*'s extended world on my own merits (I worked too hard; I was *from Newark*), by the early 1960s was enjoying a wonderful dose of desirability by association. And it was just as good as the real thing.

Even better—a great perk of being *of Vogue* was that you didn't have to have money to live like the people in *Vogue* lived. *Vogue*'s larger world seemed to have a vested interest in making sure you lived up to the *Vogue* name and, given the fact that we at *Vogue* were grossly underpaid, made the best things in life available to us *on the cheap*. I bought the latest clothes at or below wholesale cost from the best manufacturers because I was an editor at *Vogue*. I lived in a charming brownstone apartment, with high ceilings and French windows just off Fifth Avenue, and paid half the rent it was worth because it was leased by someone affiliated with French *Vogue*.

It was a delicious life, and socially, by the early 1960s, it was moving in a lot of interesting directions. Vreeland's friends—the Duke and Duchess of Windsor, Mona Bismark—were still just names to me, voices on the phone. And what I'd seen so far on my own of European aristocracy hadn't really thrilled me. I'd met the Rothschilds in France one summer through Françoise de Langlade, who was then editor of French *Vogue*, and my prevailing impression of their party, assembled for a weekend in the country at one of their châteaux, was of people who couldn't even lift their heads from their bridge game to show some visiting Americans how charming they were.

But then, they were the old world, an older generation. I was making friends my own age, the kinds of friends who had houses in Newport and would invite me up for dinners and dances and weekends in the fall and for swimming at Bailey's Beach in summertime. I'd stay with Patsy Green, a friend who moved through the fashion world with a rather lackadaisical sort of ambition, in the big house she owned with her husband, Fitzhugh, on Bellevue Avenue. Their crowd, in which the Bouviers stood out as Catholic "ethnics," was more all-American, more purely WASP, than any other I'd ever encountered in New York. I never felt so very Italian as when I went to balls at Newport, never so much a native Newarker as when, to the great amusement of my dinner companions, I misread my silverware and turned down the main course of dinner by thinking that it was an appetizer.

All the intersecting circles started coming together then: Oyster Bay and Dale Turnbull and Newport and *Vogue*, Tish and my Italian friends, who were still floating in and out of New York, working on Wall Street, dining at the Stork Club and El Morocco, and who found a semipermanent rallying point in the city when my friend Cathy Murray divorced McManus and married Alessandro, becoming the Marchese di Montezemolo. There were evenings at the Park Avenue apartment of my *Vogue* pal Denise Lawson-Johnson, a divinely zany young woman who eventually married the fashion illustrator René Bouché; her home was always filled with young Englishmen and Italians. There were also nights out with Seventh Avenue men like Bob Goldworm, who hung out in restaurants with names like Danny's Hideaway and went to football games and casinos and in every way reminded me of my father's gambling crowd. People weren't yet all coupled up and hosting formal dinners at home, and it was easy and fun to be a single woman in New York, dating various men, tied down to none.

There was no question that along with its raciness the Seventh Avenue crowd had its seedy side, and it was known to regularly claim a certain number of female casualties. Sad to say, my good friend Sheila Kilgore was one of them. She was an extremely pretty girl who always had a beau or two or ten and lived a kind of quadruple life of secrets and odd assignations and lies, many of which would ensnare me on the weekends when, before I had my own place in town, I would stay over with her in her apartment in Murray Hill and field phone calls from her boyfriends. It was an almost painful job: the manufacturers I knew as calm and professional men by day were calling, tears and rage in their voices, to track Sheila down. Eventually she came to a very sad end. I heard, a few years later, that she'd had a kind of breakdown and had been found in a motel in the Hamptons lost and destitute. It was the kind of cautionary tale that mothers told their daughters then about life alone in the city. No one needed to tell it to me.

I always had a soft spot in my heart for racy, nightclub-hopping men. I met them everywhere in those years—up and down Seventh Avenue and at the Town Tennis Club, a place that was equal parts social and sports club, and which had become a kind of second home for me in the late 1950s. The Town Tennis Club drew a wonderful crowd—tennis players like Sidney Wood and Don Budge and Dick Savitt—and it was the kind of place where you would show up to play tennis on Saturday morning and then hang around all day—partly for the gossip, I always used to say, and partly because you didn't dare leave, lest the tongues turned on you. Through the Town Tennis Club, I met and dated Hank Greenberg of the Detroit Tigers, who, like many at the time, had friends who showed up at The '21' Club with a box of hot jewelry which they hoped to sell cheap. I also found a great companion in Bud Sweeney, who was sales manager of a film distribution company owned by his former father-in-law, George Skouras, and was plugged into a racy, sports-minded crowd with Irish-sounding names like Reynolds and Riordan who hung out in places like Toots Shor, and were always in and out of all the good restaurants in New York. They were the kind of people who, when I lived in a studio on East Fifty-fourth Street, could arrange to have food sent up from Sardi's if I was home sick. I loved their style, their swagger. But I also knew how to keep my distance. It was as though I had absorbed from my mother the lesson of knowing that there were men you had fun with and men you wanted to marry. And so far, I was coming up short on the latter.

The glamour of *Vogue* followed me everywhere. It guaranteed me a first-class seat on transatlantic flights (themselves a glamourous event in those days) and ushered me with special care into the plane's dining room, where dinner was served by candlelight. It followed me overseas—to Italy, where I still spent many of my vacations, and to London, where Vreeland sent me a few times a year as her ambassador to the city's flourishing new fashion scene.

Before the 1960s, British fashion had been a matter of cashmere sweater sets, shapeless tweed skirts, and mufflers. But then Beatlemania hit, and the mods (short for moderns) took over the fashion scene and brought with them a sense of irreverence, a passion for their own youthful energy, and a feeling of mobility, freedom, and fun. Vreeland called this the "Youthquake"—it was youth as she liked it, extravagant and wildly attractive, and with notably little to say about the issues of the day—and she found it much more attractive than its angrily ugly American counterpart. "There is nothing against which to rebel," Vreeland said of the fashionable British youth. "Therefore, they are relaxed and happy."

The look of the "Youthquake" was fashion as fun: miniskirts and tights, short vinyl slickers, tight ribbed sweaters, pale lipstick, and false eyelashes. Its epicenter was King's Road and Carnaby Street in London, in shops like the Biba Boutique and Quorum and Mary Quant's Bazaar, which Mary described as "a kind of permanently running cocktail party." As Vreeland's emissary I was a kind of permanent party guest. I'd fly over and stay at the Connaught, a grand old hotel whose concierge treated me as though he were my own doorman back home and where, if I wanted to take the pulse of the London scene, all I had to do was spend my first evening in the lobby and dine at the restaurant, and I'd be sure to see everyone I wanted to see. Anyone I didn't see at the Connaught I'd find the next day at Vidal Sassoon's salon, where all the models, actresses, and photographers of London were in and out every day.

Sassoon's signature cut was revolutionizing hairdressing: it was geometric, like a wedge, cut long at one end and ending at a point at the chin. It took its shape from precision cutting, not from the "set," which created a look that was young and free and very much of the moment. Girls used to line up in the street outside Vidal's salon. Watching him cut hair was a spectacle. His assistants were spectacular too. They modeled themselves on Vidal so closely that when they cut hair they struck all his poses, made the same grimaces and gestures as he did. Their training sessions were like lessons in mimicry. Vidal tilted his head, they tilted their heads; he frowned, they frowned; he flicked a shock of hair out of his eyes, they did the same. Add to this the scene by Vidal's juice bar—the first of its kind—and you had a sort of circus, an ever-moving feast of the young and very attractive. And everyone was smiling.

After a morning at Sassoon, I'd go visit Zandra Rhodes or Mary Quant or Thea Porter. They were working on romantic, rather Edwardian clothes: slender pants with shirts with ruffled sleeves and long narrow jackets that were made of flimsy, hard-to-identify fabrics that were supposed to take the "stiffness" out of British dressing. The clothing wasn't always spectacular, as might be surmised by the fact that virtually none of the designers of that moment have survived to this day, Vivienne Westwood, Jean Muir, and Zandra Rhodes being notable exceptions. But even if the clothing were lacking, the London scene was terrific. The Angry Young Men were putting on plays that made Broadway's efforts seem like children's theater. Anabelle's was taking off as a place to see and be seen. The crowd I always loved, fashionable people contributing to and taking pleasure from life, was perpetually in and out of the city. Through good friends in the fashion and publishing communities—Felicity Green with *The London Daily Mirror*; Melanie Miller, originally from *Glamour*, then with British *Vogue*; Bettina McNulty, formerly of *Vogue* New York and then also with British *Vogue*; and Fleur Cowles, founder of a fanciful magazine called *Flair*—I was introduced to everyone I needed to know. I met Vanessa Redgrave, perpetually in character for her opening in *The Prime of Miss Jean Brodie*, and with Norman Parkinson did the best sitting of my career of Vanessa dressed in white ruffled blouses on the grounds of an old palladian estate outside London. Through Felicity, I met a man named John Addey, a publicist, who lived at the end of Bond Street in a wonderful old house called the Albany. John Addey quickly became my chief unofficial reason for returning so frequently to London. And he almost became a reason for my staying there permanently.

Diana Vreeland liked to call 1962, the year she began working at *Vogue*, "the year of the jet, the Pill." "A completely different social world was being created," she used to say. And, on the surface, at least, her *Vogue* seemed to embrace that changing world. Vreeland sought out a new, young, what we would now call "multicultural" look for *Vogue*. She brought sex into the magazine, she brought rock 'n' roll, and the drugs, of course, followed on their own. And for the first five years of her reign, youth and newness bounced off *Vogue*'s pages. The magazine was alive, buoyant, and charmingly fresh, in a way that perhaps it had never been before.

But then, somehow, it wasn't enough. The Vietnam War protesters were raging, and women were marching, and "flower children" with painted faces and Penelope Tree dancing around in a white wig just didn't seem to be enough anymore. Women were protesting the Miss America pageant in Atlantic City and throwing their bras and girdles away in a trash can (none were actually burnt), and suddenly Twiggy in a tiny T-shirt dress didn't seem so wonderfully liberating anymore.

The problem was that Vreeland's hold on history, her take on society, was all style. Woodstock, in *Vogue*, was concert pictures juxtaposed with a reprint of Manet's "Le Déjeuner sur l'Herbe"—an effect that was charming, very clever, very beautiful, and, ultimately, completely missed the point. Black nationalism was wonderful afros and models wearing dashikis. Third World-ism was girls in djellabas and harem pants, rajah coats and Nehru jackets. Sexual liberation was a nude Veruschka in body paint, and something purple called "The New Love Hair." The so-called sexual revolution was a reason to encourage women to spend more time and money on perfecting their bodies.

When Vreeland found out that American women were de-manding equal treatment with men, she put them in "unisex" clothing and discovered pants, namely, Yves Saint Laurent's mar-velous new pants suits. Pants didn't signal anything new that Vreeland was feeling or thinking about masculinity or femininity. They were just a stunt, another game, playing off a fantasy version of one of the major issues of the day. But then, Vreeland *didn't* think about the issues of the day. For her, the 1960s were mini-skirts, maxi skirts, love beads, flowers on the face, gypsy dressing, psychedelia à la Emilio Pucci, false eyelashes, go-go boots, and *youth, youth, youth*. And she loved the moment so much and found the spirit of youth so intoxicating that she was the last one to notice when it became old.

She herself was becoming older—approaching seventy—and the fantasy of youth and exuberance seemed to blind her. When, in 1968, the moment of dressing up like a Native American ended, and "street" dressing fell to gutsy, bold, and serious designs from a new generation of designers like Halston and Bill Blass, Vreeland closed her eyes and continued serving up a now silly-looking stew of flower children and fantasy. When Yves Saint Laurent intro-duced a new way of dressing in pants, a kind of precursor to warm-ups done in cashmere and shown with flat gold sandals, she turned up her nose at the new, chic, and modern way of dressing and continued seeking out her fantasy styles. Although *Vogue*'s readers had long made clear that they didn't really like the bizarrely pretty, child-woman faces of the Twig and the Shrimp, Vreeland kept them on the magazine's covers. Makeup artists started refusing to draw flowers on their faces, and hairdressers started begging her not to ruin their reputations with more blue hair, but she persisted. Even her slang became dated. Her trademark outrageousness became passé.

Vreeland had always liked to call *Vogue* "the myth of the next reality." It was her way of convincing herself that her inventions were meant to exist. But the real world was changing in a way that had nothing to do with Vreeland's myths. Women were changing, their needs were changing, *Vogue* was becoming more and more out of touch with their lives. Women were entering the work force for the first time in record numbers. They needed something to wear. And they wanted something they felt good wearing, something that, they could feel, expressed *them*. Mary Quant once summed up the moment very well, I think: "Until that stage, either women would be their father's little daughters, their clothes paid for by their fathers, or they were the wife of the doctor. This was probably the first time women had their own careers—and therefore dressed for themselves."

What Vreeland had to offer them was purple vinyl raincoats, see-through blouses, silver ankle boots, and body stockings. The message was: she didn't care about the "new woman." And *Vogue*'s readers took that message to heart. Animated by the anti-fashion hippie spirit of the time, and the message from the women's movement that fashion magazines were The Enemy, they turned their backs on *Vogue* and simply stopped buying the magazine. Newsstand sales plummeted. The women stopped shopping. And, in the first three months of 1971, sales of advertising pages at *Vogue* fell nearly forty percent.

The problem, of course, wasn't just Vreeland. Similar drops in readership and ad revenues had been reported at *Harper's Bazaar* and the entire industry had been hit by the country's general business recession. But when Si Newhouse (now in charge of the Condé Nast magazine empire) and Perry Rustin, Condé Nast's president, looked at the numbers, they saw Vreeland's face. Alex Liberman had by then had enough of Vreeland too. He had for years been begging her to rein in her spending, to strive for a more "accessible" look in her fashion pages—work that burned him to the very core of his being. For Alex was allergic to money talk; he thought it was crass, inappropriate for a "class" publication like *Vogue*, and, in normal circumstances, a needless cause for worry. He had always been backed up by management in his belief that *Vogue*, as Condé Nast's flagship publication, could afford to lose some money to the cause of remaining on the cutting edge of art and style. The problem was, Vreeland's *Vogue* was losing so much money that even a Condé Nast cash cow like *Glamour* couldn't sustain it anymore. And *Vogue* wasn't on the cutting edge, Alex thought, as the back-to-basics 1970s dawned. It was simply decadent.

Vreeland's behavior was starting to seem decadent too. When she traveled to Paris for the couture, she refused to work in the *Vogue* offices on the Place du Palais Bourbon and insisted instead on converting her suite at the Hotel Crillon into an office, moving furniture out, running in phone lines, setting up big working tables for herself, Paris bureau chief Susan Train, Susan's assistant, and her own two secretaries, and sending bike messengers around the city with film at all hours of the day and night. She insulted some of *Vogue*'s best French advertisers by refusing to go to their collections, and attended only the fashion shows of her favorites, like Saint Laurent and Balenciaga.

She sent David Bailey to India to photograph white tigers for a spread that never ran. She rejected another series of pictures he took of Penelope Tree on the grounds that there was "no languor in the lips."

Her work habits were incredibly expensive—something that only a strong economy could sustain. Inventing a look like "Queen

Christina" or "Scheherazade" meant drawing up a Concept, finding fabric swatches, commissioning the clothes, working out the accessories and hair with all the different fashion editors, dress rehearsing the look in the office, sometimes with the actual model, and Polaroiding it, so that every detail would be absolutely perfect on the day of the sitting.

Vreeland had always sent editors on extremely expensive trips to exotic locales for *Vogue*'s special Christmas issue. These trips took a tremendous amount of planning. They often had to be arranged through the State Department, which, despite travel editor Despina Messinesi's wonderful connections, could take months to approve visas. Then, to clear customs, we had to put together a carnet listing every single blouse and dress and shoe and earring and bead that we were taking out with us, and make sure that we had every single item upon our return.

Usually, Susan Train would be sent out on the trips from our Paris office. Susan was very disciplined but Vreeland had no faith in her creativity. So we'd Polaroid every single aspect of the sitting for her in advance: we'd write out every step and fit every skirt and hat and shoe on the model, often redressing her and re-Polaroiding the clothes late into the night as Vreeland found last-minute inspiration. The model bills and the Polaroid bills were gigantic. The transportation costs were too. For if Vreeland insisted, as she once did, that Susan Train use an enormous hat for a particular sitting in the Himalayan mountains, then that hat, in its box, was carted uphill, by car and by Jeep and by camel and by donkey, until it reached the top in one piece. Irons and ironing boards also had to be carted around. Which meant more expense, and more time spent, on the top of a mountain or in the middle of the desert, keeping the model standing around preparing for a shoot. I recall traveling once to Iran with Henry Clarke and spending my every evening untangling and smoothing out hundreds of old French curtain tassels that I'd brought along to create an ornamental look. The glamour of these assignments faded very quickly.

As time went on, the trips grew wilder, and expensive glitches became more common. Perhaps the most expensive came when Babs Simpson traveled to Peru with a couple of models, the photographer John Cowan, and the hairdresser Ara Gallant. They were taken by helicopter to a mountain peak in the Andes, where Cowan, an English photographer of the abrasive *Blow-Up* variety, planned to get pictures of the models in evening dresses and chinchilla coats looking like they were floating on the clouds. Their helicopter pilot told them they'd have to leave the mountaintop by five o'clock, or else an army search team would come out after them. Five o'clock came, though, and Cowan refused to stop, and the pilot took off, leaving the group at the top of the mountain at nightfall. Babs, who had vertigo, found a path down the peak and led Cowan and the models, climbing down in their high heels and Maximilian furs. After a while they found a little hollow and lit a fire, and spent the night huddled together under the furs. The next morning they found the Peruvian army waiting, absolutely furious, and pointing to the ground. It was covered with mountain lion tracks.

It was up to me to explain to Alex that Vreeland didn't arrange such disasters on purpose. That wasn't easy. For Alex didn't trust Vreeland with anything anymore. I was eventually sent to Paris in her place. I was in charge of explaining her exploits to Seventh Avenue. And I was the one who had to worry about saving Vreeland from herself, once Alex made it his mission, in the early 1970s, to "save" *Vogue* from Diana Vreeland.

I might have seemed an unlikely person for the job of saving Vreeland from Vreeland, given the fact that I had been, at the beginning, one of the most anti-Vreeland people in the office. But that was years before—years before our first conversation, years before our lunch, long before I began working hand in glove with her and discovered what the Vreeland legend was *really* all about.

When I'd first met Diana Vreeland, her legend had preceded her, and so, when she walked into the office at *Vogue*, I saw hair and nails and cheeks and galloping stride and understood little else. I heard the voice issuing what I thought were sheerly arbi-

trary, wasteful orders and I resented it. Diana Vreeland wasn't real
to me—and I disliked her unreality. But when I started working as
her associate, I began to hear the thought behind the fantasy. I saw
the process by which her creations were born, and I could appreciate the enormous thoughtfulness, the real intelligence that went
into the dream scenes she created. I realized what should have
been obvious and, due to Vreeland's own cultivation of her per-
sona, wasn't: that developing such outlandish schemes demanded
a real commitment to hard work and a meticulous attention to
detail. I also saw that the woman I'd twice half perceived and mis-
trusted—the straight, honest, perceptive woman I'd talked with in
the hall and at lunch about my job future—*was* real, more real,
in fact, than the frothy concoction she whipped into action every
morning to keep the game of being herself going.

Perhaps I had a privileged relationship with Diana Vreeland.
She'd hired me to be straight with her, she'd said; in return, she
was unfailingly honest with me. I never realized how much this
relationship mattered to her until one occasion when I let her
down. She had decided that it would be a great idea to photograph
a model getting a haircut. So she assembled the model and a hair-
stylist and a photographer and all her senior editors, and we stood
around in her office in our usual hawkish way, crossing our arms
and taking notes, as the poor girl was subjected to what I think
was the worst haircut that I've ever seen in my life. It got shorter
and shorter, and as we watched, I saw the girl's next modeling
assignments go straight down the drain, until finally I couldn't
take it anymore and walked out. At the end of the day, Vreeland
poked her head into my office, which was next to hers and, as she
always did, asked me if I'd like a ride home.

In the car she asked me, "Where'd you go earlier today?"

I said, "I just couldn't take it. That hair—the whole scene—it
was just too awful."

A look of exasperation and—something else—bewilderment,
perhaps, or even hurt came over her face.

With my mother,
Florence Mirabella,
at my graduation
from Skidmore
College, June 1950.
*(Photo courtesy of
Grace Mirabella)*

In Rome in the late
1950s. *(Photo courtesy
of Grace Mirabella)*

With Enid Haupt and Alex Liberman in Warren, Connecticut, in the early 1970s. *(Photo courtesy of Grace Mirabella)*

Choosing photos at *Vogue* in the early 1970s. *(Photo courtesy of Grace Mirabella)*

The legendary Diana
Vreeland. *(Photo courtesy
of Priscilla Rattazzi)*

With Bill Cahan in New York in the late 1970s.
(Photo by Pierre Scherman)

A front-row seat at the
Paris collections in the
early 1970s.
*(Photo courtesy of Grace
Mirabella)*

With Bill Cahan in
New York in the 1970s.
(Photo by Nancy Holan)

A wedding gift from Dick Avedon: a photograph of the newlyweds, 1975. *(Photo by Richard Avedon)*

With Leo Lerman (middle) and Joel Kaye, 1978.
(Photo by Alan Lewis Kleinberg)

With Arthur Elgort at the New School, 1982. *(Photo by Arthur Elgort)*

My portrait, by Hirschfeld, commissioned by Bill Cahan as a birthday gift and later used for the *Mirabella* launch, 1989.

With Yves St. Laurent.
(Photo courtesy of Grace Mirabella)

With Tipper Gore, Hillary Clinton, and Jerry Levin at the White House. *(Photo by Neshan Naltchayan)*

With Giorgio Armani, 1994. *(Photo by James R. Brantley)*

With Eli Wallach and Jerry Orbach at the Great American Smoke-Out, 1994. *(Photo courtesy of Grace Mirabella)*

With Hillary Clinton and Ralph Lauren, 1994. *(Photo courtesy of the White House)*

"Why didn't you tell me?" she said. "Why didn't you say something?"

For a moment her perfect posture fell. She slumped against the back seat. "What do I have you around for, if not to tell me what I need to hear?"

I never wanted to see that look on Vreeland's face again. Disappointing her was just too terrible. For I had become a real devotee. I'd become one of Vreeland's all-time greatest fans. I still didn't love her idea of fashion. And I never loved the Vreeland legend— the amalgam of curious details and wild statements and gestures and sayings: "Pink is the Navy Blue of India . . . The bikini is the most important thing since the atom bomb"—that people invoked breathlessly to sum her up, and which Vreeland once dismissed in exasperation, when an interviewer asked if it was true that she wore five coats of nail polish: "Don't you think this is tacky, discussing my fingernails at *length*! . . . I don't arouse interest in *anything* except how I have my nails done. I *hate* this stuff . . . I'm not a little . . . *fashion editor!*"

I don't believe that Diana Vreeland "reinvented herself" every morning, as some wag once said. To the degree that she was self-invented, she was constant and solidly so. The solidity of her invention was, I think, in part what sustained her. For her life was not the glorious carnival that she made it out to be. She suffered for having been born far from beautiful into a family of great beauties. She'd never had the wealth of her friends and began working as a fashion editor at *Harper's Bazaar* for the unglamorous reason that she needed the money. Although she adored her elegant husband, Thomas Reed Vreeland, and had lived an enchanted life with him among the smart set of Evelyn Waugh and Cole Porter in London and Paris in the early years of their marriage, in later years the rumor was that he was unfaithful to her and begged for a divorce. And although Vreeland liked to say, "Divorce is as glorious as caviar," she seemed not to really believe in it.

Diana Vreeland the woman needed Diana Vreeland the fashion

legend, and worked at her with the same passion, the same intense attention to detail that she brought to her professional life. Until, finally, the world came to view the woman and the legend as one and the same. And, sadly, since Vreeland's death in 1989, thanks to the work of such official guardians of the Vreeland memory as *The New York Times*'s Carrie Donovan, *Allure*'s Polly Mellen, both formerly of *Vogue*, and *Vogue*'s Andre Leon Talley, the fashion community has seen to it that the legend is all that remains. It's been heartbreaking for me to see Vreeland reduced to a caricature, her humanity lost in public memory. But that seems to be what fashion demands.

I did not love the image Vreeland felt she had to present to the world to make herself lovely and keep it loving her. But I loved, I absolutely adored, with what I can only describe as the passion of a schoolgirl crush, Vreeland the woman. I loved the fact that she depended so utterly and thoroughly upon me, that she put all her faith in me. I loved the fact that she made me so central to her life, and herself to mine. She was the first person I talked to in the morning and the last one at night. A day never came where we didn't speak at least twice. When I went on vacation, I called and cabled her. When she went into the hospital with gallstones, I wrote and called her constantly. She invited me to Sunday lunch with her family, and treated me like one of her children. When her husband died, she asked me to stick by her through the funeral. She gave me things of hers that she loved and that I had ad- mired—a Van Cleef watch made of teak, a rosewood and gold bracelet. She included me in absolutely everything—her every let- ter, every meeting. And I included her in my every waking thought. I wanted to do things for her, to please her, to anticipate her demands and alleviate her anxieties. I wanted to protect her.

By 1971, however, protecting Diana Vreeland had become al- most impossible. Things at *Vogue* were going from bad to worse. We sent a group out to Newfoundland one August to do a sitting of Shetland sweaters and kilts and flat shoes. The editor on the trip was supposed to be Mary Russell, a freelancer. But Mary got sick just before she was to set out, and Vreeland cabled me from Europe, where she was looking at collections, to tell me she'd replaced her with Anna Piaggi, a wonderful editor from Italian *Vogue*. Anna Piaggi had agreed to go to Canada on short notice, provided she could just finish the Paris shows, then stop off at home in Italy to get some warm weather clothes. I didn't worry about the shoot. As always, we had Polaroided everything in advance, and the Polaroid book was as detailed as a film's storyboard, and annotated down to the last detail. So when, a few weeks later, Alex phoned me one morning with real desperation in his voice, I assumed he was just trying to drum up trouble for Vreeland.

"What kind of clothes were sent to Newfoundland?" he asked. "I thought it was supposed to be sportswear."

"That's right," I said.

"Really?" he answered. "You surprise me."

"Sportswear classics," I said. I was annoyed. I thought he was about to suggest that Vreeland didn't know what sportswear was.

"Why don't you come down to the art department and take a look at these pictures?" Alex said then, very calmly. "I think that they might be of interest to you."

So I went down to the art department. And then I understood why Alex sounded the way he did. The pictures *were* of very stylish, gutsy classics. But Anna Piaggi, when she'd gone home to get her warmer, more "sportive" clothes to do the sitting in, had also brought with her a bunch of feathered boas—and she'd flung them all over everything! So these girls, in their Shetlands and kilts and good thick woolen stockings, were swathed in huge, bright-colored boas. The whole thing had become a "pastiche."

I looked at the pictures and my heart dropped. Alex, of course, thought the whole thing was Vreeland's idea. I convinced him that in fact it wasn't. I knew it was altogether possible that Vreeland had said to Anna, "Listen, dear, when you go home, if you have things that would amuse you to add to this, of course go ahead," but I didn't think Alex needed to know that.

And the boas were simply awful. In the end the pictures were unpublishable. And Vreeland, despite my best efforts, did take the rap. At that point everything she did was suspect.

Alex's attempts to save *Vogue* from Vreeland became more frequent and more ardent. He said she needed to start showing clothes at different price points. She'd come up with trendy junk and try to pass it off as charming. He started telling her that life could not always be lived on the level of *Aida.* He'd say Si Newhouse was distraught about newsstand sales. He'd stand before her desk and talk lower and lower until his voice was little more than a whisper. "Please, Dee-anne," he'd say, "listen to me. Hear what I'm saying." And she would take a phone call, or look at layouts, or laugh, very clearly, very dramatically, not listening. And not saying anything, either.

I used to beg her to go before Alex and Si Newhouse and speak her piece. Because I knew that there was an inner logic to Vreeland's apparent chaos. I knew that she had clear visions and solid plans. I also knew that Alex Liberman, for all his new talk about money, knew absolutely nothing about the business of running *Vogue.* Vreeland, I knew, had a much greater grasp of business than he did—if she chose to use it. And I knew just how close she was to being fired.

"Why don't you just go to management," I would say, "and give it to them straight, the way you tell things to me."

"No, Gracie," she'd answer. "I wouldn't do that. *You* tell them."

It was the Vreeland legend that ultimately did Diana Vreeland in. Because she simply *could not*, being Vreeland, allow herself to present herself to the outside world as someone who could hold a conversation about money. She could not allow the world to see her intelligence, the method behind her madness. She preferred to remain true to her image, to sink with it, than to compromise it by defending her vision.

To the end Vreeland laughed off Alex's attempts to control her. She'd return from Si Newhouse's office scoffing: "Well, the men have been complaining again, but I pay no attention to them."

And then she was fired.

CHAPTER 6
REMAKING
VOGUE

When the call came, I was in California, working on a sitting with the actress Sally Kellerman. Perry Ruston, the president of Condé Nast, left a message telling me to come back to New York and be in his office at nine o'clock the next morning.

I called my good friends Dick and Betty Dorso, and broke off our dinner date for that evening. I was sad to do so. We'd been friends for a decade, and before Dick and Betty had moved to California, we'd spent every Saturday and Sunday morning together, playing tennis and gossiping at the Town Tennis Club over by the Queensboro Bridge. Betty always loved hearing my Vreeland stories. She was a former model and fashion editor at *Glamour*, a very beautiful woman who had been featured as one of the twelve top models Irving Penn immortalized in a famous 1947 portrait for *Vogue*. Dick was a vice president of Ashley Famous and a very important player in the television world.

"I have to go back," I told Betty. "There's some kind of emergency."

"I suppose," she said, "that they're going to make you editor in chief."

"Where'd you get that from?" I asked, laughing. "In your dreams."

"Maybe," she said. "Good luck."

I caught the red-eye back to New York and arrived at the *Vogue* offices at 9 A.M. sharp. When I walked into Perry Ruston's office, I saw Alex Liberman was there too.

"It's been decided we'd like you to be the next editor in chief of *Vogue*," Perry said. My jaw dropped.

"Does Vreeland know?" I asked.

"Yes," they said.

I had my doubts. In fact, I felt as though I'd stabbed my best friend in the back. And as the days went by and the announcement was made official: "To relieve Mrs. Vreeland of the many responsibilities and duties of the day-to-day operation of *Vogue*, it is a pleasure to announce that Miss Grace Mirabella has been appointed editor of *Vogue*," I didn't feel any better.

Alex arranged for Vreeland to be kept on for six additional months, and to retain the title of consulting editor. This was partly for what the Italians call *bella figura* and partly, I've been told, so that she would have worked long enough at *Vogue* to qualify for her pension. Though she later made disparaging comments about red, white, and yellow Russians, she had no choice at that point but to be grateful to Alex, and she went quietly. She packed up her things and was moved into a smaller office upstairs, which she painted bloodred and stayed out of as much as possible. I sent pages her way that she'd worked on, sent up black and white photographs for retouching, and cowered, ashamed and afraid that I might one day run into her in the hallway and have to look her in the eye and *say something*.

So far, neither Vreeland nor I had said anything. And I knew that she wasn't likely to start. Her sense of etiquette, her pride, and her inbred feel for the right way of doing things would tell her that it was my place to make the first stab at communication. She was right. But I simply couldn't do it. I didn't have the heart, and my solution to the problem was to act as though Vreeland didn't exist. And Vreeland, knowing full well that only one person can be the head of a magazine, kept her "consulting" to a minimum. She might, in giving me back a photo spread, say something like, "I don't understand why you girls insist on showing those boxy handbags with those dresses," and I'd just say, backing out of her office without making eye contact, "I think it's okay."

She soon stopped offering her opinions at all. She knew that no one was listening. When her requisite work time was up, she kept her title but left the *Vogue* offices and took a four-month vacation in Europe. After that, she returned to New York and was asked to be a special consultant to the Costume Institute of the Metropolitan Museum. There, in her seventies, she had another landmark career, putting together exhibits on Balenciaga, Hollywood fashion designs, and Russian costume, to name a few. Her legend grew even larger. And she disappeared entirely from my life.

I am not proud of that particular chapter in my history. But in my defense, I have to say that, professionally, I had no choice but to make Vreeland disappear. Her legend was so great, and the resistance to me as her successor so widespread and so insidious, that I had to push on, at whatever personal cost, to establish myself, because there were just too many people gunning to bring me down.

The combination of simply being myself and not Vreeland was a deadly one. Since I wasn't a flamboyant fashion type, neither a socialite nor a raging clothes horse, it was easy for fashion insiders to write me off as something of a dud. John Fairchild's *Women's Wear Daily*, gearing up for the incessant nastiness that would make its name in the next decade, had begun oiling its guns as early as 1967, when it ran a dual interview with me and China Machado, a senior editor at *Harper's Bazaar*. The article was headlined "The Heiresses Apparent." China, a former model, had been born in Shanghai. She spoke seven languages and, in addition to maintaining her brilliant modeling and editing careers, painted, sewed, designed, cooked, hostessed, and had mothered "two fantastic children." Richard Avedon was quoted calling her "probably the most beautiful woman in the world." I, on the other hand, was described as a Gemini from New Jersey, best known to my bosses as being "keen on working" and "practical." The message was clear.

When I became editor of *Vogue*, the barbs continued. A colleague told *Newsweek* that I was a "nine-to-five girl." My old soulmate, Andy Warhol, let out the word that I'd been hired to succeed Vreeland because "*Vogue* wanted to go middle class." Hebe Dorsey, in an article about the editor switch that read like an obituary for Vreeland and barely mentioned me at all, summed up the mood: "The resignation of the high priestess of the fashion world in some ways marks the end to the era in which haute couture and its accompanying snob appeal ruled what people put on their backs . . . most insiders believe fashion will never be the same."

It was as though I was threatening to turn *Vogue* into the Sears Catalogue. Bulgari jewelers' Gianni Bulgari came to see me to share his concern about how the "vulgarization" of *Vogue* would affect his advertising. Even at *Vogue*, it was hard, at first, to establish my legitimacy. There had for years been a number of pretenders to Vreeland's throne, and I was never really counted as one of them. Cathy di Montezemolo always seemed a more likely choice. Carrie Donovan, who had trained with Vreeland at *Harper's Ba-*

zaar, hoped to get the job and worked hard to position herself as the only true heir to Vreeland's legacy. But wild accessories and crazy statements did not a new Vreeland make, and it was precisely this sort of outrageousness that Alex and "the boys" upstairs were trying to get away from. I think that Vreeland follower Polly Mellen, a great sittings editor in her own right, understood this. But Carrie Donovan, who had developed a kind of specialty doing gossipy fashion features on glitzy glamour, seemed so miffed when I was named editor that when she left *Vogue* for *Harper's Bazaar*, I always felt it was because of my promotion. And Babs Simpson always gave me the impression that she wondered how I'd been able to grab the editorship. She had protested soundly the first time that Vreeland had wanted to send me to the couture in her place—so soundly and so loudly in fact that Vreeland had backed down and sent her instead. I don't think that I ever measured up to her exquisite sense of taste and social acceptability. But she, at least, was too well bred to tell me so to my face.

Society editor Margaret Case was another story. Miss Case, who had spent forty years reporting on royalty for *Vogue*, then, when the 1960s threatened to put her out of business, had reinvented her career by chronicling the Beautiful People for Vreeland, came into my office just after I was named editor and, in a cold and disapproving manner, grilled me about what I was planning to do with society coverage in the magazine: "I want to know *how* you intend to change the magazine and *what* you intend to do with *me.*" Then Dick Avedon called me up and charmingly—he thought—invited me to lunch at his studio, where he proceeded to interview *me* about his prospects at the new *Vogue*.

It was annoying. But it was also a sign of the fact that *Vogue* was going to change and that people like Margaret Case and Dick Avedon were sitting up and taking notice. And they weren't just skeptical. They had real doubts about me. Their jobs were on the line—the way of life, the way of seeing, the way of talking about fashion and talking to women that they'd lived off of in the past decade at *Vogue*, was about to profoundly change.

I didn't want to read about the Beautiful People anymore. In an age of Gloria Steinems and Barbra Streisands, they were passé. I didn't want to showcase women who had no other credit to their names *but* their names. That was an old-world sense of society; in modern America, society now was talent. The anemic look of WASP ascendancy was passing from the New York social scene. Sunday lunches with the Rockefellers were no longer the only great game in town; I was going to dinner parties now where the most desirable guests on the invitation list were Elie Wiesel and Henry Kissinger, and the conversation around the dining table sizzled. I wanted to get that new-world kind of talent into *Vogue*.

I had for years been watching the example of Leo Lerman, the editor in charge of arts coverage at *Mademoiselle*, and though I'd never worked directly with him, we'd both always had fond feelings for each other that dated back to the very first time we'd met, in the elevator of the Graybar Building. I had been a very junior editor of *Vogue* and it had been very early (for me) in the morning—about 10 A.M. As we went up in the elevator, I closed my eyes and leaned against the car's paneling.

"You look tired," Leo said.

"I am," I answered. "I've been up dancing all night."

Leo liked that answer and had always shown an interest in my career afterward. And he was someone whom one wanted to impress. In the 1950s and 1960s he had made *Mademoiselle*'s name by filling it with the era's most talented writers. His friends included Julie Harris and Maria Callas and Beverly Sills and Audrey Hepburn, all of whom regularly gathered in the salonlike living room of his brownstone on Lexington Avenue for cocktails and conversation with other luminaries from the worlds of the arts and publishing. Leo, who would come over to cover culture at *Vogue* in 1972, inspired me to turn the magazine into a showcase for the new society of talent. It wasn't a big leap. The talent was waiting, the photographers were ready; we only had to leave the past and step forward.

Margaret Case was incapable of doing that. A few months after

I became editor, she killed herself by jumping out the window of her Park Avenue apartment. She was sick with cancer. She also, people said, simply felt like there was no place left in the world for her anymore.

Richard Avedon was another one who I thought was stuck in a passing era. He was still presenting clothes through fantasy and stage effects which, no matter how well they were done, seemed outdated in 1971. I wanted to bring *Vogue* a sense of ease, a sense of motion, a sense of life. And I wasn't getting that from Avedon's monumental effects.

The age of the Beautiful People was over, I felt, gone the way of Aquarius. I wanted to give *Vogue* back to *real women*. And even though I'd repeatedly been told that my idea of reality, "as seen in *Vogue*," bore no resemblance to the real thing, I still wanted to create a new image of reality, a "heightened reality," as I always called it, that would show women working, playing, acting, dancing—*doing things* that mattered in the world and wearing clothes that allowed them to enjoy them. I wanted to give *Vogue* over to women who were journalists, writers, actresses, artists, playwrights, businesswomen. I wanted to make *Vogue* democratic—not "middle class" in the sense of being pedestrian or narrow-mindedly moralistic or downmarket, but in being accessible to women like me. I wanted the magazine to be something that a woman like me—educated, reasonably well cultured, discerning in her tastes, attractively social, but not necessarily a socialite—could pick up and read and be both entertained and enlightened by. I wanted her to be surprised by *Vogue*, to learn things about fashion, politics, personalities, travel, and the arts that she never knew before. I wanted her to come away from *Vogue* with her eyes opened. And never to feel that she was smarter than the magazine. This meant raising the level of the text, and putting more of a demand on the intelligence of the magazine.

We also had to put a different kind of demand on our fashion coverage. By the early 1970s, it was clear that fashion magazines had lost their authority with American women. We could no longer count on the old prestige of *Vogue* to allow us to tell women what to wear. There had to be a rationality behind our fashion pages. We had to give the new woman of the 1970s what she needed— clothes that could carry her from work to cocktails to dinner and home, perhaps with a quick business trip thrown in for good measure.

Fortunately, we had fashion history on our side. For the moment when I became editor of *Vogue* was a wonderful moment in fashion. It was the moment when the sportswear revolution of the 1950s reached its zenith: new fabrics, new technologies, and a generation of new designers stripped the idea of casual dressing down to its barest ingredients and came up with a new style of separates dressing that was so pure, so light, and so true to the move and contour of a woman's body that they redefined the entire notion of clothes. It was as though whatever energy was sending shock waves through society was revolutionizing the fashion world as well. Clothes no longer shaped the body, as they had through the stiff-fabric designs and industrial-strength undergarments of prior decades. Now, the body gave shape to clothes, and the result was pure gutsiness, sheer ease, and thoroughly modern beauty.

It all had started with Yves Saint Laurent who, in the late 1960s, had revolutionized the idea of day dressing with the introduction of the pants suit. "Formal" day dressing before this moment had been filled with mediocrity: it was shirt dresses and more shirt dresses, for every season and at every price point, which meant that women basically dressed in a uniform. What Saint Laurent did with his pants suit—his wonderful summer suits, his khaki suits—was to introduce a way of dressing that was stronger, more singular, but also avoided the cliché of putting women in gray flannel trousers. The look of Saint Laurent's pants suits was anything but casual: it was worked out to perfection, from the fabrication to the accessories, to the stockings and the shoes. It was a more finished look than separates dressing, yet with none of the stodgy formality of the traditional day suit or dress.

The look of Saint Laurent's women set a new standard for the fashion industry. It marked the beginning of a new concept of what constituted sophisticated daytime dressing, a push for an unstructured, uninhibited kind of clothing that a new generation of designers—Calvin Klein, Ralph Lauren, Giorgio Armani—would later make *the* look of modern life. And though these designers would, it could be argued, go on to commercially eclipse Saint Laurent, there's no doubt that his vision for years remained the reference point for everything that they did. Saint Laurent took the emphasis in suit dressing away from lapeled jackets and square shoulders and turned it instead to interesting fabrication and marvelous cut and proportion. Strength and simplicity were the hallmarks of his design, as was shown beautifully one season when he produced an entire couture collection of clothes cut on the bias. They were perfect clothes that didn't rely on ruffles or sequins or beads or army boots to give them a reason for being. Their fabric, their cut, and the *body* that carried them were all that really mattered. It was woman-centered, not fashion-y, dressing. And it was the start of a revolution.

Emanuel Ungaro came on the scene with bold, gutsy clothes and models who looked, as they strode down the runway in their bias-cut pants, long jackets, and remarkable shawls, like harbingers of a new, heroic age. Emanuel's clothes spoke of courage: his fabrics were beautiful and strange and he broke all the rules of fashion convention by layering them pattern on pattern. He was someone who could put a pin-striped jacket against a floral print skirt with a lace blouse and make it work—even make it "seductive," as he liked to say—because the sheer beauty of the separate pieces was so much greater than their combined strangeness. Appreciating Ungaro wasn't easy at first for many fashion mavens. They were slow to embrace the idea that sportswear could be considered great fashion—a prejudice that for decades kept the European fashion press from giving American designers their due. (Even today, Ralph Lauren, perhaps the best sportswear designer of our time, is not considered a "real" designer by many members of our own fashion press. His clothes, with their solid basis in menswear design, are just *too* wearable.) Some editors, like the *Herald-Tribune*'s Hebe Dorsey, who always made a point of very snottily and very noticeably *not* attending Ungaro's collections, didn't come around to endorse him until years later, when he began designing the tame shirred-waist dresses that made his fortune with the "ladies who lunch" crowd. I, however, early on had a marvelous opportunity to appreciate what Ungaro was all about.

It happened in Paris, couture week one July, and came about through a lucky fluke; I'd arrived late for an Ungaro show with fashion editor Niki de Gunzburg and found that our seats had been given away. So Ungaro's assistants put us in a little passageway between the *cabine*, where the models dressed, and the little runway in the salon. And there, we had a marvelous vision of girls coming and going and changing—or rather *evolving*—from one Ungaro look to another. We saw a girl go out in a white-on-white coat, then come back in what she was wearing underneath. The under layers had no obvious relation to the outer ones, but their layering produced the most remarkable combination of pattern on pattern and texture on texture and color on color that I had ever seen. And what we realized, Niki and I, looking at this glorious parade of color and patterns was that the perfection of the collection came from the fact that its pieces could be almost endlessly combined. Presentation was unimportant; versatility and wearability were all. And we decided to show that collection in *Vogue* in just the way we'd seen it standing next to the *cabine*, and we gave Emanuel pages and pages. I remained a fan for years afterward.

Geoffrey Beene was another designer now offering up exciting surprises. He had begun designing for his own company in 1963, and in the late 1960s had made a very poor name for himself at *Vogue* by coming out with what we called his "cookie cutter" dresses. They were absolutely impossible clothes, little baby doll dresses in sequined fabrics, chiffon, and taffeta that were so stiff and sharp that they nearly stood up by themselves. This was

Beene's idea of dressing. His idea of glamour at night was a gray flannel evening dress with rhinestones.

We at *Vogue* used to scramble to arrange who was going to go back to the *cabine* to shake his hand after a collection showed. Somebody had to do it—it was a staple of fashion show etiquette—and no one wanted to, because none of us ever had anything good to say. It was terrible. The man who handled sales for Beene used to stop us at the end of a collection and ask, "All right now, which numbers do you want me to hold for you?" meaning, which did we plan to photograph, and we'd squirm around trying to find a way to say that there weren't any numbers we wanted to hold. Which always brought on a slightly threatening reaction, a "What do you *mean*. . . !" that was pure Seventh Avenue theatrics and terribly embarrassing.

Then, in the very early 1970s, Beene had a major turnaround. He came out with a collection that was as fluid and modern as his earlier clothes had been rigidly conventional. It was a collection of tunics—big and strong and attractive in a heavy corduroy and double-knit wool and crêpe de chine and hammered satin, shown over silk and cashmere turtleneck sweaters and strange, unexpected pants, some in a sumptuous wool. When I saw them, I turned to Polly Mellen and asked, "Is Geoffrey Beene the same man?" because the clothes were so new, so utterly unlike anything he'd ever done before. His new clothes, like Emanuel Ungaro's, broke down the barriers between what was considered day and night dressing, and between "dressy" and "sportive." They did this not by bringing "up" a completely undressed look, as so many women in their diamond earrings and sweatpants do today, but by relaxing the look of night dressing, widening the dress code from jackets and dresses to tunics and pants suits or pajamas. Part of what made Beene so very powerful a designer was his unique appreciation of, indeed his pleasure in, the potentials of new fabrics. Beene loved to work with fabric. He would fold a piece of fabric, crush it in the palm of his hand, to show you what he expected it to do. He'd explain how it was to have real resistance, real ease, plus real style. And his innovations matured well, giving him great staying power. By the 1980s he would emerge as the grandest and most distinct voice in American fashion, the only designer willing to sound a note of reason in that "anything goes" decade.

In the 1970s, though, the greatest scene-stealer was Halston. Halston had been discovered in the 1950s by Diana Vreeland when she was still working for *Harper's Bazaar* and he was doing custom order millinery for Bergdorf Goodman. I'd never felt much interest in him then—I always hated hats, and the fussing and froufrou and conversations that began, "My dear, you look wonderful . . ." that filled his milliner's studio had always been a bit too precious for me. Going over to watch him drape something at Bergdorf's was the sort of thing I just couldn't bear. But then, in 1968, he founded his own firm, and from his rattan-and-sisal-decorated showroom on East Sixty-eighth Street started to show the best day-to-night dressing, the most uncomplicated, dashing clothes that American fashion had ever produced.

Halston was the perfect designer for the anti-fashion 1970s. He took the demand for simpler, real-life clothes and made high art out of it. He had a pared-down, almost modernist sensibility. His custom-order clothes were dressy but never flashy and derived their decorative appeal from their fabrics and their pure bias cut. Halston's proportions were perfect. His clothes followed the shape of a woman's body without being tight; they held the body while still retaining a certain languor. Some of Halston's designs were downright revolutionary, like his day-into-night pants and tops, in suede, cashmere, or matte jersey for day with wonderful Lurex gold-wrapped tops for night. Others were just challenging enough to win over the kinds of women who had never before really worn sportswear to a "sportive" style of dressing. His ultra-suede shirt dress, which came on the market in the early 1970s, became one of the most successful dresses ever made. It attracted the kinds of women who until that time had only dressed in the designer clothes of Oscar de la Renta or Nina Ricci and initiated them into the livelier, more modern world of sportswear.

I always wore Halston. I wore it all—the cashmere dinner dresses, with their wide boat necks and great cuts, quality weights and colors. The cashmere zip-front jackets over cashmere trousers for daytime. The lamé pajamas at night. When I'd make my plans for going to the couture in Paris, Halston would sit me down and make a list of what I had and what I needed, then show me swatches and sketch out a plan for my trip, and about ten days later, I would have a perfectly planned, perfectly fitted complete wardrobe, simple and compact enough to fit in one suitcase.

I can still remember what I had in that suitcase one season, all Halston's, all custom-made: three V-neck cashmere pullover sweaters, one in white, one in beige, and one in black, then a beige woven cashmere trouser and a gray cashmere trouser; a pair of black matte jersey pants for day, and for night another pajama made up of a black, bias-cut charmeuse shaped T-shirt with bias-cut black charmeuse pants and another very simple, unstructured, thin, black charmeuse top and very simple, unstructured gold lamé jacket that wrapped and tied with a sash. It added up to sets of pajamas which would vary just in the degree of dressing. If I wanted to be more dressed, I'd wear gold and charmeuse. If I wanted the look to be less dressed, it would be matte jersey. If I wanted it bare, I would take the jacket off and the top would be bare down the back. And if I wanted ornamentation, Halston would provide a perfect little drop of some accessory designed by Elsa Peretti. I always found this to be my core wardrobe, traveling or not. The organization carried me through everything I did.

The early 1970s fashion moment, the moment of Halston, of Ungaro (in whose custom order I also dressed), of Beene, was about more than a look: it was about a feeling—and it was a feeling that the reader was made aware of through our pages. When you wore one of Ungaro's twelve-foot shawls, you strode, you *swept* down the street, feeling like a heroine from another century. When you wore Halston's pajamas to a dinner party in New York, heads would turn. Seas of short, poofy skirts would part to consider your soft, bias-cut pants. You'd be treated like someone uniquely in-the-know. And you'd be the most *comfortable* woman around. A modern woman, feeling fantastically feminine, in her pants.

The Ungaro woman, the Halston woman—comfortable, dashing, supremely self-confident—they were the heroines I wanted the women of *Vogue* to be. I wanted to remake *Vogue* in their image.

To do this, I needed help. I needed the full force of my editors behind me. I needed to trim the fat from the magazine, to prime the talents, to bring in some new blood, and to nurture rising stars. And I needed Alex Liberman. Only Alex, I knew, could give my visions full dignity on the page.

Diana Vreeland had been right when she'd told me, the first time I went in her place to the Paris couture, that I was "too approachable" and needed to put some distance into my manner. My approachability was partly what reminded Hebe Dorsey, seeing me in my custom-made Halston separates, of "the girl next door." And it was partly what allowed people like Margaret Case to let me know that they didn't quite think I was up to the job of editor. Now, I pulled rank. I decided that there would be no more nonsense. I called a meeting for all the key editors of the magazine: Carrie Donovan and Kate Lloyd, Priscilla Peck and Rosemary Blackmon, Cathy and Babs and Niki and Polly and all their associates. We gathered in *Vogue*'s big reception room, the green and white garden room designed by Billy Baldwin, and with Alex seated beside me, I began.

"Times have changed," I said. "Fashion is different and women are different and this magazine has to be thought about differently."

There was silence.

I tried to take a light tone. "There'll be no more running off to the seashore after you've finished an assignment," I joked. "No more spending Friday afternoons at the hairdresser."

When people worked at *Vogue*, they worked very hard and they didn't count hours. But nearly all the editors had developed the habit of calling it quits at lunchtime Fridays. And everyone was allowed to take as much time off in the summer as she wanted.

"We must change our focus," I concluded. "From dress-up fantasy to real life."

Polly Mellen raised her hand. Dress-up fantasy was her stock in trade. She loved it. She believed in it. And she was very good at creating it. "Would you mind going through all that again, please?" she said. "I want to understand what you mean about fantasy. And I need to know what you see as real life. Because I know that of everyone sitting here I'm going to have the most trouble with this." She was, after all, someone who, in later decades, would show up at a major fashion awards ceremony wearing little silver go-go boots and a chemise made of pressed soda cans.

"We must relax the look of the magazine," I said. "We're going to take the stiffness out. We're going to make it move. We're going to lose the pomposity. We're going to lose that let-'em-eat-cake attitude that says that if a woman isn't Wallis Simpson and can't afford to dress like her then she has no place reading our magazine."

"Well," Polly said, settling into her seat. "I'm not at all sure that I get this. But I certainly will try."

It was a tribute to Polly's great talents as an editor that she got it on the first shot. She set out to do a sitting at night in the street with Gianni Penati, a difficult and irascible but very talented photographer from Italy that captured the pulse and tone of the look we wanted just perfectly. For Polly, it was a big triumph. And for me, it was a great moment. It proved that change was possible. Talent like Polly's could make it happen. She proved that again—stupendously—when she went to Florida to do a sitting of active sportswear with the photographer Kourken Pakchanian. What emerged—pictures of Emmanuelle and Susan Schoenborn racing on bikes, slim and slick and muscular in white bodysuits, strong and perfectly dressed for exercise, without looking like exercise mavens on TV—summed up everything we were trying to do in that period.

Not only did we change our fashion coverage to fit the changing times, we were changing the look of the magazine: filling it with text, changing layouts so that the pages were more eye-catching, clean and direct and information-packed. We were changing the look of our covers, translating my convictions to make *Vogue* more accessible into cover lines that invited the reader to look at stories about fashion and beauty and health, and cover girls whose wide eyes and open smiles beckoned and whose all-American looks shouted stylish informality. It was an entirely different effect than the exquisitely elegant, but coldly stylish covers that Alex and Irving Penn had devised in the 1950s. We did away with the look of cool and aloof cover models who warned readers that *Vogue* was a rich persons-only magazine. Those attitudes went with couture thinking, the culture of exclusion, and they had no place in an expanding, democratizing *Vogue*. We simply couldn't afford to push women away anymore.

So we looked for girls who welcomed readers, models with great looks, marvelous young women like Lisa Taylor, Patti Hansen, Roseanne Vela, Lauren Hutton, and Karen Graham—one of the greatest cover girls ever, whom no one wanted to use for fashion sittings because she was a "tiny" five-foot-five. It was a time of models with blue eyes and blond or red hair and tiny noses and big white teeth. A notable exception, of course, was Beverly Johnson, the first black model ever to appear on the cover of *Vogue*, but even she was all-American in her healthy good looks. We weren't running images of dyspeptic, anorexic-looking models anymore. Exotic, *"interesting"*-looking girls were not for me. The word of the day was "pretty." Everyone was always on the lookout for pretty girls. Eileen Ford traveled around the world looking for them; Alex Liberman would watch the TV news at night and come in the next day with the name of anchorwomen on a slip of paper. And we would call them.

It was not easy changing the aesthetic of a magazine. What we were after was a new ease. A new informality. It was the chic informality of a Lauren Hutton, a beautiful tomboy type who even today runs around town in white sneakers and easygoing Armani suits. It was an informality that suited the 1970s, reaching its peak (publicly, if not fashionably) in the sweaters and shirtsleeves of the Carter White House. Everything had to change: hair, makeup, photographic technique. Makeup could no longer look like a mask. Hair could no longer be sprayed into an unmovable helmet. We were advocating a change in the entire concept of hair care to bring it in line with the active life of the new, modern woman, and by featuring cuts like Sassoon's or Kenneth's—cuts that while keeping a shape moved on their own—we hoped we were showing the way.

We were also looking more and more to photographers like Arthur Elgort who knew how to capture a sense of movement. Arthur Elgort, more than any other photographer to me, stands out as marking the last turning point in the history of American fashion photography. He'd begun taking pictures while an art history student at Hunter College and had trained as a "street photographer" in the tradition of Henri Cartier-Bresson. He came into his own with a wave of relaxed, spontaneous picture-taking that announced the modern era. Arthur wasn't the first to take fashion photography out of the studio, of course; Richard Avedon and others had traveled the globe taking heroic pictures of girls lurching out of great temples and on mountaintops for at least a decade. And he hadn't discovered spontaneous fashion photography: we had the paparazzi of the 1960s to thank for that. But what Arthur Elgort innovated was outdoor photography that *wasn't* operatic, and wasn't flashy (and often shoddy) like the work of the paparazzi. Arthur knew how to photograph three girls walking together and to catch not only the movement and sway of their clothes, but their stride, their gestures, the trivial details of their movements—a hand to the mouth, a sideways glance—that were true and fresh and present. For a beauty feature, he took a marvelous picture of Lisa Taylor driving in a Mercedes convertible over the George Washington Bridge. In the close-up, you see the detail of her sweater, her hair whipping back, her watch half-raised in a gesture of commuter impatience. It was a wonderfully stylish, wonderfully *real* shot, and like the best of his work, it captured the sense of the moment, of the transitory, which Baudelaire identified with modern life.

I always felt there was something wonderfully modern about Arthur, something wonderfully American. He was from the Midwest, and though he couldn't have been more sophisticated, enjoyed cultivating a homespun style of talking. Whenever he used it a lot, you knew he was displeased and was trying to talk his way out of a big argument. If he wanted to complain about the way his work was being handled, for example, he would say, "Well, my mother isn't going to like it." I appreciated his code and responded to it much more readily than I did to Avedon's angry outbursts.

We were moving away from the classically stylish, black and white still lifes of Irving Penn and John Rawlings. Rawlings had taken one of my all-time favorite pictures, a still life of things that might empty from a man's pocket: keys and change and a pencil, all spilled out on the floor around the most perfect pant leg and ankle and shoe. The foot and the shoe happened to belong to Niki de Gunzburg, a man very much of a passing era, as, I felt, Rawlings's sort of stylized elegance was too. Now, if we ran a still life, it needed to have a bit more thrust, like a very memorable picture Irving Penn once took of a woman's pink sandaled foot nuzzling its way up a man's pant leg. It was a picture that was perfect in its form and balance and used the pink shoe as an almost ironic token of femininity, creating the image I was always after of the feminine woman *as agent*. But then, Penn as early as 1949 had shown he was a master at capturing the perfectly beautiful casual moment. His picture of Jean Patchett, sitting in a café in Lima, Peru, and vacantly chewing on her pearls while slipping one tired foot out of a high-heeled shoe, was a classic.

We were changing the content of the magazine—getting away from visions of loveliness and running articles on Woodward and Bernstein, diary entries from Gloria Emerson, a *New York Times* correspondent in Saigon, printing portraits of great performing artists like Leonard Bernstein and Alvin Ailey and Tina Turner, running health stories on abortion and the new birth control pills. The magazine had to have diversity and bite, I felt. Reading it couldn't be like driving down a long straight road that lulled you to sleep. You couldn't have all the articles written at a fever pitch. Or all the fashion shoots taking place in Tahiti. There had to be texture, a mix: light stories and serious ones. We started bringing wonderful new voices into the magazine: Susan Sontag, Anne Roiphe, Calvin Trillin, Ada Louise Huxtable, just to name a few. On another level we were changing the way we talked to *Vogue* readers. The editorial tone of our Fall Forecast of July 1971 (my first issue) summed it all up: "What we want to say first about the clothes you're going to find in these pages is: just that. You-are-going-to-find-clothes!! And you are going to find the kinds of clothes you've been looking for—clothes you can see your lawyer in or your lover in or go to the park in when the rest of the company is wearing 3 to 6X. Clothes to enjoy your life in."

We no longer were suggesting that women dressed for men. We no longer were telling them to exercise because it would make them more adorable and alluring. We told them to exercise because they needed the extra stamina and energy for life. We no longer felt that we could get away with running diets that forbade desserts but allowed two martinis a day. In the past we had rationalized that as a realistic way of letting women have some pleasures without giving in to them all. But I always had known that we couldn't expect readers to take us seriously when we treated serious subjects like nutrition and health in such a cavalier way. In fact, in later years, I had problems with the notion of our printing diets at all—not that I ever could have considered doing away with them. Alex always argued that diets, advertised by cover legends, sold magazines—a lot of magazines, and so the diets stayed. But I always thought it was unfair to tell a woman she could lose thirty pounds in thirty days without telling her she'd probably gain those thirty pounds back just as quickly. Proper diet, I always thought, was a worthwhile topic. But I felt the word "proper" had to be in there, and that wouldn't have been a sexy sell.

Making articles on subjects like health and fitness be informative *and* look good on a page was easier said than done. Vreeland had gotten around the problem in the past by making beauty spreads be all about their own beauty. This created some marvelous visual effects—like an image of Veruschka crowned in a halo of blond braids—but gave readers little or no information about real-life beauty products and how to use them. The serious topics that I now wanted to tackle simply did not lend themselves to taking those kinds of creative liberties. And so, I just crossed my fingers and counted on Alex, who was a genius for getting around art and layout problems. He once, for example, put together a photographic montage on health that featured Patti Hansen running on the beach in a bikini next to slides of a CAT scan and a bone scan, to introduce those new diagnostic techniques in a visual way.

It isn't possible to make such substantial changes to an institution as venerable as *Vogue* without *somebody* complaining. And there were plenty of complaints. The fashion-y fashion crowd found our new "real life" fashion boring. Oscar de la Renta, Vreeland's protégé, who was turning into a major star and a major pain, made no effort to spare my feelings in telling me so.

I was visiting him in his showroom, listening to him tell me that *Vogue* was no longer a very fashionable fashion magazine. It was a year of hats: Karl Lagerfeld had presented his entire fall collection for Chloé with cocktail hats and the idea had been picked up by Seventh Avenue, with the result that everyone, Oscar included, was showing collections with terrible little hats. And all the fashion magazines except *Vogue* were following suit. We'd shown Lagerfeld's best hats—on Brooke Shields, for that matter—but not the others. And, as I said, I had always hated hats. I had celebrated women's liberation from them. Oscar loved them that year, and found the fact that *Vogue* didn't a sure sign that we were out of step with the times.

"What kind of fashion magazine could possibly not have had a hat in its entire September issue?" he said. "Certainly not one that was fashionable."

I found that a very unattractive kind of comment.

"Oscar," I said, "the fact is, women *aren't* dressing in hats anymore. Hats are uncomfortable. They're constraining. They're just not right for our readers. I think that the woman we want to talk to strides when she walks; when she's driving, she's in a small car. She's in motion. She doesn't want to worry about losing her hat."

"Well, your woman may be in motion, but you're not," he said. "You're a still magazine, not moving pictures"—a typically inane sort of comment, which proved that he had absolutely no idea of what I was talking about.

"Well," I said, "a woman needs to look good, she needs a certain ease when she gets dressed," and I gave him my usual little speech about modern women needing to live in their clothes.

"Well," he said, "I imagine you're quite right, but it's so boring."

Women looking good in life was "boring." I thought this was unforgivable. And that was the last little fashion chat we ever had.

If *Vogue* was now too tame for Oscar, we were becoming too risqué for some of our readers. The clothing we showed had become sexier: bathing suits, for the first time, were manufactured for the most part without breastplate bosoms, and a new generation of fabrics permitted designers to create weightless, stretchy bodysuits that left nothing to the imagination. The so-called sexual revolution had hit the fashion world in full force. It was propelled in large measure at *Vogue* by Alex, who, with his typically European disdain for what he called American puritanism, had seized upon the new "liberated" age as an opportunity to inject some sex into the magazine. He liked the look of *Playboy* and *Penthouse* and began combing their pages for photographers, eventually hiring *Penthouse* photographer Stan Malinowski to work for us. He encouraged Helmut Newton, who had impressed me so in Australia a decade earlier, in his new specialty: turning fashion spreads into stories about sexually ambiguous scenarios.

In the hands of Helmut Newton, the new body-bearing clothes became an opportunity to show off the body in motion. There were sometimes unexpected and remarkable results, as in the case of the motion of a girl photographed in the first bodysuit by Warner's straining to pull away from a man holding her on a leash. As Helmut knew, I often found some of his work to be offensive. But its technical quality was so brilliant and the humor and the sophistication he brought to his pictures were so dry and delicious that I felt he got away with things that in the hands of a less skillful photographer would simply have been soft porn. Throughout the 1970s I felt he walked a fine line, but I almost always came down on his side.

In any case, there's no arguing around the fact that as was true throughout most of the American media, the sexual revolution at *Vogue* was about putting long-repressed male fantasies on paper, and not about revolutionizing or liberating our female readers. It was chiefly about a rise in nudity and a kind of obsession with finding sex in every topic: in the early 1970s our version of this was travel features with titles like "Sex on the Go" and "Eroticism of Hotels" or fitness articles with the spin of "Nakedness vs. Nudity."

I didn't find increasing the amount of sex in *Vogue*'s pages particularly inspiring. I did think, though, that in working with the best photographers of the era, we had a unique opportunity to use sexually charged imagery to turn the tables on who seemed to have the power in an encounter between a man and a woman. Penn's pink sandal shot, I always thought, did this very subtly. And one of my absolute favorite pictures from this period was a Helmut Newton: a picture of Lisa Taylor sitting in a very pretty, soft cotton dress with her legs spread apart, absently playing with her hair and coolly checking out a faceless man walking in front of her in tight white pants and no shirt. That picture, like Helmut's "Story of Ohhh . . ." set in Saint-Tropez in the same issue and suggesting the erotic adventures of a man and two women, didn't go over well in the Bible Belt—and brought a spate of angry letters and canceled subscriptions. In an odd coincidence another photo story in that same May 1975 issue also made readers rage: it was a series of pictures by Deborah Turbeville shot in a public bathhouse down on Twenty-third Street in New York. The girls weren't naked in this picture: they were modeling bathing suits. But they were so thin and so pale, and the location was so spare and so spooky, that some readers said it made them think of women in gas chambers. It made others think of anorexia. Or of death generally. The fact that one of the models looked like she was masturbating made them think of still other things.

Deborah Turbeville, of course, appears to have had none of this in mind when she put together the shoot. "All I was doing was trying to design five figures in space," she later said when the angry reaction reached its peak. Polly Mellen, who was the editor on the sitting, certainly never would have had such thoughts. Serious things tended, I think, to edit themselves out of her mind, and she'd been so caught up by the difficulty of shooting in the location that she'd never thought about what it was or how sinister it looked. Which perhaps explains how, upon leaving the baths one Friday afternoon, Polly was able to cast an eye over the crowd waiting out in the street for a bath and say, "My! I'm surprised to see so many people still in town!"

It wasn't easy to bring an old-world magazine into step with the times. More often than not, *Vogue* moved out of the past in fits and starts. An Avedon photo fantasy set at Johnson and Burgee's new Fort Worth WaterGarden that ended with Tony Spinelli giving René Russo a slap that sent her flying (in her white John Anthony jumpsuit) brought letters from readers who wondered just how pro-woman the new *Vogue* really was. It was true that in the early years we took one step back for every two steps forward as far as feminism was concerned. *Vogue* was very slow to embrace the more far-reaching implications of the women's movement and the sexual revolution—I was too—and for years we sent mixed messages about feminism. Our June 1971 issue on "You, the American Woman . . ." featured an article on Gloria Steinem, an essay by Bella Abzug, and an article on "wife power" with a photo of Mrs. Alfred Vanderbilt captioned "This was worth fighting for . . . the pleasure of going back to the kitchen." Our January 1972 issue on "How We See You—the Woman of Today" proclaimed, "In 1972, we'll continue to address her—you—as Miss or Mrs. rather than Ms. because we see her as we think she sees herself: a modern, small-l liberated woman who doesn't need labels to show who she is . . ."

That small-l was still too big for some of our old-time readers. A certain number of them began defecting from *Vogue*. They couldn't read about their friends in the society pages anymore; they didn't get the body-hugging fashion, and they didn't like the sex. But a whole other generation of women felt they could be part of our new world. And they signed on in the hundreds of thousands, offsetting our losses and burying them. The results were colossal: from 1973 to the end of the decade, circulation skyrocketed, rising from just over 400,000 to just over a million. In that same period, the magazine's gross revenues also rose from $9.1 million to $26.9 million.

Our message was getting out. We had to have been doing something right. Readers were responding to our heady mix of articles and real-life clothes and advertisers were following suit. *Vogue* was once again considered the undisputed leader of the fashion press. And it wasn't because we were reinventing fashion, or stoking our need for glory by creating glorious fantasy looks. It was quite the opposite: *Vogue* was on the cutting edge of fashion precisely because our sensibility was so firmly in tune with that of Seventh Avenue. We were all moving in the direction of ease, of classic beauty, of comfortable chic. In this, we were simply following in the march of history.

"The Queen Is Dead. Long Live the Queen!" Eugenia Sheppard had crowed in the pages of the *New York Post* shortly after Vreeland was deposed and I was installed as editor of *Vogue*. It wasn't long before I understood what she meant. Memories—and loyalties—are short in the fashion industry. The editor of *Vogue* is the editor of *Vogue*, no matter what anyone may think of her state origins. The resistance to me quickly passed as *Vogue*'s ad revenues rose. Before long, *I* was the celebrity editor du jour. I had my own trademark office, all painted in beige, my limousine, my custom-made clothes, my front-row seat at every fashion show, obsequiously saved for "Miss Mirabella of *Vogue*." I was living now on Park Avenue, in an apartment decorated by Angelo Donghia. I'd bought the apartment with an interest-free loan from Condé Nast and at Alex's urging, and there, with my herringbone-painted floor, black, white, and yellow living room, and voluptuously blue bedroom, I lived in the manner expected of a woman of style. I held cocktail parties and dinners for all the people that "everyone" (read: Alex) thought I should know. I entertained. I *presented*. It was my job. I was expected to be out and around. I was "Miss Mirabella of *Vogue*."

It wasn't always easy. I'd made some wonderful new friends: Sandra Kasper, who was then married to Richard Feigen, a well-known art dealer, and Joanne Cummings, whose husband, Nathan, was an art collector and the chairman of Consolidated Foods, which later became the Sara Lee Corporation. Although they did everything they could to introduce me to people I needed to know and invite me to everything that I ought to do, from formal dinners to casual suppers to the opening of the Metropolitan Opera, I never felt entirely comfortable in their wider social worlds. And being a single woman in her early forties at a time of big dinner parties wasn't much fun. Though I wasn't altogether happy with the situation, I contented myself in thinking, as did so many hardworking women of my generation, that it was just the way things were meant to be. But that was soon to change.

CHAPTER 7
EVERYTHING COMES TOGETHER

M y mother had for some years been calling up, every now and again, with a worried word from "a friend" or a distant relative or the very interested neighbor down the street: *Wasn't there anyone? Anyone at all? Was there something wrong with me after all this time?*

Or, as Bob Goldworm less charmingly put it, in his Seventh Avenue-ese: *Was I just "queer" or something?*

I laughed—always laughed—and pleaded not guilty to all of the above. Sure, there had been plenty of *someone*s: Bob himself, for one, and Dale Turnbull and Hank Greenberg and Bud Sweeney just to name a few, and I'd come very close to actually marrying John Addey, my dashing-about-town London friend. I'd gone so far as to have him come to New York and meet my mother, which he did, posthaste, but once I had him here, the luster of London all worn off and the lightness of dating dulled by the prospect of marriage, I'd had second thoughts. The thoughts were disappointing enough that John Addey had gone back to London alone, and we'd never really been friends again.

Was it just that the right man hadn't come along? Or did I simply not want to get married? The truth was probably a combination of the two. I hadn't yet met a man who had interested me for any extended period of time, nor had I met one who seemed to offer a life that could be any more enjoyable than the one I was leading on my own. The problem was that married life seemed to me likely to be a lot *less* enjoyable than the one I'd built for myself. I loved to work, loved the energy and excitement of running back and forth to Europe, the thrill of meeting new people, and had, with the full responsibility of *Vogue* on my shoulders, become as exacting and perfectionistic as Vreeland had been at her very worst. I *was* married to *Vogue*, and because I was so faithful to the magazine, I didn't mind the long hours at the office, the evenings and weekends spent socializing for work, all of which would have been impossible, I thought, if I'd been married, much less married with children. The successful women I'd always seen around me at *Vogue* were either multi-married and divorced (Mildred Morton), or had given up on marriage altogether and were living alone or trying out new and untraditional arrangements (Babs Simpson). So, with no truly charming prince on the horizon, I decided to stick with a known quantity, and work.

My mother worried, but she consoled herself with the fact that I at least hadn't married an Italian. That had always been her deepest fear—a worry of much greater consequence than that of whether or not I'd marry at all. Italian men were to her way of thinking a bit suspect. She drew little distinctions between Mafiosi straight off the boat from Sicily and Italian noblemen working on Wall Street: both types were suspect, and neither would be allowed anywhere near me, if she could help it. We once had dinner together in an Italian restaurant near her home in New Jersey where some neighborhood fellows sent me some rather interested glances and offered wine. After we were done eating, she sent me out of the restaurant first, then lagged behind long enough to tell those local toughs that if they knew what was good for them, they'd stay away from me, saying, "My daughter is not for you." And when I went down to the docks once with Cathy di Montezemolo and her husband, Alessandro, to see my mother off to Europe, I received a letter about a week later, which began with the worried words, "Who was that *Italian*? . . ."

I did my best to find my mother's worries just charming. I myself didn't have time to worry, which was probably all well and good. And is probably why I met my romantic destiny so simply and unexpectedly one Saturday morning on the shop floor of an antiques shop in bucolic Bedford Village, New York. My husband, Bill Cahan, who was then sixty, likes to say that I "went looking for an antique and I found one."

On that fateful morning—a rainy one, I recall—I was in Bedford visiting my friend Sandra Feigen, keeping her company in the Bedford Green Antiques Shop, which she owned with another friend, Jeannie Amory. I was standing and vaguely wondering what my apartment would look like entirely redecorated in antiques, when in walked Bedford's most eligible summer bachelors: Dr. William G. Cahan and his college-age son, Anthony. Bill Cahan was a star in the New York social firmament of the 1970s. He was a brilliant cancer surgeon at the Memorial Sloan-Kettering Cancer Center and a professor of surgery at the Cornell University Medical College. He was internationally known within his specialty, thoracic surgery, at a time when nearly everyone smoked, and people from all over the world and from all walks of life called him for consultations. The first time that I'd ever heard his name, in fact, had been in the art department at *Vogue*, when I'd walked in to find Alex Liberman on the phone with a friend in Europe, saying, "Why don't we get him to come over here and see Dr. Bill Cahan? He's the noted authority."

Through his first wife, Pamela Gordon-Howley Cahan, or, more properly, through his first mother-in-law, the actress Gertrude Lawrence, and from his own involvement with the wartime production of Moss Hart's *Winged Victory*, Bill Cahan was intimately acquainted with the big talents of the theater world. His second wife, Mary Arnold "Sisi" Sykes Cahan, was the type of woman who is generally referred to as a "socialite." With her, Bill had grown to know people like my friends the Cummingses and the Feigens, friends who would help bring us together, plus a whole world of others that included women like Brooke Astor. Despite his "good" marriages, though, he was really as much a newcomer to their world as I was. He had grown up in the unfashionably middle-class Jewish neighborhood of Washington Heights to a family distinguished by talent, not birth. His cousin, Abraham Cahan, was the founder and editor of the Yiddish-language *Jewish Daily Forward*, and a writer whose 1896 novel, *Yekl*, was made into the movie *Hester Street* in 1975. His father, Samuel Cahan, had been born in Lithuania and worked as a quick-sketch artist for the newspaper *The World* for thirty-two years, depicting scenes of street life, peddlers and rabbis, markets and religious holidays, in the immigrant neighborhoods of the Lower East Side where he'd grown up. Bill had gone to Harvard, and to Columbia University's College of Physicians and Surgeons, and then into residency at Memorial Hospital, battling Jewish "quotas" and institutional anti-Semitism and emerging triumphant through it all, and thoroughly without bitterness or anger. He'd emerged, in fact, emblematic of the new society of talent that had gained ascendancy in post-war New York. Dr. Cahan, the preeminent cancer surgeon, went everywhere and was welcomed by everyone. The Jewish boy from Washington Heights *was* the heart and the soul of the new New York.

I had met Bill Cahan twice before, with no fireworks. The first time had been at a dinner that Joanne Cummings had put together in order to try to match me up with a Wall Street banker whom I had met once or twice and had found attractive. For the occasion, she'd pulled together a crowd that included Oscar and Françoise de la Renta, Diana and Egon von Furstenburg, Warren Avis, and Bill and Sisi—little suspecting, as we would learn from the gossip columns shortly thereafter, that the Cahans were on the verge of divorce. We'd met a second time at another dinner party, a party this time given by Bob Skull, the taxi magnate and modern art collector, and his wife, Ethel. It was one of those unbearably "with it" New York dinner parties where I always feel that no one quite knows why he or she is there, or perhaps just isn't telling me. Bill Cahan seemed entirely at ease, and we made pleasant conversation.

I'd been struck by the good-looking, self-assured surgeon, with his silver hair, aquiline nose, and blue eyes. But I'd never really looked into those eyes before. Perhaps I hadn't allowed myself to pay that much attention to a married man. Now, word was out that he and Sisi were, in fact, separated. He was said to be living in a room in an apartment at the United Nations Plaza, owned by the Lasker Foundation and made available to him by his good friend the philanthropist Mary Lasker. And the Bedford summer house was very clearly a father-son bachelor pad.

When I came back to New York that Sunday evening, I ran into Dr. Cahan on the street where I'd gone to return my rental car while he was returning from parking *his* car. It was as though the hand of fate was working furiously to bring us together. I went home, laughing to myself. It was love at first sight. I'd never felt anything like this before. All of a sudden, I was forty-two going on sixteen.

A few days later Bill called and invited me to come out to dinner. We sat down, and I put a pack of cigarettes on the table. I lit one and brought it to my lips. Bill's face fell.

"How much do you smoke?" he said.

"About two packs a day," I answered. The truth was something more like two and a half. I smoked constantly, smoked any cigarette that I thought looked classy and attractive. In that, I was like nearly all my colleagues at *Vogue*.

"Two packs a day?" he said. "Really. Let me tell you something about my work."

I learned that he called his operating room Marlboro Country. I learned that at that time, 1972, fully thirty percent of his hospital's adult patients would not have been there if they had not smoked. Deaths from lung cancer in women had nearly tripled in the past two decades, he said.

"And to top it off," he said, "I can't stand the smell of smoke in a woman's hair and on her clothes. Now, tell me something about *your* work."

The next day I found myself throwing my last pack of cigarettes into my wastepaper basket. "That's it!" I shouted. "No more!"

It was easier said than done. I was sleepy all the time. I had headaches. I worried that my career was over; I'd never make it through the smoke-filled couture shows in Paris again. I probably screamed at my secretaries and tortured my closest colleagues. Then, a few days passed, and I felt fine. I was human again, and I hadn't eaten more than usual. And by the next time I saw Bill Cahan for dinner, I was smoke-free.

Nate Cummings gave me an added incentive to stay that way. A few days after the worst of my nicotine withdrawal, after I'd had a chance to recount my date with Bill Cahan in detail to Joanne, he called to make me a little business proposition.

"Listen, Grace," he said, "don't let this one slide. I'll give you a thousand bucks in a year if you'll have stopped smoking as of today."

I laughed at the thought of multimillionaire Nate pulling out his wallet and giving me a cool thousand at a cocktail party. I bit my tongue to keep from telling him that maybe I'd already quit.

"Take the money and run, Grace," Joanne, who knew the truth, shouted into the phone. So I agreed. And then they both began telling me what a nice man Bill Cahan was and how well suited he was for me. And Nate warned me not to forget our bet and hung up.

I'd gambled well; Bill was touched when he learned, at our next dinner, that I'd given up smoking just for him. We began seeing more and more of each other, going to dinners and parties and even fashion shows and medical lectures together. I started, for the first time, to run frequent and hard-hitting health pieces on the dangers of smoking. People noticed the articles and noticed Bill and nodded knowingly at the connection. And when they asked him if I was having an influence on *his* work, he began to say, "Now, when I make an incision, I cut on the bias."

Being with a man who was so firmly entrenched at the top of his profession that he couldn't in any way be threatened by my professional life was a new experience for me. So was being with someone outside of the fashion world who took my work completely seriously. I sometimes felt that next to Bill's life and death procedures, my work was thoroughly and pointlessly trivial. I told him so one evening, when he came home tired after a nearly day-long operation.

"While you were operating," I said, "I was choosing between different shades of lipstick."

"Lipstick is important," Bill said. "I always tell my residents to notice when a female patient recovering from major surgery starts to wear her lipstick again. It's a sure sign that she's feeling better and is getting ready to go home. So you see, your world is no less significant than mine, Grace," he said. "It's just forty-eight hours later."

Sometimes it seemed like the whole city was watching the progress of our romance. We were "holding hands through the best parties of New York," as the *Herald Tribune*'s Suzy Menkes put it. Our relationship felt about as private as a runway show. *Every-one*, I realized, knew Bill Cahan. And if they didn't know Bill, they knew his still-wife Sisi, and if they didn't know either of them they probably knew me; and even if they didn't know me, they probably had an opinion on the breakup of the Cahan marriage and the speed of my entry into the thick of it. The truth was, Bill and Sisi had formally separated a good year before I'd met him in Bedford, and their marriage had been on the rocks for quite some time before that. But they weren't yet formally divorced, which made them think I was the spoiler or the "other woman" to some of Bill and Sisi's old friends. Some, like Arthur and Betty Houghton, simply dropped out of Bill's life. There was some tension too with Bill's younger son, Chris, who had been living at home through his parents' breakup and had emerged with a number of unhealed war wounds.

I, who had always lived such a private and quiet life, wasn't used to the pressure of the public gaze. It made every seeming setback in the relationship, every uncertainty, into a public mortification. Bill lived his life in the public eye. He was very much in demand. He was constantly being invited everywhere, for weekends in country houses in Connecticut and in the south of France, not necessarily with me. I never quite knew where he was or what he was doing or who he was doing it with. And since he had just extricated himself from a long marriage, he wasn't overeager to tie himself to another consuming relationship.

I was completely sold on Bill; I was "hooked" in a way that I'd never thought I could be, and the fear that nothing permanent would come of it had started to haunt me. As our relationship entered its second year and Bill's divorce seemed nowhere nearer to being finalized, I began to get antsy. The gossip columnists, honing in on what was promising to be a good story, were starting rumors of new romances every time that Bill escorted a female friend—or a friend's wife—to a dinner or charity ball. It would be bad enough to be left heartbroken, I thought, if I could at least have a chance to recover privately. But to be made a public fool of would be just unbearable. I started wondering if I should make the first move and pull out.

I called Joanne Cummings and invited her to have lunch.

"I'm not going to be left looking like an idiot," I said. "This had been going on now for years."

Joanne studied my face.

"Are you ready to say good-bye?" she asked.

I said, "He said to me, 'Give me a little time.' He said, 'I just need a little time.' What does that mean?"

"Were those his exact words?"

"Yes," I said.

"Then he means it, Grace," Joanne said.

"How can you be so sure?"

Joanne smiled. "He's a nice Jewish boy if I know one. I'll vouch for him."

And we went on with our lunch.

I later learned that Joanne called Bill up and warned him that I was at wit's end. "I gave you my *Good Housekeeping* seal of approval," she said. "You'd better come through."

She wasn't the only one to put her two cents in. Soon I had another unexpected helper as well. In 1973, shortly after my title had formally changed on the *Vogue* masthead from editor to editor in chief, Estée Lauder, the charismatic founder of the cosmetics empire, called me up and invited me to lunch. I had never lunched with her before. I assumed she was calling about business, that the punching up of my title (my job had stayed the same) had somehow caught her eye and convinced her that I was someone worth talking to. I went to lunch at La Goulue, expecting a Margaret Case-like grilling by a cold and imposing woman, and instead was surprised when Estée, as warm and friendly as could be, started straight off asking me about her old friend, Bill Cahan.

Was I seeing him, she asked. Yes, I said.

Did I like him? I said I did, very much.

"Well then, let me tell you how I think you marry a nice Jewish doctor," Estée Lauder said. "Can you cook?"

I admitted that I couldn't. In fact, my lack of ability in the kitchen was legendary. Betty Dorso had once given me a recipe, but I'd never gotten around to making it. And what I had made was not generally considered highly edible. Bill had already named my version of caramelized carrots "Princeton Carrots" because they matched the school's colors—orange and black. He liked to say I was the only Italian woman he'd ever met who couldn't cook. I thought he liked that about me, actually. Estée wasn't pleased. For about an hour she talked to me about chicken. I kept waiting for a word to drop about the cosmetics business. It never came. Instead, Estée gave me a couple of easy chicken recipes, and offered some pointers on entertaining. And she talked about the importance of being centered and how she felt about her husband, Joe.

I was touched. And, chicken recipes aside, I found getting to know Estée Lauder a real gift. I found her to be generous and vibrant, an unpretentious grande dame. She's someone who can't stand still to make conversation with you at a cocktail party, but will pull you into her guest bathroom in Palm Beach for a half hour to do your makeup. I know, because she did it to me. Her husband, Joe, was a very quiet man with a wry and dry wit, as laid-back as Estée was tightly wound. He ran the production side of her business, and generally brought life down to earth. He made me laugh uncontrollably one night at a dinner at Mildred Hilson's apartment. Mildred Hilson's, in the late 1970s, was a place where you'd be likely to find people like the Nixons and the Buckleys and a general of some sort, and the conversation was always very labored and very heady. After dinner one evening, when everyone was having their coffee and standing around, Mildred said, "Let's play a game where each person makes believe and names the place where he or she would most like to be." Everyone came up with exotic and amusing locales, until, when Joe Lauder's turn came, he yawned and said, "The place where I'd most like to be is at home, asleep, at just this moment." I loved him for it.

Estée was a dynamo. But she was off the mark about Bill. The truth was, he needed no love potion. He just needed to sort out the financial details of his divorce. And that, in New York, where couples fight over visitation rights for dogs, can be more troubling and time-consuming than falling in love and marrying in the first place. Finally, Bill decided simply to force the matter to a crisis. On my birthday, June 10, 1974, he gave me a Cartier watch, with a card that read, "Let's spend the rest of time together."

I looked at the watch, at the card, then back at him and, choosing my words carefully, said, "Does that mean what I think it means?"

He said it did, and I said yes.

Bill hadn't had too many doubts on what the outcome of his proposal would be and had assembled a surprise birthday/engagement party for me at Ballato's, an Italian restaurant down on Houston Street. All our closest friends were there, plus my mother, thrilled beyond all possible limits, not just because I was getting married but because I was marrying a Jewish doctor—the highest human life form, in her book. We made our announcement and everyone toasted us, and Bill kissed my mother.

"I guess this is okay," she said, "but if there are any children, I want them brought up as Catholics." And as I looked sternly at her, Bill said, "Ma, I don't mind them being brought up as Catholics as long as they vote Democratic."

So we were engaged, an established couple, traveling together to Paris and to Italy and to Moscow. We set our wedding date for November 24, 1974. After our well-attended courtship, we wanted a relatively low-key wedding. Nate and Joanne Cummings kindly offered us the use of their New York home, a cavernous apartment in the Waldorf Towers in which Nate's incredible collection of Impressionist art was hung on every wall. We readily accepted, relishing the idea of getting married under a canopy of Monets, Bonnards, and Cassatts. Instead of buying a traditional wedding gown, I asked Karl Lagerfeld to design for me a very pretty dinner dress that I might wear again, and he came up with a dress of wonderful heavy blond crêpe embroidered with pearls.

Three weeks before our wedding, Bill's father died. He was eighty-eight years old and had been in declining health for some time, but it still was a terrible blow. I immediately wondered if we should put off the wedding. Bill's mother, however, told us her husband would have wanted us to go on. To bring his presence to the ceremony, Bill asked Nate Cummings if he could hang one of his father's paintings over the fireplace in the dining room where we were to be married. Nate agreed and took down a Picasso, and Samuel Cahan's "The Tulip Tree" was hung in its place.

We were married in front of it by Owen McGivern, presiding justice of the New York State Supreme Court's Appellate Division, before a small audience of our closest friends. Bill's teenage sons, Anthony and Chris, actually cut their long hair to serve as best men. Sandra Feigen, who had, after all, played such a key role in our meeting, was my matron of honor. Her husband, Richard, the art dealer, at one point looked at Bill's father's painting over the mantel and whispered to her, "I didn't know Nate had bought a new Pissarro." Bill wouldn't have wanted his father eulogized in any other way.

Nate Cummings felt that even though Bill isn't religious, he ought to have some aspect of the ceremony remind him of his heritage. The Jewish custom at weddings is to step on a glass and break it. So, after we'd kissed, Nate brought out a glass wrapped in a napkin, and Bill had to stomp on it. Nate then picked up the pieces, still wrapped, and had them affixed to a canvas background, which he framed. The collage now hangs in our home, like an abstract painting.

A reception for about one hundred people followed the ceremony. The Lauders were there, of course, and Mildred Hilson, plus friends like Geraldine Stutz, Nan Kempner, Bill Blass, Bob Wagner, Franco Zeffirelli, Helen Gahagan Douglas, Walter Cronkite, Barbara Walters, and Marie Fauth. Diana Vreeland was notably not present. I hadn't had the courage to invite her.

After the wedding we went up to Bedford, where we'd rented a house for our honeymoon. When we came back, took up residence in Bill's town house on East Sixty-second Street, and began our daily routines once again, I was immediately struck by what a difference in my life being married to Bill had made. I felt moored. I felt as if I had a real home. I had a center from which to operate, a best pal with whom to commiserate, a companion to take me out on the rounds of parties that were my lot in life, and with whom I could come home laughing, or complaining, and then stay up with for hours, conducting a postmortem of the evening.

I felt, for the first time ever, perhaps, that I *belonged*. Everything was so much *easier*, so much more pleasant. The people who, for years, Alex had been trying to force me to get to know were now our friends. Going out among them wasn't just a late night at work anymore; it was part of my married life.

Bill loved all the aspects of my job that I didn't—the need to socialize, to be "out," to know everyone—and he had a talent for it that I envied. I'd never been a great success on the New York social scene. I wasn't a collector of people. I didn't have a good ear for light small talk; I wasn't charmingly devil-may-care. I couldn't "work" a room, or circulate through a party with a kiss and a good word for everyone I saw because I often, when nervous, failed to recognize people in a crowd. I was basically rather shy. Before I married, I rarely entertained, after a fiasco once when I'd invited twelve of the most attractive people I knew to a dinner party, only to find that the conversation was about as thin as the consommé. Once I was editor of *Vogue* and Alex and Si were pressuring me to make use of my Angelo Donghia living room, I invited people like Felix Rohatyn and Laurance Rockefeller or Leonard Lauder over for cocktails. But it was a stretch for me.

Bill, on the other hand, was the kind of person who mapped out long nights with multiple party stops, and if he could make it to four parties in one evening, with each party filled with a totally different group of people, then he'd go home satisfied, thinking he'd had "a proper New York evening." He could plan wonderful surprise parties, transport people to unthinkable locations and have them pop out from behind a door singing some song he'd written just minutes before. He organized everything from the phone in the surgeon's lounge, sitting and waiting to be called into the operating room, with a little slip of paper in his hand and his phone numbers. Like this, he could make twenty-five calls in one sitting—while I, in my office, with my assistant, was lucky if I could remember to make three or four in a row. I was more than happy to follow his lead.

The world suddenly seemed so rich, peopled with rare jewels. We vacationed in Palm Beach with Douglas Fairbanks, Jr., and Marylee. We dined with Elie Wiesel and Baryshnikov. I became friends with talented women like Carol Channing and Beverly Sills and Barbara Walters. Having these kinds of friends made my work immeasurably easier. When we wanted to do a really special fashion sitting and decided to try to send a crew to China, an impossible-seeming feat at that time, all I had to do was to ask Nancy Kissinger if I could talk to Henry. And as a result, not only did I get a direct line to the State Department, I got Henry's wife, Nancy, to come along and model clothes for the trip. The result was that just months after Kissinger had been sent by Nixon on a secret diplomatic mission to Beijing (in July 1971), his wife was walking through the streets of China modeling clothes, with Arthur Elgort photographing and a stream of excited Chinese children following her, laughing and shouting in her wake.

Even going to Paris for the couture, which I'd always treated as the worst possible chore, became with Bill a great pleasure. Paris couture week used to be a city-wide fiesta. There were banners flying everywhere and ballet in the courtyard of the Louvre, special art exhibits and endless cocktail parties and dinners. It could have been extremely charming if you liked Paris—which I didn't. I wasn't comfortable with the French and I didn't speak their language, and I couldn't understand why, *in July*, the only place in the entire city that was air-conditioned was the Ritz bar, which was closed. The air was sweltering, the cigarette smoke at the couture shows was sickening, and the "ladies" who hung around those shows, lunching in the garden of the Plaza Athenée and hosting parties, were cloying. One year our office at French *Vogue* was so unbearably hot that Alex demanded that Condé Nast Europe buy us an air conditioner for our group of rooms. They did, but stored it as soon as we'd left, evidently not wanting the staff of French *Vogue* to get any such extravagant ideas.

And, to top it off, we worked at night. Every night. The major working challenge of the couture in those years was that the designers showed their clothes to buyers during the day and the magazines weren't allowed to borrow them for photographing. Which meant that after a full day of salon visits and lunches and cocktails and shows, we had to start doing our sittings, which generally would last all night. This inconvenience was, unexpectedly, how I found something about Paris that I especially loved: sunrise in the city, a moment when the blue-gray new light softened the glare of the streetlamps, when the streets were freshly sprinkled and glistening and the smell of bread drifting out from a thousand invisible bakeries followed us back to our hotel.

After a few hours of sleep, I would join Alex to go to work on reviewing the pictures from the night's sitting and starting to put together layouts. It was often not a terribly glamorous existence. And what glamour there was, was generally not so great. Alex knew a great many people in Paris, both wealthy social types and writers and artists, and included me whenever he went out with them. I often wished that he hadn't. My discomfort with the French was epidermal, and I found these people precious and superficial. The worst crowd of all, I thought, were the guests at Yves Saint Laurent's dinners, which I found torturous. They were held in his lavish town house, which, in the 1970s, he'd decorated in line with the current vogue of third worldism. There were Buddha-like statues everywhere and tasseled cushions and a crowd that you expected at any moment to begin pulling out pipes and smoking opium. The presence of the celestial Catherine Deneuve aside, it was a ridiculously flaky crowd, filled with fashion victims and hangers-on and would-be actors and writers, and some aristocrats—all swingers of the refinedly degenerate type that you found around Europe in those years.

As the years passed, from party to party, you saw the signs that substance abuse was destroying Yves Saint Laurent. If you caught him in his studio at an off hour when he wasn't expecting you, you often found a rather lost-looking man with a bottle and a glass in his hand, looking like someone who couldn't remember anymore how or where he'd started. The pain of seeing his genius decline was another reason why I preferred to keep my distance.

Once Bill started coming to Paris with me, things changed immeasurably for the better. He had his own set of friends—couture-shoppers like Deeda Blair, wife of William Blair, a former U.S. ambassador and former aide to Adlai Stevenson, and Mary Lasker, whose car, we liked to joke, was the only place *other* than the Ritz bar that was air-conditioned in July. We'd go to concerts or to the Louvre or to some funny hot-as-hell little restaurant with Helmut Newton and his wife, June. We struck up a good friendship with Emanuel Ungaro, and spent long hours visiting him in his very white, very clean salon. Emanuel always said he felt a special affinity for Bill. He liked to work in a white coat and referred to his work space as his "laboratory," and felt that what he did in his "lab" was not, in essence, so very different from what Bill did in surgery. In fact, one summer he told Bill that he would like to change his work uniform to dress as a surgeon did. Bill, compliantly, went home and sent him over a set of green scrubs. Emanuel stuck to the white lab coat.

Once, when the Paris collections fell over Bill's birthday in early August, Alex and I organized a dinner for him with all our visiting American friends. We searched and searched for a restaurant with air-conditioning and finally ended up reserving at the Lido, which, thanks to the constant presence of busloads of American tourists, *was* air-conditioned. We took a long table at the foot of the stage and put together a good mix of people, and we giggled all through the evening. Our friend Bill Blair amused us to no end by telling us the story of how, when on his way to London once to meet Adlai Stevenson, and, staying over briefly in Paris, he had sat at this very table at the Lido and his pant leg had gotten caught in the mechanism that raised and lowered the stage. The fabric had been completely shredded—ruining the one blue suit he'd brought to Europe to wear to a meeting at 10 Downing Street.

After couture week was over, I'd secure a few days off from *Vogue* and we'd go on vacation. We might go see Alex and Tatiana Liberman in Ischia, where Alex horrified Bill by taking radiation baths. We might go to Italy to see Bill and Beverly Pepper, or to Venice, or to stay with Mary Lasker at La Fiorentina, the house in Saint-Jean-Cap-Ferrat that she rented from Mary Wells Lawrence. La Fiorentina was one of the most beautiful houses I'd ever seen. It had a saltwater pool and a freshwater pool, which had a stone terrace running around it from which you had an unobstructed view of the Mediterranean. At every corner of each pool were stacks of fabulous blue towels. And the house was so well run that the moment you came out of the pool and grabbed a towel and were done with it, a member of the staff grabbed it and removed it, and another towel was added to its place in the pile. This was Bill's idea of heaven. Constant perfection.

There were dream moments in different places: dinners at La Fiorentina with Madame Rochas and Madame de Rothschild, Sao Schlumberger and Grace Kelly. There was an absolutely magical benefit party for the Wafa Wal Amal Center for the handicapped in Egypt, organized by Madame Jihan Sadat, in the desert near Cairo, with tables set up on rugs on the sand, the moon rising, lanterns and candles glimmering in the darkness, and Frank Sinatra emerging from the shadows to sing to us under the gaze of the Sphinx. I had tried, as was my habit, to beg out of that magnificent party, for which Si Newhouse had bought an entire table and had flown us to Cairo in a private jet. But Bill hadn't let me. As always, his social instincts kept me afloat.

It was a rare stroke of luck, in midlife, to find both love and a modern marriage of the type that I never, in my youth, would have dreamed possible. Marriage—the thing I'd so feared as a burden, a career-buster—had opened up a whole new world of challenges and adventures. I was happier than I'd ever been in my life.

Everything was coming together.

It was too good to last.

CHAPTER 8
FALLING
OUT OF
VOGUE

"If you take away the light in the individual eye, can there be fashion at all?"

KENNEDY FRASER,
The New Yorker, January 14, 1980

By 1980, for the first time in United States history, more women were working outside of the home than were staying in it.

And what did they have to wear?

Well, if they wanted to "dress for success," there were three options: vampy, tailored "Girl Friday"-type suits, short, tight skirts with slits worn with teeteringly high-heeled shoes, and straight, knee-length skirts, worn with padded-

shoulder jackets. And if they didn't want to look like Rosalind
Russell or Rosalynn Carter, they could simply play dress-up and
choose a costume from yet another era. If they wanted to be Victorian, they could dress in Laura Ashley. They'd find vestiges of the
1930s in Yves Saint Laurent. Bill Blass was doing the 1960s again,
and Oscar de la Renta had reinvented Balenciaga.

Basically, working women were on their own. Nobody had a
clue as to what they should look like. And virtually no one was
coming up with any good suggestions.

Where had the creativity, the glorious energy of the early 1970s
gone?

Into chocolates, sunglasses, lingerie, cookware, luggage, sheets
and towels. Into sex, drugs, and Studio 54.

Taking control of their own businesses in the late 1960s had
made the designers their names. Licensing, in the 1970s, had
made them rich. By the 1980s they were very, very rich. In 1982
Bill Blass, Halston, Perry Ellis, Oscar de la Renta, and Geoffrey
Beene earned in the neighborhood of 2 to 4 million dollars each.
Ralph Lauren earned an estimated 12 million; Calvin Klein, 15
million. Or so reported the now-ubiquitous *Women's Wear Daily*.
And in the culture of money, glitz, and celebrity that gripped the
country as the seventies turned into the eighties that turned into
the Reagan years, they all became celebrities.

Halston, under the influence of drugs and a massive licensing
agreement he'd signed with Norton Simon in 1973, grew grandi-
ose. His personal manner got grander and grander, and his offices
grew bigger and bigger. He settled into a gigantic space high up
on Fifth Avenue with panoramic views overlooking Saint Patrick's
Cathedral and Rockefeller Center. He was haughtier than ever,
especially when he was high on drugs, which I could always per-
ceive anytime I went backstage to shake his hand after a collection
and received a cold, clammy hand and a few words of welcome
directed somewhere over the top of my head.

It was terrible to watch a genius like Halston go down. It was
torture to go to dinner at the beautiful town house he'd bought on

the Upper East Side with his boyfriend and see it ransacked by the spooky, wicked-seeming crowd he'd gathered around him. They were guys he'd picked up, club types of indeterminate gender, nationality, and age, various bits and pieces of New York demimonde, including a character who always lurked in the background looking like an old movie villain, plus the hottest fashion editors around. People would regularly disappear from dinner and sneak off up the huge, banisterless stairway that led up to the bedrooms. You never knew exactly what they did up there, or how they came down without holding on to a railing, because when they came back to the table their eyes were red and unfocused, and the table conversation moved down yet another notch toward incoherence. No one cared. Incoherence was almost de rigueur at an evening at Halston's. People cultivated it, like they cultivated the contacts that got them their invitations.

By the 1980s everyone now was a *personality*. Everyone was *presenting*. The friendly, gritty world of the Seventh Avenue manufacturers was gone. Ralph Lauren was living in great style. Calvin Klein, once a kid from the Bronx I used to see running up Seventh Avenue with a garment bag of clothes on his shoulder to show Mildred Custin at Bonwit Teller, was now a superstar. He was a Studio 54 regular, a real king of the social scene, so busy experimenting with everything the eighties lifestyle was about that he no longer had the time to show swatches or sketches to the editors with whom he once worked so closely at *Vogue*. We at *Vogue* had always worked a great deal with him because we loved his sense of ease and his very modern, unexcessively designed clothes. But now he lost interest in communicating with us. He acted as if he didn't need us. Which, in reality, by the mid-1980s, he didn't.

Bill Blass was playing the role of Cole Porter. He showed his clothes at the Pierre Hotel, Bobby Short music playing in the background, and with his "babes" and his "dames"-studded speech, he sounded like a character straight out of Noel Coward. He maintained an aura of glamour around himself that made women feel, when they were out with him, as though they were with Fred As-

taire, dancing through darkened black and white streets. Doing
this well, *being Bill Blass*, was how he built up his business.

Blass was the first designer to travel around the country with
his clothes, presenting them in small "trunk shows" at department
stores like Neiman Marcus and I. Magnin to a select group of ladies
who stayed around after the show to meet The Designer. These
were wealthy ladies and they were usually so taken with Blass's
clothes that they bought dresses and pants suits and jackets and
skirts, and invited him to the opera or to the opening of the ballet.
It wasn't too long before Blass had become a very key player in the
San Francisco social scene and the Chicago social scene. Blass always managed to be showing his clothes in San Francisco in time
for the opening of the opera, and to be back in New York for the
start of the winter social season. Traveling in this way, he built
himself a constituency among wealthy ladies all around the country. His ladies all looked more or less the same: blond and pretty
with names like Missy and Cordie, all Waspy and leggy and draped
in Bill Blass. As had been true with Emanuel Ungaro, though,
there was a price to be paid for Blass's popularity with the "ladies
who lunch" crowd: The more successful he became, the less racy,
the less bold, his clothing grew. Blass was a designer with unrivaled talent for what Diana Vreeland used to call "Toff Tailoring"—a man capable of making the best-designed women's suit,
with the smartest, raciest cut and the gutsiest fabric. He knew how
to make clothes that moved, and could have set a shining path for
modern American design. Instead, he became a maker of evening
dresses and played the old-world role of couturier to the rich and
leisured.

Rivaling Blass in his success at bridging the gap between fashion and society was Oscar de la Renta. Oscar de la Renta, an insurance adjuster's son from Santo Domingo by way of Madrid and
Paris, had been a charming, attractive young man when he'd first
begun coming by Vreeland's office in the early 1960s to show her
his clothes. At that time he had just come from Paris to design
custom order at Elizabeth Arden, following in the steps of Antonio

Castillo. His designs were lovely and ornamental, and with Vreeland's encouragement he'd eventually set up his own business on
Seventh Avenue, first under the auspices of the very talented businessman Ben Shaw, and finally on his own. He'd hung on by the
skin of his teeth, until his perfume, Oscar de la Renta, had made
his fortune. With his wealth had come a taste for high society,
which Oscar pursued so effectively, particularly after marrying
Françoise de Langlade, formerly the editor of French *Vogue*, that
by 1981 *The New York Times Magazine* had labeled the de la
Renta household "a latter-day salon for *le nouveau grand
monde*—the very rich, very powerful and very gifted" and had
crowned the de la Renta couple the "barometers of what consti-
tutes fashionable society."

Oscar's closest society was a group of particularly wealthy ladies who'd become his regular clients. They were the kind of ladies
who began all their sentences with "My dear . . ." and set the tone
for much of what passed as conversation in the fashion world during the early Reagan years. I recall one such conversation particularly: I was sitting with an empty seat beside me, waiting for one of
Oscar's fashion shows to begin. It couldn't start until that empty,
important seat was filled. Finally, the grand Lady Dudley swept
in, fifteen minutes late. Once seated, she turned to me and, like a
sergeant calling her troops to attention, bellowed into my ear, "My
dear! You can't imagine where I've been!"

"No, I can't," I murmured, craning my neck to watch the first
dresses.

"I've been up at Memorial visiting a friend who was operated
on by Dr. Bill Cahan. She showed me her incision, and, my dear,
Vionnet couldn't have done it better."

Vionnet was a great designer in the early twentieth century who
was known as a genius at cutting on the bias, and in appreciation
of this very clever joke, I interrupted my work to smile at Lady
Dudley. "Thanks," I said, "I know Bill's been trying to perfect his
bias work."

An atmosphere was building that made me seriously wonder what the future of the fashion world would be.

The balance of power was shifting, and in a very disturbing direction. Whereas manufacturers had once been thrilled to find themselves featured in the editorial pages of *Vogue*, designers didn't have to depend on the good favor of magazines like *Vogue* to get their clothes shown anymore. Designers now had so much money that through heavy and well-placed advertising they could "buy" the look of a magazine, or reach an even wider audience by buying spots on television, as Calvin Klein did so very powerfully with his Brooke Shields ads for his jeans. What the designers looked to us for now was the prestige that a positive mention in *Vogue* could confer. And, increasingly, they were willing to use their ad money to try to force us to give them that good mention.

The problem, which had always been present when dealing with Italian designers like Valentino (in Italy, the boundaries between editorial and advertising space were far weaker than in the U.S.), had been building and worsening for about a decade. In the 1970s, though, it was still sometimes possible to cut through the strong-arm tactics with a little direct give and take. When Ralph Lauren called me once in a rage and chewed me out because he didn't think we had reported a spring collection of his well enough, I apologized, listened for a few minutes while Ralph really laid me out flat.

"Okay, Ralph," I said, "let's cut this short. We didn't design the collection, you did."

Ralph was so surprised that he laughed and always said afterward that he appreciated the fact that he could count on me to talk straight to him. But soon, there wasn't much chance of that happening. By the 1980s no one was speaking directly to designers anymore; editors spoke to assistants and publicists and received responses by letters and faxes. Communicating with a designer was like playing telephone. Approaching Giorgio Armani meant first getting past a troika of absolutely miserable women whose purpose in life seemed to be doing everything and anything they could to torpedo Armani's relationship with *Vogue*. When I cabled once to say that I had been called home from Milan a few days early and would have to miss Armani's show, the three furies threatened *Vogue*. When I telexed another time saying that I thought I would have to miss a preview, I received *orders* saying that "Mr. Armani" demanded my presence. It was all simply appalling, though the worst was to come later, when we criticized a ghastly collection that Armani had done and received a hailstorm of letters and phone calls threatening us never to count on being able to photograph Mr. Armani's clothes ever again. (We, of course, being great fans of Armani's, did photograph them, time after time.) I often wondered afterward, and still do wonder, whether Giorgio was even aware of all of this. In any event, it did not prevent him from going on to change the way an entire generation looks at fashion design. Armani's influence, as the 1970s turned into the eighties and nineties, cannot be underestimated. His clothes were more than "fashion," they were a *style*, a school of thought. Were it not for him, the fashion-following women of Los Angeles would still be running around looking like Barbie dolls.

The era of sustained, close working relationships between editors and designers was over. No one cared about working together to better fashion anymore. In fact, the people working for a designer like Armani didn't really care about what *Vogue* thought of the clothes. They had no creative pride at stake; what they really wanted was a mention in *Vogue* that would boost name recognition and status and bolster the sales of the designer's licensees. That was all that really mattered. Fashion was first and foremost about big business and only secondarily about design.

With bigness, wealth, and celebrity came gossip, self-promotion, and nastiness. And there was no greater single source of it than John Fairchild's *Women's Wear Daily*. *Women's Wear Daily* had once been a rather straightforward trade newspaper. But as the designer moment began, in the late 1960s, Fairchild devoted more and more of his pages to gossip and star gazing, profiting

from it so much that in 1972 he created *W* as a sister publication
to *Women's Wear Daily. W* obsessively chronicled the ins and outs
of New York society through articles like "The Beautiful People,"
"The Fashion Victims," "Nouvelle Society," and "The Tribes of
New York." Like Oscar de la Renta, whom Fairchild always harassed in print, implying that the noble *particule* in his name was a
fake, Fairchild built his power and his fortune by living off people
obsessed with seeing their faces in print. He lived off scandal, off
competition, and off fear. He whipped up momentum behind the
fashion "star wars" that supposedly went on between Halston and
Calvin Klein in the 1970s, and between Calvin and Ralph Lauren
to this day. He turned market reports into scandal sheets, unable,
for example, simply to do a feature on Calvin Klein and Halston
without accusing Calvin of being a knockoff of Halston, because
he knew the latter tack would set off fireworks. Everything became
political. The gossip and intrigue, and constant in-and-out group-
ings of designers and socialites, poisoned the atmosphere of the
fashion industry and spread like a cancer. The buzz up and down
Seventh Avenue became quite mean-spirited. The industry became
full of people haggling for space and attention and trying to outdo
each other in image—and not in design. And that, as far as I was
concerned, was the worst thing of all about the moment of John
Fairchild and Oscar de la Renta. Fashion came to be about personalities and not creativity, and the competition in the fashion world
came to be built all around who was in and who was out, and not
around who was designing well and who wasn't.

The demands of being celebrities and maintaining big businesses sapped the creativity of the best fashion designers. Very few,
like Ralph Lauren, could manage to remain grounded and maintain a proud level of quality across the board in the products they
licensed their names to. Halston's clothes got worse as his drug
problems got worse and his taste for money got all the more pressing. His licensing deal with Norton Simon, Inc., had given that
company the right to use his name on any product. I would have
been all for bringing Halston's greatest clothes to a wider customer

base. But that didn't happen. Instead, Halston's clothes at every price point started to look mass-produced, candied. They lost their spontaneity. There was no sense of glory in his work anymore, not even in his custom order. And Halston himself was clearly going down on drugs. I watched his decline with a real sense of loss, frustrated that the days of being able to march up to a designer and say "I know you can do better" were so far gone. Finally, when it became too much to bear, I called Hillie Mahoney, a friend of mine who was married to David Mahoney, the head of Norton Simon, and asked her to talk to David. Choosing my words carefully—after all, you couldn't go tell the parent company of Halston that their boy was on the wrong track, if on *any* track—I tried to send out a warning. "Something's getting lost," I said. "Go see him."

But my warning seemed to have fallen on deaf ears as far as Norton Simon was concerned. I had the impression that all that company wanted to do was keep Halston going well enough that they could continue to sell him. His name, for them, was written in dollar signs. He was eclipsed by it. In 1987 he signed a licensing agreement with JCPenney that brought his clothes to mail order. Halston thought it would allow him to "dress America." And while he pursued his lofty (and lucrative) goal, high-end stores like Bergdorf's dropped his line, sure that the JCPenney connection would scare away their customers. By the time Halston died of AIDS, in 1990, after a series of corporate takeovers that had moved his name further and further out of his reach, he was virtually prohibited from selling fashion items he had designed under his own name.

Ironically, as the designers reached a greater number of customers, they lost a sense of the women that they'd begun designing for in the first place. At their prime, in the early years of the 1970s, Bill Blass, Halston, and particularly Yves Saint Laurent were obviously designing with their clients in mind. Blass had his "ladies" and Halston was always busy in his Sixty-eighth Street salon meeting with women like Babe Paley or me, working out compassionate designs to meet our needs. Yet, once their businesses became truly big, they seemed to lose interest in their clients. Perhaps they found the thought of designing for a range of women too frightening. Or perhaps the thought of so many women was just too overwhelming. Whatever the reason, the result was that just at the moment when women of all social classes were developing a need for the *same kind* of good quality, stylish work clothes, these designers decided to limit their sights to designing for the tiny number of women who formed their core constituencies. They decided to design for the "ladies"—the wives of wealthy men whose fashion needs hadn't really changed since the 1950s. And that left working women haplessly in the dark. Not to mention the young women who thought fashion was fun, but couldn't get near it because of the price.

The retrospective clothing and dress-for-success jokes of the late 1970s were harbingers of an era where fashion design basically died. A few consistently vital designers aside—Calvin Klein, Ralph Lauren, and Armani chief among them—the new cult of personality in the fashion world ushered in a decade where fashion came increasingly to be not so much about real clothes as about the image they projected of the designer who had created them. The culture of celebrity was partly to blame for this. The need to generate fantasies that could attach themselves to licensed products and sell a designer's name was important too. So was the increasing need to reach a wider and wider audience. Fashion in the late 1970s and 1980s could no longer whisper its suggestions of style to a select group of customers. It had to scream: wealth! class! clout! to the millions and millions of women shopping for Halston dresses in the JCPenney catalogue and for Ralph Lauren sheets at Bloomingdale's and squeezing themselves into Calvin Klein jeans in the dressing rooms at Macy's. And it also had to meet the peculiar demands of the latest blight to hit the fashion industry: the runway show.

In the past the couturiers had shown their clothes to a relatively small group of clients, store buyers, and fashion editors in their beautiful, intimate salons in Paris. Then, in the late 1970s, as time went on and his business became big, Yves Saint Laurent moved from showing in his salon to the ballroom of the Intercontinental Hotel. The room quickly filled, and each season became fuller and fuller, and Yves began doing runway shows, because the runway was the perfect way of making a big splash on a room filled with 500, 800, 1,000 people. Suddenly fashion shows weren't so much about fashion anymore as they were about creating a spectacle. You knew, when you saw those 500 people, that they weren't all going to buy at the couture; you knew that some of them were the cousins of the cousins of a woman who once, fifteen years ago, bought a couture dress . . . and you knew that others in the crowd were, perhaps, Madame de Whatever's favorite hairdresser, who knew Yves when he was a boy and had brought along his own little crowd of followers. These people came to the couture for the sake of the show. And soon the paparazzi came too and the full court press, and media from every corner of the globe. More and more interests started converging on the couture. And, soon, it was happening in ready-to-wear as well. Today's fashion scene was born.

From the dawn of the runway eventually came the ruin of clothes. Because the emphasis in fashion went from design, which is the sort of thing that can really only be appreciated up close, to presentation, which involves keeping a crowd of 500 (and more) people amused and entertained. Entertainment of that sort takes grand gestures, exclamations, styles that shock. In the 1980s the culmination of it all was Christian Lacroix.

In 1986 Christian Lacroix, formerly a designer for the House of Patou, introduced his first clothing line in Paris. Titled his "baby doll" collection, featuring bubble skirts for women who wanted to dress up as dolls, it ushered in a moment of crinolines, taffeta, tightly laced waists, miniskirts, poufs, and bustles. Lacroix's clothes were magical, musical, and ultimately set the fashion world back a good half a century. His fashion shows were the hottest tickets around in the mid-1980s in Paris. They were always held on a Sunday, traditionally a dead day for fashion, when only

Ricci showed his clothes. And they drew out whole arrondissements of rich ladies who couldn't think of a more splendid way of spending a Sunday afternoon than in passing *chez* Lacroix. I used to imagine them thinking: "What could be more charming and entertaining than to spend a few hours viewing Lacroix? My friends will all see that I'm here. I'm being entertained, I don't have to buy anything, and it's certainly better than any movie."

Lacroix's fashion shows were held in rooms marvelously decorated with flowers, mountains and mountains of flowers, always selected to match the colors of the collection and suited for the current season. The flowers were arched to form canopies over the stage entrances where Lacroix's models came out on the runway, and in their exuberant ball gowns, bouffant skirts, and exquisitely embroidered jackets, they looked like ladies resurrected from eighteenth-century illustrations of drawing-room life. One of the models even had white hair, and came prancing down the runway waving a little fan, looking for all the world like Marie Antoinette with her head sewn back on. When she reached the foot of the runway, I always expected her to stop and begin to perform a piece of light opera. And I was disappointed when she didn't. It would have given me a little something to distract me from the fact that despite all Lacroix's glitter and beauty and glitz, he wasn't giving women a damn thing to wear.

Christian Lacroix was from the Pyrenees, the mountainous region where France meets Spain, and his clothing, at its best, had a certain gaucho quality, "French Western" you could call it, romantic and cultivated with a flamenco frame of reference that came through in bolero jackets and beautiful embroidery, sunburnt colors and drama. Lacroix's creations, while exquisitely rendered and beautifully made, were more costumes than clothes. They were wonderfully well suited for the stage, magical when used by the New York City Ballet in 1988 for its performances of the American Ballet Theater's Gaieté Parisienne, but utterly unwearable in everyday life.

If I had not been in the fashion business, but merely been a spectator at one of Lacroix's shows, I'm sure that I too would have sat back in enchantment, thinking what a wonderful way it was to stay out of the dreary Paris rain. And I'll admit that there were times when Lacroix's magic did sway me. But when I started to realize what he was doing to fashion, I sobered up. Especially once I realized what Lacroix's impact was on the folks back home.

The ready-to-wear manufacturers on Seventh Avenue had jumped on the Lacroix bandwagon almost overnight. Victor Costa, for one, was making a fortune reproducing his fantasies and selling them in department stores like Saks at very approachable prices. Soon, at every price point from the couture on down to discount, the stores were flooded with Lacroix look-alikes. I thought it was a disaster. For what was truly glorious about Lacroix—the quality and vividness and extraordinary detail of his couture designs—was entirely lost when his ideas were watered down into ready-to-wear. Lacroix's confections were meant to be one-of-a-kind pieces, not trends. They weren't meant to be copied and adapted. And Christian Lacroix knew that. When I'd said to him once, at breakfast in New York, "You have done more damage to Seventh Avenue than any other single designer I've ever seen"—he'd laughed, proudly, and agreed. His partner, however, Jean-Jacques Picart, never spoke to me again. Perhaps he knew just how deeply I really felt about what I said so lightly.

I always felt that Lacroix's was a profoundly anti-woman moment. So it amazed me to see how avidly women fell for his clothes. They fell in droves, sometimes at $45,000 a pop. I'd see them all turned out at the Metropolitan Museum's Costume Institute ball wearing his costumes—or other similar confections by Ungaro or Scaasi—and I remember thinking how absolutely tortured they looked. And often they *were* tortured; their crinolines didn't permit them to sit down and they had to turn sideways to fit through doorways. When I saw this, and I saw the glee with which so many women swallowed it up, I realized that it wasn't Lacroix, it was I who was falling out of step with them. Lacroix's success told me that there was something widespread going on in society and that his clothes were just the tip of the iceberg. It told me, very clearly, what these women, flaunting in their froufrou, were really all about: wealth, and display, and excess. And in that, they weren't unlike anyone else in New York in the 1980s.

In the 1980s everything that I had ever loved in New York was falling sway to money-grubbing and glitz. Nothing was about anything anymore. Theater was all spectacle and no content— Madonna in David Mamet's *Speed-the-Plow*. Literature and art and architecture were "post-modern," as self-reflective and narcissistically bound up in their own self-creation as were the people who consumed them. Fashion was about gilding the lily until it died: it was the moment of tasteless wonders when even sportswear companies produced clothes that were like elaborate ice cream sundaes onto which someone put more and more and more cherries until the whipped cream bled red.

I was used to being around people who *did* something, created something, and derived their power from their accomplishments; these people were out of style in the 1980s. A "new aristocracy" had been born of investment bankers and their skinny wives, a new generation of society ladies whose good works for charity were performed, I always thought, more with an eye to a mention and a photo in the Sunday *New York Times* than with any sense of duty or compassion. As Elinor Wylie wrote: "Down to the Puritan marrow of my bones, there's something in this richness that I hate."

In the 1980s everything that was once considered wrong was now right, when what was once crude was now polite, and money talked, unabashedly, everywhere you went. The gloating, the excess, the *bad taste* of it all was revolting. Newly wealthy people began employing publicists to get their names and faces into the newspapers. One-pound gift tins of caviar circulated up and down Seventh Avenue, into the Condé Nast offices on Madison, and ended up in our Upper East Side kitchen so frequently that we started to plan our entertaining schedule around them. It was an Emperor-Has-No-Clothes era, and the new privileging of show over real style in the fashion world was altogether typical of it.

I was disgusted by much of what I saw of 1980s society. And I was sickened by the changes I saw overcoming the fashion industry. The old manufacturers weren't angels; they were businessmen, and pursued success often rapaciously. But they weren't mean-spirited and pretentious and socially exclusive either, and when they grew rich, they didn't suddenly reinvent themselves as new world aristocrats. They also didn't lose sight of their constituents.

My troubles with *Vogue* started at just about the time that Christian Lacroix burst onto the scene. Up until that moment, it had been possible, by keeping our sights focused on great designers like Saint Laurent, Armani, Geoffrey Beene, Calvin Klein, and Ralph Lauren, to continue to produce fashion coverage that I felt really remained true to our goal of "real life" clothes. But the Lacroix moment was so totalizing and so widespread within the fashion industry that it was impossible to ignore. And the sensibility that created it, reflected it—the wealth worship, the elitism, the disdain for the real lives of working women—was so thick that in the mid-1980s it was virtually impossible to find anyone willing to create images on a page that suggested other values. I couldn't get an easygoing look pictured in *Vogue* both because the clothes in the marketplace didn't allow it and because the "hot" photographers wouldn't—or couldn't—shoot it. A new generation of photographers like Patrick Demarchelier and Bruce Weber had bankrolled their way into prominence on the star-studded, glitzy eighties, and had no interest in—or ability to—turn their sights on alternative ways of seeing.

Arthur Elgort was a notable exception, and Helmut Newton, with his formidable talents, could have been, but wasn't. Instead, something tawdry had crept into his work, and as the new money culture had bled into his tales of seduction, themes of sexual exploitation and prostitution had crept in too. It seemed to me like such a terribly *cheap* way to show clothes: women in spike heels, panty hose, and bras running around a spa in Tuscany; Daryl Hannah in a Fiorucci bikini in Malibu, lying on a magenta bed with a shirtless young man before her, while in the mirror the faceless image of her husband, in polo costume, appears. This ridiculous scene of a beautiful rich woman's adultery was, according to Helmut, "My romantic notion of what America is or should be like." But what this and other pictures made me wonder was what Helmut was saying *women* were like.

That question may have been partly answered one summer when we sent Jade Hobson to Paris just before couture week to do a series of pictures of furs with Helmut Newton. Jade checked in with me at 10 P.M. every evening to let me know how things were going. The first night she called and said that everything seemed fine except for the fact that the model had quit. Not to worry, she said, she had arranged for another one for the next day. The second night, the same phone call, the same report. And then the third. She started running out of models.

"What's going on there?" I asked. "Why are they quitting?"

"I don't know," Jade said. "There's got to be something about the sitting they don't like."

When I arrived in Paris I found Helmut waiting with the developed film. I took one look at the pictures and instantly knew why all those girls had quit.

Each picture showed a model standing under a streetlight, almost nude under her fur coat. A short distance behind her was a male figure who looked, unquestionably, like her pimp. She looked, unquestionably, like a street walker. The pictures were technically perfect, absolutely beautiful. But they were also profoundly, inexcusably offensive. I told Alex he couldn't possibly use them.

"You can't publish this kind of thing in America anymore and not have people wonder what we're doing to women," I said.

And Alex, who normally stood by everything Helmut did, for once didn't say anything. He told Helmut that the pictures wouldn't run and tried to peddle them to French *Vogue*. Helmut was unexpectedly understanding. He was preparing a show in Los Angeles, and took all of this as a taste of what might happen to him there.

"Do you *really* take these things that seriously?" he asked Alex.
"Well," Alex said, "Grace does."

French *Vogue* took one picture out of eight, and *Vogue* took a
rather substantial loss. And I was left feeling like a square.

It was a feeling that was coming over me more and more now,
as the eighties progressed and Alex Liberman and I began profoundly to clash in our views. Alex had been interested in my idea
of "real life" dressing in the Vreeland years, when it was new and
radical, and through the 1970s, when it was fashionable, but in
the eighties, the words seemed to him to be too pedestrian, too
banal. I tried to make the argument to him that no matter how
hard we tried, *Vogue*'s version of reality would never bear much
resemblance to the real thing, but he wasn't interested.

"You have such a *seventies* way of thinking," he said.

Alex always wanted to follow what was new. And he always
favored European designers over Americans. When Christian Lacroix's baby dolls appeared on the scene and were screamingly
embraced by *Women's Wear* and the rest of the fashion press, Alex
loved the opulence and the tartiness and urged me to support Lacroix. When I resisted, and gave Lacroix news coverage in our couture report but not in the pages where we showed what we thought
was best, Alex was furious.

It was the first time that we'd ever, in twenty years of working
together, had bitter, irreconcilable differences, and I found it very
painful. It was, also, however, probably unavoidable. I had become the editor of *Vogue* with a rather unusual caveat; I was to
exert my role, the official announcement said, "Under the over-
all guidance of Mr. Liberman, Editorial Director of Condé Nast."
Keeping a watchful eye on *Vogue* under Diana Vreeland had been
the purpose of promoting Alex to Condé Nast editorial director in
the first place. When I became editor, it was only natural that his
control would extend to me.

Alex supervised the redesign of my new office into shades of
beige and insisted, before Diana Vreeland had left the magazine
and against my protests, that I move into that office right away so

that everyone would know who was in charge. He then divided up
the magazine, putting me in charge of fashion and beauty, and he
began to consult on and assign features and arts coverage. I didn't
question this; in fact, I was grateful. I knew that I didn't have the
broad knowledge or cultural background that Alex did, and I
didn't have the kind of eye to be able to translate ideas into wonderful visuals, as he did. So, while other editors at Condé Nast
struggled to minimize Alex's presence in their lives (Ruth Whitney
of *Glamour* refused to work with him altogether), I welcomed his
input. I was, I think, rather in awe of him, and I felt blessed, in the
early years, to have him for a boss.

We were collaborators, friends. We had a light, slightly flirtatious working style that made our time together a pleasure. We
enjoyed being in each other's company. We loved our occasional
grand lunch together when we'd spend half an afternoon at La
Grenouille, Alex in his perfect gray suit and me in my suit from
Saint Laurent couture, very attractively drinking wine and eating
sole and guiltlessly enjoying ourselves on work time.

By the 1980s Alex had become a kind of mythical figure in the
Condé Nast empire. He was a gray-haired gentleman in his seventies. He had enormous power. He'd grown up at Condé Nast, he
knew everyone and everything, and as editorial director of all the
magazines, he was everyone's boss. He was one of the most perfectly organized people I'd ever met, and it fascinated me to see
him moving from floor to floor and art department to art department, using everyone's phone as if it were his own, traveling, like
Bill, with a slip of paper in his pocket, and being able to get twenty
calls made as he moved between his office on the fifteenth floor
and all the others throughout the building.

Alex ruled like a benign dictator, asking everyone who crossed
his path for opinions on major decisions ("Keep Alex off the elevator," I always used to say, "or he'll be asking the elevator men
their opinions too") and issuing his orders so solicitously that an
unseasoned ear might have mistaken them for suggestions. "My
dear Penn, let me send you a drawing of how that's to be done . . ."

Alex would begin an assignment for Irving Penn. "My dear Richard, surely you . . ." was his mode of address for a recalcitrant Dick Avedon. Alex never said "no" directly, either. Instead, it was: "What do you want to do that for?" an old Condé Nast line that I'd first heard from Vreeland when I was still a fashion editor and had asked her if I could join the little group on the masthead who were called senior editors.

"What do you want to do that for?" she'd asked me, a convincing tone of surprise in her voice. "It sounds old to me." And she'd left me feeling that maybe she had a point.

Behind Alex's honey-soaked delivery was an iron will, a tin ear for dissension, and an ego the size of the Newhouse fortune. He would regularly make mincemeat out of art directors, redoing their work in front of them, reassigning their stories, humiliating them before their assistants. He drove Ruth Ansell, our creative director, up the wall. Art director Roger Schoening was reduced to a quivering mass of frustration. If and when I disagreed with any of Alex's decisions, I used to exhaust myself finding ways to cradle his ego while working toward making him see my side of things. For starters, I never disagreed with him in front of anyone else. If he worked out a photo spread that I thought was atrocious, I'd never say, "This is awful," but rather would wait until we were alone together in his office and then would carefully wind my way around the words: "You know, somehow I don't feel this is working. I can't get my mind around the fear that it isn't quite what we intended." And as though in recognition of my not-insignificant efforts, Alex would listen. He wouldn't say anything while I spoke, nor would he acknowledge when I'd finished, but more often than not, a few hours later, I'd find him in the art department reworking an idea. His pride in his craft, his need for perfection, was more powerful even than his ego. Or so it seemed to me then.

Until the moment of Christian Lacroix, Alex and I never lost our sense of pleasure in working together. But after Lacroix, our relationship started degenerating. Alex was often cross, wandering through the art department changing things. I started arguing with him more and more about the look of the magazine, particularly criticizing the nudity and what I saw as the anti-woman imagery in the work of photographers like Helmut Newton or even Deborah Turbeville. I hated it when we did fashion pages like the ones entitled "Hidden Delights" in our March 1987 issue, which showed two models blindfolded, one binding herself tight in her corset strings, and another with her ankles tied together. We started fighting over everything: whether a sleazy sex piece by Mary Russell was worth running because it was "modern" (Alex) or "poor" (me); whether or not Le Cirque had surpassed La Grenouille briefly as *the* place to eat at that moment (I said yes, Alex said no), and whether it mattered at which restaurant the food was actually better. All of Alex's opinions, no matter how trivial the topic, appeared to have been handed down to him by the highest authority. When I wanted to do a story on breast cancer, Alex told me "*Vogue* readers are more interested in fashion than breast cancer." I replied, "Alex, I've been a woman longer than you, and they're interested in both." In the past I had grinned and borne them. Now, I couldn't bear to acquiesce anymore. I was exhausted with trying to feed Alex's ego. And I was tired of being perceived as a pushover just because I believed in collaboration.

It was an unexpected side effect of my marriage: the happiness, the new grounding that life with Bill Cahan had brought, had given me an entirely new kind of self-confidence. Bill was making me think hard about my role as a fashion editor. When he saw me coming home, night after night, demoralized and complaining about *Vogue*, he asked, "What, exactly, do you think you're supposed to be doing? Are you a critic or a player? Is it your job to protect women from fashion? Or are you meant to reflect fashion in the best way possible?"

For some time I wasn't sure how to answer him. In my heart, of course, I'd always been a critic. But my job as a journalist was ostensibly to report. Advertising concerns *demanded* that I report. And, in response, I'd always sat on the fence between the two roles of reporter and critic. That hadn't been difficult in the 1970s, when I'd felt that a good deal of the clothing being designed was in step with modern women. But in the 1980s, with clothing veering toward the abyss of the utterly reactionary, I felt that position put me in bad faith. And as the years passed I grew more and more convinced that it wasn't enough just to report fashion, or to *rationalize* it into some larger than life phenomenon, as the fashion press always does—most outlandishly of late with the waif phenomenon of 1992. Now, I began to feel sure that fashion editors had the responsibility of playing the role of critics, that they did, indeed, have to "save" women from fashion, when fashion was bad for them, by offering them better choices. And if that meant neglecting Christian Lacroix a bit, I decided, so it was. It was better to weather the blast of Alex's criticism than to be in bad faith.

Another area in which Alex and I were constantly at loggerheads was over our health coverage. Life with Bill Cahan had made it impossible for me to see fashion and beauty news as the most important information we could pass on to our readers. I felt more and more strongly that we had to provide hard-hitting, awareness-raising health coverage. Alex agreed in theory. But in practice he balked. His attitude toward women and health was, in many ways, like my elderly mother's. My mother came from a world where you never wanted anyone to know your unpleasant "business," and where things like breast cancer, for example, simply weren't talked about. Some women she knew never even went to the doctor because it violated their sense of privacy. In Alex's world order, good manners prevented any discussion of cancer—and probably, if practiced stringently enough, could have fended off its occurrence as well. The end result was a see-no-evil, hear-no-evil approach to all that was unpleasant.

"For God's sake, who needs to read about cancer?" Alex would say. "Nobody wants to. It's too depressing."

Aging was another topic that Alex found too unattractive for words. Aging at *Vogue* had traditionally been covered through a column called "Over 40," which had later been renamed "Mrs. Exeter." "Mrs. Exeter" showed larger-sized clothes with high necklines and little cap sleeves to hide drooping arms, modeled by gray-haired ladies who looked seventy and were supposed to be about forty-five. I suppose the advantage of this was that any forty-five-year-old woman reading *Vogue* could look at "Mrs. Exeter" and feel that she looked a good thirty years young for her age; the downside was that the very real question of aging all but disappeared from the magazine. As I passed the fifty-year mark and realized that I was older than "Mrs. Exeter" and still not ready for cap sleeves, the question of aging—psychologically, physically, aesthetically—began to interest me. I called a staff meeting of all my editors, and together we plotted out a special issue on age, with beauty, fashion, health, and feature articles all addressing different aspects of the topic. We all were excited about the idea— until, after our second meeting, Alex knocked it out flat.

"Nobody wants it pointed out to them that they're older than anyone else," he said, killing the aging issue. "It just isn't modern."

"Not modern" was the worst thing that anyone at *Vogue* could have been. I was silenced. And I was furious.

After the aging debacle, I began to fight Alex in earnest. I'd been tethered to him for more than fifteen years and I was beginning to chafe at the bit. I'd finally had what in the early 1970s the women's movement called a "click," a moment of lucidity in which the injustices of my everyday life suddenly became crystal clear.

I started thinking about the fact that although the vast majority of Condé Nast employees were women, putting out publications for women, only one senior company official, Mary Campbell, the head of personnel, who had started out as Condé Nast's own secretary, was female. I thought about the fact that at *Vogue* the men were all on the "business side" while the women were in editorial, and the men earned decent salaries while the women earned debutante wages. I thought about the fact that Alex, who knew far less about the business of fashion than I did, was the only person from the editorial side of *Vogue* with whom Si Newhouse shared his thoughts about the financial operation of the magazine. I thought about the fact that Alex—not I—controlled all decisions on hirings and firings at *Vogue*. This meant that I was stuck with staff members who were out of synch with the *Vogue* I wanted to edit. And it meant that as editor in chief I didn't have the right to redesign even the masthead without Alex's blessing.

I thought about the way that Alex Liberman had adopted my pro-woman line as a way of selling the magazine to new readers. And then I thought of his favorite line about the women's movement: "Clearly the woman of the future will be bald," how he dismissed story ideas: "No, you don't want to do a story on the pro-choice movement. Nobody cares . . ." and how he reacted when we wanted to do a story on the changing roles of women: "You don't need to do another story about working women. Women are cheap labor and always will be."

I'd never been any great kind of a feminist. In fact, I'd never been any kind of feminist at all. Condé Nast was such a sheltered environment that I hadn't had much contact with day-to-day sexism. Sexism in the larger world was like background noise, a nuisance that was so constant and so *normal* that I never thought to name it or even take it all that seriously.

Sure, I used to get annoyed. When I was in the marketing department at *Vogue* in the early 1960s, I used to periodically go out to the General Motors Tech Center in Detroit to check out the new cars and note those which we might eventually want to photograph in fashion sittings. The men in the showrooms would very seriously and politely take me around to the cars and would show me the new vanity mirror on the back of the sunscreen where a woman could check her lipstick. They showed me glove compartments big enough to hold a pair of gloves. They acted as though car design had to be explained to me on the level of the design of a handbag. I was disgusted. I finally went up to the office of one of the G.M. executives and said, staring down at the flow of traffic in the streets below, "Do you think there's not a single woman in any of those cars? Do you think women don't drive? Or own their own cars?

Or participate in the purchase of a family car?" I told him G.M. wouldn't be able to ignore female customers forever. Which, of course, they couldn't, though they tried long and hard. As the saying holds: As General Motors goes, so goes the nation.

I didn't have to go to Detroit to be condescended to in those days. Condescension began at home, right here in New York, at the very best dinner parties. It wasn't uncommon then that after everyone had made the effort of speaking politely to one another, one man would turn to another with real interest and say, "What happened on the stock market today?" and then turn to me and whatever lady happened to be on his other side and say, pseudo-sheepishly, "Forgive me, but I just want to ask him because I know he's an expert. I know *you're* not going to care."

Which isn't to suggest that I walked around in a state of noble outrage. I didn't. If I was annoyed by G.M., or if I was bored after dinner, as the men and women separated, the boys to smoke cigars and talk politics and the girls to chat about clothes, I didn't protest, I just tuned out. These were the annoying, nonnegotiable facts of life for me, and I accepted them almost unquestioningly.

I accepted the world as I found it through the 1950s and 1960s and even into the early 1970s. And when Brenda Fasteau of NOW held forth on the women's lib cause at Sandra Feigen's in the late 1960s, I dismissed what she said. When Gloria Steinem showed up at Lally Weymouth's for lunch, I avoided her. She was a woman whom I'd admired, on a personal level, right from the start. But I always suspected that given half a chance she and the likes of Brenda would start pointing their big guns at me. And I didn't buy into that. I always felt that from the moment they stopped talking about equal rights and equal pay and got into the broader ideological arguments about power and patriarchy, the women's rights movement lost its relevance for women like me.

I did not consider myself part of a patriarchal power structure. I'd always worked for such tough, demanding women—Ballard and Morton and Vreeland. I'd worked with the kind of women who had been choosing professional ambition and personal gratification over traditional marriage for decades before "women's liberation" told them to. I'd always identified myself with these women, and never with the broader mass who had given up their careers for husbands and children.

I didn't understand what these women were up against at home. I didn't understand what office conditions were like in other places. When a *Newsweek* editor called me once for some information and, while he waited for us to find the material he needed, asked me if anything unusual was going on at Condé Nast, I remember being shocked to learn that female researchers at *Newsweek* were holding a protest meeting and announcing they were filing sexual discrimination charges against the magazine. And I was very surprised *Vogue* was singled out as an enemy in the war for women's equality. I had thought that *Vogue*, by its very nature, was a pro-woman institution. It took many years of having a male boss for me to see otherwise. Working for Alex Liberman radicalized me.

After Alex had announced, as though he had it on the *highest authority*, that women would always be cheap labor, I decided to take him to task for it. Editors' salaries at Condé Nast had lagged despicably behind all the pay increases that women were earning in other fields. In the mid-1970s I began an all-out campaign to get Alex and Si to change that.

"Alex," I would say, closing his office door behind me and taking a stern pose before it, "you are going to end up with a talentless magazine. Women who fifty years ago wanted to work in fashion and had nowhere to go except department stores or magazines can now work anywhere they want. You're not competing just with other magazines anymore. You're competing with the whole world. And if you want to attract the best people, you simply cannot expect to continue paying these salaries."

After about five years, Alex got the message and began, slowly and fitfully, to relate it to Si Newhouse. By the early 1980s salaries had started to go up at *Vogue*. As far as my own job was concerned, I by then wanted more power than money. I wanted corporate clout, a voice on the business side of the magazine and a seat at the table when important decisions were made. I was tired of being, in some essential ways, a figurehead. I'd learned, for example, that *Vogue*'s newsstand price was rising not from Alex or Si but from the publisher of another magazine. This was humiliating, and it was bad both for my image and for *Vogue*'s. It was a travesty for a corporation that was ostensibly all about women.

I went to Si Newhouse and asked to be made a vice president of Condé Nast.

"I've been here for years," I said. "I've played a very active role in every aspect of this publication. I have a successful magazine. I deserve a voice in its future."

"Oh, what do you want to do that for?" Si Newhouse drawled. "We don't really even *have* vice presidents."

I'd received the same kind of brush-off from him, many years earlier, when Mack Baldrige, Tish's brother, who would later become Secretary of Commerce, invited me to be on the board of his company, Scoville Zippers. Like a fool, before accepting, I asked Si for permission. Without more than a moment's thought, he said no. And when I asked why, he didn't even struggle to produce a convincing excuse.

"Women don't really mean anything on boards, Grace," he said. "And nobody pays any attention to their boards, anyway. It's a waste of your time."

Now, Alex chimed in, "You've got the biggest title in the place. You're editor in chief of *Vogue*. That's as big as you can be."

I remembered that comment recently when I saw Alex quoted in a *New York* magazine story on the appointment of thirty-six-year-old James Truman as his successor at Condé Nast. Truman was chosen over several long-term job aspirants, including Condé Nast vice president and former associate editorial director Rochelle Udell, Anna Wintour, and *New Yorker* editor Tina Brown. Alex said, "I think it is better for a man to be in this job, because you deal with other men. You know, the business side is all male, and you deal with the engravers, printers, all those things. And I think the women editors are more receptive to something from a man, and there may be female resentment, jealousy . . ." Alex refused to admit that I might have any role on the business side of the magazine. And Si, seeing me working with shoulder pads and lipstick shades, simply assumed I couldn't do anything else.

I had learned the meaning of the words "glass ceiling." I'd never in my life been aware of such limits.

And yet another battle was still to come.

Ever since I'd married Bill and had begun to educate myself on the dangers of smoking, I felt that the best thing *Vogue* could do for its readers was to get them to quit smoking. Right away, I banned smoking in fashion photographs. We put together a symposium of doctors discussing what was most important for a woman to know about her health, and each and every one of them said that the most important thing for any kind of healthy living person was to stop smoking. We reported every new study that spoke out against smoking. If we did a beauty feature on lips or teeth we made a point of mentioning smoking and nicotine stains. In doing this in the 1970s, *Vogue* had been a trendsetter. By the mid-1980s we were right in the middle of a great upsurge of anti-tobacco activism. In fact, I now felt that we weren't doing anything nearly enough.

In 1986 *The New York Times* reported that while the number of adult smokers in America had declined by nearly a fifth in the last decade, the number of women who smoked had actually increased, and now more than twenty-four percent of female smokers smoked more than twenty-five cigarettes a day. A growing chorus of opinion now held that cigarette advertising targeted specifically to women was in large part to blame. In 1985 the National Advisory Council on Drug Abuse had recommended to Margaret Heckler, secretary of the Department of Health and Human Services, that legislation should be implemented to eliminate cigarette advertising in the United States. Two years later Canada did ban all cigarette advertising in the media. But in the U.S. in the late

1980s the tobacco lobby had grown much too strong for government or the media to dare such tactics.

In 1985 the tobacco giant R. J. Reynolds, owner of Canada Dry, Del Monte, Chun King, and other brands, took over Nabisco, whose products included Oreo cookies, Inglenook wines, Smirnoff vodka, and Kentucky Fried Chicken. Overnight, the company controlled 961 million dollars in advertising revenues. Marlboro maker Philip Morris then acquired General Foods, the nation's largest food company, and gained control of $1.2 billion in ad revenues. In the wake of these mergers, *Reader's Digest*, which had begun refusing to carry cigarette ads, turned down a proposal for an advertising supplement on heart disease because it would have mentioned the dangers of smoking, and the editors worried they wouldn't be able to find sponsors because their major advertisers were food companies now owned by tobacco companies. Media watchers were warning that television and radio stations too could expect to see their ad revenues from such big accounts as Birdseye frozen foods or Fleischmann's margarine threatened if they reported on the health hazards of smoking.

I'd long felt that our editorial policy of denouncing smoking while all the time accepting millions of dollars each year in cigarette advertising (3.25 million in 1986 alone) made us look foolish, to put it mildly. I'd been embarrassed when one of our reporters, Janice Kaplan, had interviewed Stanford Medical School Professor John Farquhar for a health feature and, upon being asked if *Vogue* accepted tobacco ads and having to say that we did, was sent back to me with the message: "Tell Grace she can do more for women by cutting cigarette advertising in *Vogue* than by anything else she can do."

No one should have had to tell me that. I had raised the issue of refusing cigarette ads with Si Newhouse at various times during the 1980s and had always been met with either silence or bleak refusal. But there'd never been any interference with our editorial campaign against smoking. All of that changed, however, in the wake of the R. J. Reynolds and Philip Morris mergers.

In August 1986 I received a memo from our publisher, Richard
Shortway, saying that while he didn't disagree with my views on
the dangers of cigarette smoking, he felt he had to draw my attention to the fact that *Vogue*'s three-million-per-year patrons, the
cigarette makers, had been reading the magazine and were starting to complain. He attached a note from Bob Rose, our manager
of tobacco advertising, which said that Philip Morris was "fuming" over the fact that an article in our August issue had intimated
that cigarette smokers were downscale, uneducated, chiefly lower-
income people. A recent article we'd run commenting on the 1985
Surgeon General's report, Richard said, had been "very badly received." A skull and crossbones illustration that we had used in
a May issue to make a point about smoking had met with some
displeasure as well. "Couldn't we slow it down for a moment and
perhaps when you feel the need do it ideally without mentioning
names . . ." Richard begged me, "or without illustrations such as
the skull . . . ?"

I tried to laugh the suggestion off, and green-lighted a long
article on the dangers of smoking by the writer Judith Schmid.
When the manuscript came in and made its way up to the "boys
upstairs," another avalanche of memos began. First, there were
some proposed line changes: Richard Shortway suggested that we
"take a little of the sting out" of the piece by softening its message
with a few choice phrases added by Bob Rose. One was to temper
the assertion that women who start smoking early are the most
highly at risk for cancer with the words: "unless in their lifetime a
cure is found." Bob also suggested we note that many women who
smoke to avoid overeating "do not inhale thereby reducing health
risk." Richard and Bob demanded that one full section of the
piece, which singled out cigarette advertising as a most pernicious
form of propaganda and was subheaded "politics of smoking," be
cut altogether. Richard said that running this story would put us
just one notch above refusing tobacco ads altogether. He repeated
a suggestion made by Norman Waterman, our advertising director,
that if we published the article or any other anti-smoking articles

in the future, we would have to alert cigarette advertisers so they could cancel their ads in the same issues. Doing so in February 1987, the month that Schmid's piece was slated to run, he cautioned, would probably cost us eleven full-color ad pages, or $330,000. And Philip Morris and Lorillard had both already threatened that if we continued on this anti-tobacco campaign, they would pull not only out of *Vogue*, but out of the other Condé Nast magazines as well, costing millions and millions of dollars.

I refused to bend to the pressure. Finally, Alex approached me.

"My dear," he said, "Si and I were wondering if you wouldn't perhaps just want to be a little less *heavy-handed* on the subject of tobacco? Don't you think you might not want to mention cigarettes in every four inches of copy? Might an article on the dangers of smoking not be a bit too much in every *single* issue? Don't you think you might like to lighten up a bit?"

"*Vogue* lite?" I thought. "How 'modern.'"

"No," I said to Alex. "I don't want to lighten up."

"Oh, come on, Grace," Alex said. "How much conviction do you really have to have about *smoking*, anyway?"

"You know," I said, "with all that we do, at some point, *something* has to count. *Something* has to matter. I may not have realized that fully in the past, and I may not always have acted on my principles, but this means so much to me that I have to."

"But why *smoking*?" Alex asked with distaste. "Why *cancer*?"

I could see that he found my passion for such an unattractive subject totally incomprehensible.

"If you tell me that I cannot do articles warning women about the hazards of smoking," I said, "then I will quit."

"Oh, you wouldn't do that," Alex said.

"Try me."

It was a very seventies way to be, I was told. All this emphasis on content, on *meaning*. It was all out of style in the eighties. "Grace, don't you realize that, in our game, perception is more important than reality?" Verne Westerberg, who became publisher after Dick Shortway, would come into my office and ask me, as a prelude to a conversation about my "lightening up." "Don't you realize that perception is more important than content?"

No, I didn't realize that. I didn't want to. There was too much at stake for me. I had spent almost my entire life working for *Vogue*. I wanted to have something more behind me there than a history of raised and lowered hemlines. I wanted to be committed to *something*—whether it was fighting smoking or striving for real-life clothes or fighting Alex and Si to improve the status of women both in the pages and in the offices of our magazine. So I remained unrepentant on the subject of smoking. (Dick Shortway finally gave up smoking after having to recover from a smoking-induced cancer. Norman Waterman gave up smoking before any disease occurred.)

I believed in *Vogue*. I believed it could be a driving force to enhance the changing lives of American women. We only had to take ourselves as seriously as our readers seemed to take us, I thought. We had to be committed to doing the best for our readers.

Which was why, in 1986, when the trendy, young upstart *Elle* came on the scene and Si and Alex panicked at *Vogue*'s fluctuating circulation and ad figures, I resisted their efforts to turn our magazine into *Vogue* lite. I didn't buy into the cuteness of *Elle*. It was a magazine, I thought, that posed no real threat to us at *Vogue* because it spoke to an entirely different reader. It was a magazine for kids, a pure product of the MTV sensibility: trendy, cartoon-like, light on text, heavy on jokey fashion modeled by young and adorable girls. *Elle* made its fashion points by showing, say, an arm loaded with bracelets like Madonna's, or showing crayon-colored clothes, or browns and reds surrounded by licorice. It was cute, as far as it went. But it wasn't *Vogue*.

I thought that the way to defend ourselves from *Elle*'s encroaching circulation was by standing firm in keeping *Vogue* *Vogue*. I thought it was foolish for us to imitate a magazine that wasn't even in our league. *Vogue* was a winning bet; if we played someone else's game, I thought, we were sure to lose.

Si Newhouse disagreed—as did Alex. Whether it was on the

strength of his own convictions or just in an effort to please Si, he began leaning on me to make *Vogue* younger, cuter, jokier. It was the first time that I'd ever seen him willing to sacrifice taste and sophistication out of the fear of losing money. I think it was the first time in his life that he'd ever done so. And as the months passed and tempers flared and Alex fussed more and more in the art department, unable either to stick with what he knew how to do well or to learn another man's game, I saw a kind of panic come over him. He was, I felt, out of his league.

I was too. I didn't know how to edit a lite 'n' lively *Vogue*. I started writing Alex long letters, as I always had, to keep up contact during the summers when he'd taken off for his vacation in Europe and I'd stayed in New York minding the store and, up until the last few years, missing his presence. The letters had always been light and friendly in tone; now, they grew formal and angry. "Is *Vogue* meant to be an elite version of *Elle* (pretending quality of a sort but acting out a different message)?" I wrote. "I'd like to know everyone's thoughts! May I please?"

I was aware that more and more decisions were being made without my blessing. I was aware of the fact that I was falling out of *Vogue*. I *wanted* to get out. I wanted to become editor in chief of *Self*, which was in trouble, and asked Alex to ask Si if that would be possible. He told me that was out of the question.

It became clear that my days at Condé Nast were numbered. I'd grown up at a *Vogue* that was classy, strong, and genteel. To the end, I believed that the magazine was still, at base, a class act. I didn't see that things were changing, that the good old guys now were downright nasty, and that all the polish and gentility in the world couldn't bring back the decency of the old days. It was my great failing that I never really did get much of a handle on "real life." Instead, I kept blindly clinging to my dream world of magazine life in the better days. It never dawned on me to watch my back.

Maybe I *was* too much a woman of the seventies.

Maybe I wasn't sufficiently "modern."

Or maybe, in the end, it was all just about Anna Wintour.

CHAPTER 9
"FREE
AT LAST!"

A nna Wintour, a vision of skinniness in black sunglasses and Chanel suits, came to New York in 1976 and went to work at *Harper's Bazaar*, where she was soon fired on the grounds that she didn't understand the American fashion market. She then moved to Bob Guccione's *Viva*, a *Penthouse* for women of the seventies, but lost her job, with the rest of the staff, when the magazine folded. Eventually,

she landed on her feet at Ed Kosner's *New York*, where she produced periodic fashion supplements. Her work caught the eye of
Alex Liberman, who, upon meeting her, fell so in love with her
youth and well-born British cool that in 1983 he invented the title
of "Creative Director" for her at *Vogue* and gave her the power to
do as she wished with the magazine.

And so she was foisted upon me.

A very bizarre three years then followed, during which Anna
created a kind of office within the office, working with Alex, with
fashion editor Polly Mellen, with Jade Hobson, and *against* me.
She'd suggest photographers, locations, and story ideas and generally do whatever she could to undermine my thinking and authority. She'd sit in on editorial board meetings, shaking her head,
obviously disagreeing with everything I said or did, and biting her
lip to keep from saying so. Then, she'd go behind my back and
redo layouts, bring in new art, circumvent me and my fashion editors, and take charge of planning fashion sittings with photographers.

When she couldn't bypass my editors, she'd harass and criticize
them: demanding Polaroids, dropping into sittings, and ordering
them redone from scratch. Jade and Polly eventually got so angry
that they came to Alex and me and threatened they'd stop working
if Anna stayed on the scene. "Keep that woman out of the studio;
we can't stand her," they said, and they began, as much as they
could, to shut her out of their work.

Alex's solution was to stick Anna with Amy Gross, who'd
become features editor in 1983, when Leo Lerman was made
editor in chief of the new *Vanity Fair*. So Amy now found herself
running story lineups by a creative director.

Anna Wintour was cold, suspicious of everyone loyal to me,
and autocratic in her working style. She carved out a sphere of
influence for herself within the magazine and reported directly to
Alex. I think, in retrospect, that she was so sure she'd soon end up
in my job that she considered me more of a momentary inconvenience than a person she might have to answer to or contend with.

And I have no idea of what promises might, from the very start, have been made to encourage her. Alex absolutely adored Anna. He loved her look, her glamour. He loved the intrigue of having her clicking around the office in her high heels, trusted by and trusting no one except him. He thought that her work, which combined the glitz of the eighties with elements of street art and design, was brilliantly "modern." He'd often show up in my office and, with all the pride of a cat presenting a dead mouse to its owner, show me samples of art that Anna Wintour had brought in. "Isn't this wonderful," he'd say, breathlessly. "Look at what Anna has done."

The rumors quickly began that Anna Wintour was being groomed to succeed me. But I didn't believe them. There were always rumors flying around *Vogue*—once it had been that Françoise de Langlade was going to get my job—and I'd learned that listening to them all was the surest way to drive myself mad. Alex laughed off suggestions that anyone might be after my job. And, very solicitously, he led me to believe that keeping Anna Wintour around was in my best interest.

"Grace," he would say, "I know how you feel about talent. *Harper's Bazaar* feels that way too. I'm quite sure they're about to make Anna an offer. Don't you think that we should keep her here?"

"We can't survive without talent," I'd say, as Alex knew I would.

"Then you agree. We'll keep her here."

Anna Wintour dug my grave with my blessing. The vultures were circling and I didn't even see them. I assumed that she was being kept around *Vogue* to train before being sent back to England to work for Condé Nast in London. And when in 1986 she *was* sent back to London, it looked like I'd been right. Anna was named editor in chief of British *Vogue* and was charged with breathing life into its dowdy, exclusive, and outdated-looking pages. Once installed in the job, she started talking about bringing a sense of the modern women into the magazine, of improving its health and fitness coverage, of making it more democratic and more relevant . . . in other words, of bringing to it everything she'd seemed to disdain about *my Vogue* during the three years she'd worked there. Americanizing British *Vogue* worked. Although Anna's colleagues soon dubbed the period of her editorship "Nuclear Wintour" and the "Wintour of Discontent," the new magazine was generally considered a success. And the job established Anna as a player on the editor-in-chief circuit.

As the eighties progressed, and my relationship with Alex soured, this should have worried me. And when, in September 1987, Anna Wintour was brought back to New York and set up in the Condé Nast building with the job of remaking *House and Garden*, I should have been all the more suspicious. But I was so busy longing to get out of *Vogue* that I didn't entertain the possibility that someone could be longing to get in. Of course, I was longing to walk out, on my own terms, not to be kicked out.

But I still couldn't believe that the threat from Anna was all that real. Her makeover of the venerable *House and Garden* into the trendy new *HG* was by all accounts a disaster. She started off by rejecting two million dollars' worth of inventoried articles and photographs. She decided she was tired of the "empty rooms" that had always been the design magazine's stock in trade, and in their place commissioned pictures of celebrities' homes, did lifestyle stories on the rich and famous, and dressed everything up in such a fashion-y way that critics were soon calling *HG* "Vanity Chair" and "House and Garment."

Subscribers were less lighthearted about the changes. Condé Nast had to install a toll-free number to handle all the protest calls and subscription cancellations. Advertisers also defected, and by the winter of 1988 ad pages were down twelve percent.

In response to this fiasco, Si Newhouse decided to take action. In June 1988 he made Anna Wintour editor in chief of *Vogue*. And in the same shot he made me the latest casualty in a long and proud line of editors to have been suddenly and thoughtlessly axed.

It was two days before the long Fourth of July weekend; I should, in a sense, have seen it coming. My friend Leo Lerman, after all, had been fired from *Vanity Fair* by Si on New Year's Day, 1984. Bill and I had called him to see if he wanted us to pick him up on our way to a party at our mutual friend Betty Comden's, and he'd lightly said, "No, I have a date. I have to see Si Newhouse and I'll come after." In 1987 Si had waited until *House and Garden* editor Louis Gropp went on vacation before telling him that he'd been fired and replaced by Anna Wintour. This worked so neatly that two years later he fired *Self* editor Anthea Disney while she was vacationing in Connecticut, going so far, in her case, as to stop by her country house just for the pleasure of delivering the good news to her personally. My firing was clearly meant to have happened over the Fourth of July weekend, when it would have attracted the least media attention possible. Had someone not leaked it to Liz Smith, the tactic might have worked. Instead, it became *the* cause célèbre of a long, hot New York summer.

Si's history of firings had made him as unpopular as a man of his enormous wealth and power could be. His unceremonious canning of the highly esteemed, long-time *Mademoiselle* editor, Edith Raymond Locke, had sent shock waves through the magazine industry in 1980, and is still seen by many, in retrospect, as the blow that ushered in the new era of disloyalty, insecurity, and cutthroat competition that plagues the magazine world in our day. Edie Locke, who in the 1970s had changed *Mademoiselle* from a prim, "college girl's" magazine into a more modern book for a wider audience, was fired when she'd resisted pressure from Si to make *Mademoiselle* younger and sexier and more like *Cosmopolitan*. Her successor, Amy Levin, tried to make Si happy with stories like "Vibrators: Today's Love Toy," and was eventually fired and replaced by Gabé Doppelt, who after one year was replaced by Elizabeth Crow in 1993. At the time of my firing, Si seemed to be on a roll for particularly brutal dismissals. The year before I was dismissed from *Vogue*, in addition to Louis Gropp, Si had fired William Shawn, the beloved thirty-five-year editor in chief of *The*

New Yorker. (Five years later, Shawn's replacement, Robert Gott-
lieb, would come back from a trip to Japan to find he'd been un-
seated by British import Tina Brown.) A month after I was fired,
Si Newhouse approached Valerie Weaver at *Self* and reportedly
asked her if she'd *mind* making a change in editors in chief.

What was a constant, in all of Si Newhouse's seemingly erratic
behavior, was a kind of extreme insensitivity to the feelings of his
editors. Bill, who has known Si socially for decades, attributes this
brutality to a rather pathetic sort of shyness. Si takes a surgical
tack in his firings, Bill suggests, because he can't stomach having
conversations. I've always preferred not to give him the benefit of
the doubt. Having looked him in the eye and received his dull gaze
back as my future lay in the balance, I simply decided I didn't
care.

At the best of times, I'd never found him an engaging man.
We'd met in the 1960s, shortly after his family had bought the
Condé Nast publications. I was having dinner at The '21' Club
with a group of friends. At a certain point during dinner, one of
them waved at someone I didn't know across the room and said,
"Hey, Grace, I want you to meet your new boss." Along had come
a little fellow with a lady, and he shook my hand agreeably without saying much of anything. I found myself wondering if my
friend was really pulling my leg, and I know I didn't linger long
in conversation with him. And as the years passed, and I became
convinced that, unfortunately, Si really *was* Si, this pattern didn't
change.

I never took Si Newhouse very seriously. I never had much to
do with him, as I hadn't with his father, Sam, though for very
different reasons. Sam Newhouse had had very little to do with the
day-to-day running of the magazines, and I'd met him a relatively
small number of times. I've always remembered the first time: it
was at a cocktail party that he and his wife, Mitzi, held for *Vogue*
in their very swell Park Avenue apartment just a few years after he
had bought Condé Nast and just after I'd returned from Australia.
Someone introduced me to Mr. Newhouse and told him about my

trip. He looked at me with a nice little smile and said, "Tell me about Australia."

And I, not knowing the kind of man he was, and falling back on well-learned Condé Nast habits, said, "Well, the weather was wonderful and the sky was incredibly blue and it was warm," and as I watched as his eyes glazed over, I realized that he hadn't been looking for a weather report. He had wanted a solid answer about Australian *Vogue*. I wished that I could melt into the carpet.

Sam Newhouse, the son of a poor Russian Jewish immigrant, had dropped out of school at age thirteen to support his family and by the age of seventeen was turning his first newspaper around from near bankruptcy to profitability. Si, on the other hand, had grown up rich and privileged on Park Avenue in Manhattan. He'd been a poor student and an even worse journalist, and hadn't taken any particular interest in magazines until, in 1961, his father put him in the promotion department of *Glamour*. For years after he became the publisher of *Vogue*, the enormous power and cachet of his position sat uncomfortably on his shoulders. He didn't really move with the "right" crowd. In fact, one of his closest friends was Roy Cohn. He hadn't had the "right" sort of first wife. Or the right clothes. Or manners. That was where Alex Liberman came in.

Alex, who always knew where his bread was buttered, took the young Si Newhouse under his wing after a mutual friend suggested that he help Si purchase paintings for his apartment. He took Si around to museums and galleries, introduced him to the movers and shakers of the art world, advised him on putting together a good art collection, dined with him at the best restaurants. Before long, Si was ready for prime time. In 1973 he married Victoria Benedict de Ramel, an architectural historian who had previously been married to a French count. And Alex soldered a relationship that guaranteed him a unique sort of power: Si may have been the money behind the Condé Nast operation, but Alex would forever control its soul.

I disliked dealing with Si Newhouse so much that after a number of years, and many rather fruitless conversations, I decided to communicate with him through Alex. Alex advised me against this at first.

"You've got to make an effort," he said. "You have to get to know Si and work with him. Why don't you spend some time with him? Talk to him?"

And I, bowing out, said, "Oh, Alex, why don't *you* talk to him?"

In the 1980s, as our disagreements grew, Alex was more than happy to be doing my talking to Si Newhouse for me. Or rather, *not* talking to Si for me. I don't think that Si ever knew *why* I resisted making *Vogue* more like *Elle*. He only knew that I resisted. I don't think he knew that I had other visions for the magazine. He only knew that I didn't share his. I don't even think he knew that I wanted to go to *Self*. Alex controlled the flow of information as it suited his purposes. Which is why, on the day I learned I'd been fired, his final words to me were all the more ironic: "Talk to Si."

I phoned Si early that evening and talked to him just long enough to confirm that I was out and make an appointment to meet with him first thing in the morning. At nine o'clock the next day I went up to the fourteenth floor and took a seat before him in his huge, glumly decorated office. Si sat, shoeless. He had already been at work for four hours. This was no emergency.

"Well," he said laconically, "it's been a long time."

Too long, I reflected ruefully.

Si didn't waste words now.

"Talk to Pam van Zandt," he said, "and make the arrangements with her. And if you don't like the arrangements, Grace, come back and *we'll talk*."

Pamela van Zandt was the Condé Nast corporate secretary, and the only woman vice president since Mary Campbell had gone.

"I've been trying to warn you, Grace," she said as I came into her office and sat down. "I've been trying to tell you for years."

I looked up at her in disbelief. In Miss Campbell's absence Pam van Zandt had become the only shoulder that we at *Vogue* felt we could trust well enough to cry on, and I, over the course of the past few years, had often come up to bemoan to her the unfortunate turn that I thought *Vogue* was taking.

She had always listened sympathetically. Until once, not long before our present meeting, she had cut me off abruptly with a question: "Do you think, Grace, that you could edit *Vogue* without Alex?"

I paused only briefly, barely contemplating the question, before answering. "Oh, I couldn't even *think* of doing that," I said. "Alex is so wonderful." I thought that was the polite way to answer what I'd assumed was a merely rhetorical question. And I wanted to be loyal.

Now, in the bright light of changed circumstance, I realized that the question hadn't been rhetorical at all, and that Pam had been looking for an entirely different sort of answer. Alex was seventy-six; his health was weakening. He was already slowing down a bit, how much slower he'd grow and how soon was a question that troubled everyone. Pam van Zandt would have liked to have been able to assure Si that I could have forged into the future with *Vogue* with or without Alex. But I hadn't made that answer possible.

Pam offered me a settlement. It sounded awfully low, so I called up my friend Mort Janklow, the literary agent and lawyer, and asked for some advice, even though I knew that the conversation might be awkward for him since he was a friend of Si Newhouse as well. Avoiding taking sides, Mort suggested a formula by which I might figure out a fair compensation package according to the number of years that I'd spent, at relatively low pay, working at *Vogue*. I took his advice and Si accepted my proposal without argument, which immediately made me suspect that my calculations had been way too low. While I didn't expect to see anything like the enormous severance package that Lee Iacocca had received a few years earlier, I did think that my "golden balloon," as Tatiana Liberman called it, wasn't as high-flying as it might have been.

Si asked me to make an announcement to the staff right away. That afternoon I called all my editors into my office for a mandatory meeting. Everyone filed in: the fashion editors, the art department, the copy writers, the assistants. Taking a deep breath, I faced the packed room and said, "I didn't expect to be telling you this until the end of the year, which is when I was thinking of leaving. Unfortunately, management has seen fit to have me go earlier. Anna Wintour will be the new editor of *Vogue*."

For a moment there was silence. Some of the editors had heard about Liz Smith's broadcast from people who had seen it at home. Others hadn't heard anything at all. They were stunned. Some even had tears in their eyes.

Polly Mellen, who had actually heard the news a good twenty minutes earlier, and had already told another editor that she'd thought my firing was long in coming, was the first to break the silence. Grabbing her breast, she threw herself against the cabinet that held our TV and VCR and shouted, "MY GOD, GRACE! MY GOD! *How could this happen?*"

I thought of Diana Vreeland's line: "The stage lost its greatest actress when Polly Mellen joined *Vogue*."

When the room had stopped vibrating from the shock of Polly's torso against the furniture, Kay Hayes, our shoe editor, put in her two cents. She was a rather difficult woman with fat legs who looked very poorly in shoes and always seemed to be in an unpleasant mood because of it.

"Well, you don't need the money," she said. "You're married to a doctor." And while everyone murmured their disgust, she added something largely inaudible about "new blood."

Jade Hobson, in her typical, retiring way, hadn't said anything when I'd made my announcement. Then, when things had quieted down, she raised her voice and said, "I'm not staying here."

"That's silly," I said. "You've got to stay. You've had nothing to do with this."

"No," she said. "I'm leaving."

When the meeting was over and everyone had left, Carlyne Cerf de Dudzeele, a senior fashion editor, came back in and closed the door behind her. Carlyne was a very temperamental, difficult French woman with a great talent and utterly impossible working style. She was very high-strung, cried easily, and, because she never believed anything anyone told her, lived in a constant state of mistrust. I'd always kept my distance from her. The sight of her, chewing on the end of her long hair during fashion meetings as she fidgeted and twitched in nervous agitation, had bothered me for years.

Carlyne stopped in front of my desk and looked at me.

"This is a tough place," she said, lowering her raspy French voice to little more than a whisper. "Very tough. I had no idea." And then, with a look of sympathy, she turned around and walked out.

Later that day Si Newhouse issued two staff memos. One formally announced my "retirement." The next stated that Anna Wintour would be the next editor of *Vogue* "effective immediately"—an odd thing, given the fact that Si Newhouse had asked me to stay on through the middle of July. All the cards were on the table. There was no nicely padded "consulting editor" job for me. I was to finish my last issue and clear out.

The next few weeks were a strange and ugly time. Everyone was walking around whispering and looking over their shoulders to see who was listening. They would do what they had to with me to complete the October issue, then run upstairs with their things for Anna. Even Si Newhouse, who had never had anything to do publicly with the editorial running of the magazine, was seen walking through the halls with baskets of jewelry, carrying things out for a run-through in Anna's office. It was almost a gratuitous gesture, like a slap in the face to see him suddenly so interested in the day-to-day goings-on at *Vogue*.

Meanwhile, Anna Wintour was calling editors up one by one to her office at *HG* and asking them who was and who wasn't worth keeping on staff. Jade Hobson quit as soon as she got the call for an interview and went to work for Revlon. Amy Gross was offered a job by *HG* and quit. Paul Sinclaire, Kathleen Madden, and Susan Oberstein had already left, too.

Anna Wintour assembled her staff and produced a first issue with a tousled-haired model on the cover wearing faded jeans, a bare midriff, and a Christian Lacroix jacket jeweled with a pattern in the shape of a cross. This look was called "haute but not haughty." It was *Vogue* taking to the "street," and it was supposed to make the magazine look more hip and attractive to younger readers.

I should have been depressed. But instead I felt oddly elated. It had been at least two years since I'd first wanted to leave *Vogue*, but I'd never had the nerve to quit. Now, the angst of deciding whether or not to leave had been lifted. I was free! My friend Beverly Sills, who had not long before left a difficult post at the New York City Opera, drove that point home when she called me at home the morning after Liz Smith's broadcast. "Remember what Martin Luther King said, Gracie," she said. " 'Free at Last! Free at Last . . .' "

Free at last! At long last, I didn't have to spend the summer working. I didn't have to go to Paris for the couture. There were other reasons to celebrate too. The day after I was fired, when Bill took me to La Grenouille for a lunch that was supposed to have been a cheering-up party, we found ourselves instead cheering as, one by one, and couple by couple, people I hardly knew came up to our table and said things like "They must be crazy!" and "If it ain't broke don't fix it!" When I got back to the office the phone was ringing off the hook with friends and colleagues calling to express their outrage, encouragement, and support. After the story fanned out into the press, a woman whom I'd never seen before stopped me on the street one morning as I was coming out of the Regency Hotel's Fitness Center and she was taking her little boy to school, held out her hand, and said, "Get 'em!"

People were calling out to me at the hairdresser's: "There they go again!" People were grabbing me at dinner parties to say, "They just don't know how to do things." For a woman as "out" as she could be, I'd never felt so warmly connected to people before in my life. Liz Rohatyn and Liz Smith, who was furious with Condé Nast for allowing someone to "leak" the story to her before it had been revealed to me and has roasted Si Newhouse in her column ever since, invited me to a marvelous lunch with Diane Sawyer and Peter Jennings where we spent hours laughing off our outrage. Then, Ira Neimark, chairman of Bergdorf Goodman, and Dawn Mello, the store's president, gave a cocktail party for me at Bergdorf Goodman. As Oscar de la Renta, Bill Blass, Geoffrey Beene, Donna Karan, Herbert Kasper, Isaac Mizrahi, and every fashion writer and editor I knew stood around grinning, Jade Hobson recited a speech: "Grace, this gift doesn't have a name. You have to do that. It doesn't have a home. You have to do that too. It has tremendous growth potential, will always have the correct hair length, comes with a beautiful fur coat, has the ability to make you very happy as it simultaneously destroys your carpeting. Comes accessorized with a collar, a trainer, and a late-night walker, and last, but not leashed, it's beige and comes with all our love." And as everyone clapped, a sugar cookie-colored Labrador retriever was placed in my arms. An ivy-encrusted doghouse made by the Bergdorf Goodman display department was set up beside her.

It was fun being fired. And as the weeks went on, it became particularly amusing to see who stayed my friend when I was without a magazine and who didn't. Bill Blass called me the very day I was fired and invited me to lunch at Lutèce. Isaac Mizrahi continued to invite me to his fashion shows when I was in between jobs, as did Ralph Lauren. Karl Lagerfeld, whose clothes I had adored when he was designing at Chloé, and whom I had introduced to Kitty D'Alessio, formerly the head of Chanel operations in the U.S., when Chanel had first expressed interest in him, turned his back the moment I was out of *Vogue*.

John Fairchild, who'd barely addressed a word to me since I'd become editor of *Vogue* and had made clear, after that awful piece comparing me to China Machado, that he hardly thought I was

worthy of the post, suddenly was filled with kindness and solici-
tude. When Bill and I arrived at a benefit one evening shortly after
I was fired and found that our tickets had been misplaced, Fairchild rushed up and demanded we be admitted immediately, tickets or no. Afterward, he invited us to dinner and bathed us in his
warmth and friendship. It was as though he had never had anything against me, only *me* in that *job*. Of course, once it was announced that I was starting up my own magazine, he stopped
talking to me once more, and has never spoken to me since or
given coverage to my magazine except to circulate the periodic
rumor that we were going out of business.

When the October issue of *Vogue* was put to bed, I put on my
sneakers and white shirt and khakis and grinningly took off for
Bedford. "I am finally," I told Bill, "going to take a real, relaxing
vacation." I talked about gardening and set about answering every
one of the hundreds of letters I'd received after my firing.

"Don't get too relaxed," Bill worried. "It doesn't agree with
you. You really ought to think about what you're going to do
next." My good friends soon started pestering me to start sending
out feelers for another job while I was still in the public eye.
"You're 'hot' now, Grace," they warned. "In a few months you
won't be. Memories are short in this business."

They needn't have worried.

Within one week of my firing, I'd been called by Ed Kosner,
who asked me if I would have lunch with Rupert Murdoch at La
Côte Basque (how I wished it had been the Four Seasons in full
sight of Si!), and had been approached by nine different book
publishers about writing a memoir. I was playing tennis and answering my mail and enjoying myself. In the back of my mind I
was nursing the dream of the magazine that Rupert and I had
talked about, but as the weeks passed after our lunch and no further calls from him came, I decided not to give our conversation
too much thought. It was going to be difficult enough, come fall,
to try to figure out what to do with the rest of my life without going

out on a limb for imaginary projects. And it wasn't as though I didn't have concrete offers to occupy my mind.

Robert Dilenschneider of the public relations giant Hill and Knowlton had called, saying that he was going to try to move into representing people in the fashion world and was wondering if I'd be interested in joining him. We met and talked ideas, but decades of being on the other side kept me from accepting a job. I was also getting calls from the people who were thinking of starting up the English-language *Marie Claire*, and was having conversations with Hearst Magazines, whose president and chief executive, Frank Bennack, had called me just two days after my lunch with Murdoch to ask if I'd be interested in working as a consultant within their magazine group with an eye to eventually taking over *Harper's Bazaar* or starting my own magazine. It was very tempting—something altogether new, creative, and business-oriented all at once. It had the potential to be high profile and high status. And I liked Frank Bennack so much that I even felt willing to set aside thirty-five years of competing with Hearst and allow for the fact that its employees might, in fact, be decent human beings. Though I still felt when I walked into the gloomy old Hearst Building in the West Fifties as though I were entering the lair of the enemy, I figured that I could get over it. Condé Nast hadn't turned out to be so lofty, after all. And Frank Bennack seemed very much to be a man I could trust.

July progressed, Hearst and I moved closer and closer to an agreement, and still I heard nothing from Rupert Murdoch. The conversation we'd had still played in my mind, but it was becoming more and more of a distant—and disappointing—memory. I grew more used to the thought that the ideas I'd started to form after our lunch were only a pipe dream. As the summer progressed, Paris came and went, and as the Milan shows approached, I found myself growing nostalgic for my old haunts and my old crowd. Bill was right; as a full-time activity, answering letters and playing with my new puppy left something to be desired. I missed seeing Dawn Mello, Jade Hobson, Rosemary Bravo. I thought wistfully of the moment when we all would arrive in Milan, meet up in the lobby of the Hotel Gallia, break into small groups, and start talking and laughing and working, our excitement echoing into a crescendo. I received a few invitations to the ready-to-wear shows in New York. Not the same seat—but still in the front row, where Anna Wintour now reigned, flashbulbs reflected in her dark shades. I was welcomed, but not fêted. I was no longer "Miss Mirabella of *Vogue*." Being a civilian took some getting used to. I was eager to move on.

Frank Bennack had drawn up some papers, which were gathering dust, waiting for my signature. Something kept me from signing. And then one afternoon the phone rang at our country house. It was Rupert. He'd been busy, he said. He was sorry. He sounded so rushed and frazzled that for a moment I pictured him looking like the hero from "Get Smart," with a phone in the heel of his shoe. I knew he'd been occupied that summer buying *TV Guide*, *Seventeen*, and the *Daily Racing Form*, busy to the tune of countless millions of dollars.

"Don't give up on me," he said. "I'm going to get to this."

So I let another month go by, and then called his office. "I don't mean to nudge you," I said, "but if Mr. Murdoch really does have something on his mind concerning me, tell him that I'm about to sign a contract and I can't put it off any longer."

His office called back the same day. Mr. Murdoch, I was told, would like to have lunch with me in two weeks. "I'm sure that would be lovely," I said, "but I've got no two weeks. I have papers here in front of me that I've got to sign *now*."

So a few more phone calls were made, and duly returned, and I was asked to come downtown to see Mr. Murdoch that very afternoon, for a meeting in a ten-minute time slot he had free before dashing off to catch a plane—something, I would learn, that he did almost daily.

So I myself ran downtown, and had an audience with Rupert and John Evans, president of Murdoch Magazines. We reaffirmed our commitment to the idea that women were looking for a different kind of magazine, and Rupert, with a quick handshake, flew off to catch his plane. "Talk to John," he said, "he'll tell you everything."

A few days later, in a private room at the Box Tree, a charming restaurant in midtown, John Evans did tell me everything. He threw a pile of Murdoch magazines on the table (Murdoch at that time owned *New York*, *New Woman*, half of *Elle*, and *Premiere*) and explained when we would start, where we would work, how much we would spend, and how the magazine would be named *Mirabella*.

"Excuse me?" I said, my head snapping up at the sound of my name. "I think I missed something." And I asked him to repeat everything he'd just said.

"That's the name of the magazine," John said, almost impatiently.

"Wait," I said, "what do you want to do that for?"

"Well," he said, "the magazine's got to have a name. Yours is as good as any."

For a moment I was taken aback. I wondered aloud why anyone would buy a magazine with such a foreign-sounding name. As a little girl I'd always thought it was difficult to have Mirabella for a name, when everyone else was called things like Gray and Smith. That feeling, I realized, had stuck with me.

"It's a perfect name for a magazine," John said. "Do you know of anything we've done that's failed?"

It was true that even in 1988 Rupert Murdoch seemed invincible. From the time that he'd inherited a small Australian newspaper from his father in the early 1950s and turned it into his country's second largest publishing combine, Murdoch's media empire had never stopped prospering. In the late 1960s he'd ventured into Great Britain and resuscitated the *London Sun*. In 1973 he'd made his first incursion into American publishing, purchasing and turning around the *San Antonio Express and News* and later buying the *New York Post*, the New York Magazine Company, and launching the supermarket tabloid, *The Star*. He'd become a U.S.

citizen so that he could own American television stations, had bought the Twentieth Century Fox movie studio, and purchased the Fox-TV network.

I didn't appreciate Murdoch's brand of slice 'n' dice tabloid journalism. But I did admire his guts. And I found him a very appealing and intriguing man. His personality seemed to operate on a kind of on/off switch. On the one hand, he was charming and gracious in social settings. But when he started to talk business, his mouth tightened, his whole bearing toughened up, and what emerged was a machine-gun delivery of words, a barrage of sound at breakneck speed, so low and so fast that you had to strain to keep up and lean over forward to hear. And I'd found him very worth listening to.

I went home and told Bill all about the new plans. He was thrilled. "But do I really want," I groaned, "to start out on something like this at my age?"

"*At your age?*" Bill, who is fifteen years my senior, exclaimed. "Grace, think of your eighty-nine-year-old mother. Think of what it would mean for her to see Mirabella plastered across the top of a magazine."

I called Frank Bennack back and regretfully declined his kind offer. "What has Murdoch offered you?" he asked. "Let me match it."

"No," I said, "somehow I don't think that you can."

CHAPTER 10
M&M NIGHTS AND PIZZA DAYS: TOWARD *MIRABELLA*

In 1993, as the fashion industry was gearing up for Seventh on Sixth, the first ready-to-wear shows to be held all together in tents in Bryant Park, I approached Carolyn Wall, an executive vice president at Murdoch's News America, and asked her to donate $100,000 in *Mirabella*'s name to the Bryant Park effort. I knew it was an enormous amount of money, but I felt it was essential for us to be known as a player at that kind of event. Carolyn said no. And when I protested, she said, "But, Grace, you're not a fashion magazine."

"We're *not?*" I exclaimed. It disturbed me—until I realized that Carolyn had a point. Not being a fashion magazine was how *Mirabella* was born.

The idea, as I first discussed it with Rupert Murdoch and John Evans, was to create a magazine that focused on *style* rather than fashion. The focus would be on style in the broadest sense of the word, as the spark that informs every aspect of our lives—where we travel, what we read, how we think about ourselves, and how we fit into the larger world. Fashion and beauty would have a place in this. But so would politics, humor, business, psychology, fiction, health, the performing arts. When we covered fashion, we would separate what we considered just news from what we considered just great. When we covered beauty, we would find ways to discuss the role esthetics play in women's lives—and not tell them that cellulite cream was the answer to their prayers.

Mirabella wouldn't, Rupert and John and I agreed, try to compete with *Vogue* or *Elle* by running after trends or jumping through hoops to embrace the hot and the new. *Mirabella* would not blindly embrace whatever fantasies Seventh Avenue cooked up in any given season. It would set standards. It would have a point of view. It would demand substance. It would stand for something, something solid and immutable: a deep concern for women's lives. And that concern would save us from the traps of the flip and the slick.

We were going to break the mold for women's magazines. We were going to provide as much text as fashion, and we were going to make that text top quality. Smart. Literary. Fun. It was a unique challenge. How to show "timeless" clothes without looking out-of-date? How to be heady without being heavy? How to handle the most pressing issues of the day without becoming blatantly ideological? And how to attract fashion advertisers when we were not-a-fashion magazine?

Rupert and I finalized our contracts in November 1988, after I'd had time to disengage myself from Hearst and a while after he'd sold his half interest in the ubiquitous *Elle* back to Hachette. I was to be made *Mirabella*'s publication director, responsible for both the magazine's editorial content and for overseeing the look and content of the advertising. Rupert committed himself to putting up millions for our launch.

"We'll want the first issue for April," I was told when I went down to the Murdoch offices to sign my papers.

April would have meant closing in February.

"You've got to be kidding," I said. "That's completely impossible."

I felt a chill in the air. The ink was barely dry on the contracts.

"We'll do it for June," I blurted out, biting my tongue as soon as the words were out of my mouth. June is a nonclothes month, a nonbook month, a graveyard month for magazines. Not the month for making a splash in a start-up.

"Fine. It's a deal." A room full of Murdoch men eyed me warily.

"June. You don't change it."

I didn't dare. I switched into overdrive. I called Jade Hobson at Revlon and asked her to come oversee *Mirabella*'s fashion coverage. She came. I called Paul Sinclair at *HG* and asked him to come work under Jade. He flew over. I called Amy Gross, also at *HG*, and asked her, "Are you pryable?" I knew no one else in the magazine world with Amy's intelligence, and I told her I'd give her full autonomy for features. We had a series of secret breakfast meetings at an out-of-the-way hotel on East Forty-second Street. Amy jumped at it but also had another job offer. She hemmed and hawed. Finally, I called her and said that I needed an answer and if she still couldn't decide then it was probably better that she say no.

"I need someone," I said, "who can really put her heart and soul into the magazine. This really has to be a labor of love."

A short while later Amy called back.

"I'm yours," she said.

There was a great advantage to starting a magazine under the auspices of a mammoth company like Rupert Murdoch's News Corp. Murdoch provided everything: the structure, the office, the car service. I didn't have to run around trying to figure out how to print things and where to buy office supplies. There were circulation people already in place. We'd been given everything necessary to manufacture and distribute a magazine. If I had questions, I could bring them over to the Murdoch offices and have an entire magazine group ready to answer them. All we had to do was come up with the content.

There were advantages to the breadth of Murdoch's influence. And advantages to the fact that he took such an interest in each of his holdings, especially when it came to keeping track of the talents and whereabouts of his personnel. When I needed an art director and couldn't find one, Rupert said he'd see what he could do. The next thing I knew, in a few short days, he had produced Michael Rand, the art director of the London *Sunday Times*. He had a wonderfully straightforward, emphatic style, and never for a second thought of simply giving us visions of loveliness. It was a perfect fit.

The media right away tagged *Mirabella* "the magazine born with a silver spoon in its mouth." Working for Murdoch, though, often felt like a hardship assignment for those of us who had grown up at *Vogue*. Murdoch corporate culture couldn't have been more different than Condé Nast's. *Vogue* was the flagship publication of the Newhouse magazine empire, and it was Alex's baby. So while we did have budgets, they were loose, and if we had to take 20 extra pages in one issue and 30 more the next and by the end of the year were over by 120, no one really said anything. Murdoch demanded a totally different way of operating. We couldn't have layers of people—senior editors, associate editors, junior editors, assistant editors—as we had always had at *Vogue*. The Murdoch men—I always think of them as men, even though there are a good number of female executives among them—ran lean and mean and thrived on trimming fat. They also worked like crazy, and they demanded we learn to do the same.

We learned. It wasn't that difficult, I soon found, to run meetings without ten extra people standing around—and we worked like dogs. By the end of December, our full staff of twenty was working in an office Rupert had found for us in the Harper & Row, now HarperCollins, Building on East Fifty-third Street. It was big and rather grand—two full floors—and when we first moved in it had absolutely nothing in it. A day went by and we found two desks and one telephone. Then, another phone might come in, and another desk, and a chair, never quite enough for everyone. We'd all scramble to arrange ourselves around what furniture there was, reach over each other to answer the phones, grab each other's pens and pencils, hoard message pads.

Fortunately, we often worked in shifts. Many of the people I'd hired away from other places hadn't yet been able to get out of their jobs and came in before and after work, starting out early in the morning and working till late at night. Jade did sittings at midnight and ran around with a terrible flu, nursed, no doubt, on the hours and the stress and the steady diet of M&M's and pizza that we all swore kept us going through the long days and longer nights.

"M&M nights and pizza days"—that's how we all remember that time. When we hired new people and they asked about the hours, we told them, "Twenty-four." And we weren't joking. No matter what our workload, the Murdoch men didn't cut us any slack. One evening the assistants went home at 6 P.M. At 6:03 one of the Murdoch men who'd been assigned to make sure that we ran on scheduled stamped into my office.

"I don't know how you think you're going to launch a magazine if everyone thinks they can go home whenever they want," he said.

"Let me look into it," I answered. I was surprised. It wasn't like our group to leave early. So I investigated and found that the young women (the "kids," I called them) had left because the entire computer system had gone down and wasn't likely to be fixed before morning. Their bosses had urged them to go home. My taskmaster looked unconvinced. "They could have found *something* to do," he said.

Whip-cracking from the Murdoch crowd aside, a wonderful camaraderie soon grew up among our editors. We had no choice but to get along; we were each other's only companions. Together, we buried our fatigue. We fermented each other's ideas. We felt like heroines, creating a revolution in publishing, fighting all the odds. Our enthusiasm was contagious. Women started coming by the office just to breathe in the atmosphere and see if they could lend a hand. Kitty Hawks, Slim Keith's daughter, and Wendy Gimbel, wonderfully stylish women in their own right, drifted in and out, making wonderful suggestions. Beverly Pepper, the sculptor, would stop in and hand me a pocketful of notes filled with ideas for the magazine. Mary Wells Lawrence, a founder of the Wells, Rich, Greene advertising agency and the owner of the heavenly La Fiorentina in the south of France, would see me whenever she was in town or write me letters from overseas, filled with ideas and suggestions.

People loved the unstuffiness, the *coziness* of our desk-less, chair-less, secretary-less office. They loved the sense of adventure, of freedom. I think it reminded them of their own dreams. From the initial buzz of "You can't start a magazine in four months' time" (which is what it was once the staff really started work in January), the word now was that we were miracle workers. We bathed in the warmth of good wishes. It was a singular, momentary reprieve from the nastiness of the New York publishing world. And it didn't last long.

When we started moving from the planning stage to trying to get out and shoot pictures, strange things started to happen. Our contacts disappeared. People stopped taking our calls. It was like we were pariahs. I'd tell Bill Cunningham, the wonderful street-fashion photographer, "Here's a quarter. Give me a phone call." But it really wasn't funny. Virtually no major photographer was willing to shoot our fashion pages. Wayne Maser, who had at the outset agreed to work with us, suddenly had cold feet. First, he didn't want us to print his name with the pictures. Then, he took the pictures but wouldn't give us the film. Jade showed up at his studio and offered him a paper bag for his head, with slits cut out for his nose and eyes, and he didn't find it amusing. She finally managed to get a couple of rolls of film out of him.

Steven Meisel didn't even give us that much. He was, after Arthur Elgort, one of the first photographers I'd gone after in starting up the magazine. He'd been very interested at first, but then, as time went on, had become uncertain about everything: where he wanted to work, what he wanted to do, whether he wanted to live in the U.S. or in England. He went through a kind of existential crisis which corresponded, disastrously, with the very moment we most needed him to choose being our photographer over nothingness. We had counted on the strength of his name to help us get access to models and impress advertisers. In the end, after much discussion and many postponements, everything fell through. We never even made it to contract.

Next, models started disappearing. Some showed up on the first day of a sitting and never came back. Others would be scheduled to work with us and then find themselves booked in Bali for an extra four days. Hairdressers, makeup artists, and stylists, people we'd long considered our colleagues and friends, now avoided us like the plague. One of our editors came back from an outdoor shoot convinced that she'd seen people with binoculars and cameras spying on her group from a distance. It sounded paranoid; but then, it was obvious that *someone* was keeping tabs on us and undermining us, cutting off our access to photographers and models and stylists.

That someone was said to be *Vogue*. The pattern soon became clear: if a model was supposed to come by our studio after she'd finished a *Vogue* shoot, she'd never show up. Or she'd be held by *Vogue* and come hours late. We'd call up her agent and be told that they'd been told that if the girl showed her face in *Mirabella* she'd never see it in the pages of *Vogue* again—nor in any other of the Condé Nast magazines. There was nothing we could do. No offer we could make through the Murdoch magazines could rival the scope of what *Vogue* could offer—or threaten. Arthur Elgort put it very bluntly. "I'm sorry, Grace," he said, turning down our offer of a contract after *Vogue* tripled his salary. "But I just built a new house and I want to redo my apartment. I have a studio to maintain and a mortgage. I have to thank you, though. This is the best thing that's ever happened to me."

We started joking around the office that one call from us could make any photographer or model's Condé Nast career for life. But in fact, we were terrified. *Vogue*'s embargo could be devastating. We had a couple of very close calls. During the start-up of the magazine, we had booked a model to do a promotional film for the advertising department. There was a lot of money wrapped up in making the film, many people involved, and much time invested in bringing it all together. The day we were supposed to start shooting, we got a call from the model's agent, saying that she was stuck on another job and couldn't make it. When, outraged, I pressed for a better answer, I found out that she'd been booked for a *Vogue* sitting and had been told that if she worked with us she could forget it.

It was a disaster: there were big sums of money at stake, plus our entire promotion schedule. For a few hours it looked like everything was going down the drain. Then, Jade's husband, Martin Charnin, the lyricist and stage director, suggested we take a look at one of the cast members currently performing in his off-Broadway musical revue. She came in, and in a split second we knew that she was our girl. She was attractive without looking too polished and commercial, and she projected intelligence as well as good looks. We were so pleased with her that we started using her whenever possible. And we realized that there was a bright side to *Vogue*'s embargo. New faces guaranteed us a new look. New photographers guaranteed us a new style. And that freedom, born of necessity, made us bold.

Jade started combing through books and record album covers looking for fresh new visions. We found photographers who were willing to deal with models over the age of nineteen, who didn't have to airbrush every face to perfection, who could take pictures of women over thirty and use color film. We found photographers who hadn't been stuck in the rut of runway thinking for a decade. They were photographers who were maybe a little hungrier than some of the superstars, and as a result they were more open, even eager, to embrace our vision.

We fought on, feeling like pioneers. Sometimes, though, the swashbuckling atmosphere was trying. The Murdoch men tended to think of themselves as barbarians at the gate, getting business done at all costs. When they were happy with the way things were going, they could be charming. But if they were unhappy, they didn't talk, they *yelled*, bombarding us with words that were like a rain of bullets. At first, I was completely dumbfounded by this. Then I learned to deal with it by taking the tone and the tack one would when dealing with an irrational person or a child. "Wait a minute," I'd say. "Calm down. We can talk this out. . . ."

This was nothing like dealing with Alex Liberman—at the best or the worst of times. Some of the Murdoch people would make lunch dates and then forget to write them down. And after they'd stood us up, they wouldn't apologize—they were too busy. They were conducting business in a variety of time zones, and they made no bones about letting us know it. If Rupert called, they'd drop everything and run to him. And since everything was always happening transoceanically, at breakneck speed, they used urgency as a weapon to get what they wanted. Often I'd receive a call from the Murdoch group telling me they needed to see me that very second for a decision that had to have been made half an hour before. It was a scare tactic: a way of bullying me into making decisions I might have preferred not to have made had I had more time to consider my options. I found this out in a moment of rude awakening, which resulted in *Mirabella*'s accepting cigarette advertising.

We had started out with a policy of not accepting tobacco ads. John Evans had thought it up, and I'd been thrilled. But then, a few weeks before we began publication, he'd blown in—cheeks red, red scarf flying—and said, "I've got to see you. I've had a call from London." From the urgency with which he said it, it sounded like "London" was still hanging on the phone on hold in his office halfway across town. A major British tobacco company, he said, was threatening not to advertise in any Murdoch publication unless *Mirabella* took their advertising. I was distressed. Many of the Murdoch publications, I knew, owed their existence to tobacco ads.

I said I needed to go home and think it over.

"No, you can't do that," John said. "I've got to have an answer now." And he proposed that we make a compromise: three pages of tobacco advertising and no more per issue.

"That's what I think you oughta do," he said, "and that's what we'll do."

I agreed to it. I really had no choice. Given the fact that Rupert Murdoch is on the board of Philip Morris, expecting him to let *Mirabella* be *the* premiere anti-tobacco women's magazine was probably too much to ask.

Since then, no one ever asked us to soft peddle the health issue, and we were really able to make our mark for being a strong anti-tobacco voice.

The Murdoch people were fast. They were smart and frank and dedicated. But sometimes it seemed that they had no idea of what selling a style magazine was all about. And they were not very open to letting fashion editors tell them how to run their business. In no time at all, they put together a promotional mailing for potential subscribers made of old scrap materials that bore no resemblance to the real look or tone of *Mirabella*. After all, we had no back inventory of photographs. The subscription materials picked up readers and lost them when the real magazine came out. They stuck a big orange sticker on the first issue, promoting its special one-dollar price. The sticker made it look like it belonged in the supermarket next to the chopped meat and the chicken and not on the coffee table of our affluent, tasteful projected readers. Once again, I was sure, we'd attract the wrong sort of reader, one who would buy the magazine for the one-dollar sticker and be sorely disappointed by what was inside. "That's what you get," I told myself, "for signing on with a bunch of guys who make their living printing supermarket coupons."

But I was wrong.

When *Mirabella*'s premiere issue hit the newsstands, it hit big. It sold out—525,000 copies. The orange sticker—all I could see in my prepublication anxiety—was eclipsed by our startling, stupendous cover photo of documentary film producer Diandra Douglas. She was shown in extreme close-up, her lips, one eye, and part of her nose all that the camera could contain on the page. The intimacy of that photo, the strange beauty of it, proclaimed to the world that we were different, dedicated like no other magazine to getting beyond superficial visions of women. Beyond the cover, we had an excerpt from Phyllis Rose's biography of the legendary singer and dancer Josephine Baker, a story of former prima ballerina Suzanne Farrell's visit to the Soviet Union to teach George Balanchine's ballets, an essay on the anti-abortion movement, and a report on press responsibility. We ran an interview with Hedda Nussbaum's psychiatrist and a short story by Marianne Wiggins, then in exile with her husband, Salman Rushdie. I thought it was a glorious achievement. While some critics felt that the combination of such serious articles with visual features like a montage of lipstick shades made for rather schizophrenic reading, supporters welcomed the variation of light and dark and applauded us.

Throughout the first year, everything seemed to augur well for *Mirabella*'s future. Women stopped me on the street to say, "I love your magazine. Thank God you're doing this." Each time it happened, I came back to the office feeling like a woman with a mission. Wonderful writers were dying to write for us, saying we'd raised the level of "women's journalism" to rival the men's. In 1989, when *Elle*'s profits started to decline, the magazine was revamped, making it, with its slightly deeper articles and slightly more "real life" fashion, more like, well, *Mirabella*.

Throughout 1989 ad sales soared—so much so that the Murdoch people gave our advertising department a trip to Italy for their annual meeting. It was thought that *Mirabella* might start making money in two or three years. By June 1990 we had racked up 1,264 ad pages, and our circulation had climbed from 225,000 to 350,000.

We were considered a success story. With each issue, we shone brighter in the public eye. But on the home front, storm clouds were gathering. After about six months of issues devoted to what we considered timeless, classic style, the Murdoch men started insisting that we run stories that were a bit more *timely*. (The euphemism is "more journalistic.") And they started demanding that the magazine begin running *on time*. In that complaint, I knew that they had a point. Amy Gross was a brilliant editor, but she'd been trained, as had I, in the Condé Nast tradition of throwing budgets to the wind and holding pieces and pages for rewrites and redesigns so that they could be their very best. I sympathized. The Murdoch men didn't. When our managing editor, Nancy Comer, couldn't manage to get Amy moving, the Murdoch people took the matter out of our hands. They brought in Gay Bryant, the former editor in chief of Murdoch's *New Woman*, to act as a manager, but instead of giving her a managing editor's title, they installed her as editor in chief, above Amy. The reason, they said, was that Gay, with her background, could never have been brought in at a lesser position. The truth, I think, was that the Murdoch group wanted Amy Gross out. They felt the magazine was too serious, too heavy. Gay was a team player, and she knew where the Murdoch crowd was coming from.

I knew right away that there was going to be serious trouble. Gay was a Murdoch person through and through; weak on esthetics, strong on sensationalism. She and Amy Gross had nothing in common—aside from the fact that they were both good text editors and that Gay now had the title that Amy felt she deserved.

Amy felt profoundly betrayed—not least of all by me.

"This is terribly unfair," she told me. "I've been responsible for half of this magazine."

"Listen," I begged her. "This was imposed on me too. Please ride it out, and with a little luck, maybe the problem will go away."

The problem didn't go away; it only got worse. As soon as Gay came on board, it became clear that Amy and Gay had completely different visions for *Mirabella*. I did nothing to draw Gay in; I felt too strongly that Amy had been wronged. Gay soon stopped attending story meetings and confined herself to administrative work, doing the managing editor's job basically by default. Pretty soon, she started fighting back. Amy and I would go home in the evening and come back the next day to find that a layout had been changed or copy had been redone, or a pull quote was different— all on the premise that "something happened and they had to have it last night and we couldn't reach you." It was a highly volatile setup. I should probably have done more to defuse it. But I had other, more pressing matters on my mind. Like the fact that a bleak depression had hit the magazine industry, and it wasn't at all clear whether or not *Mirabella* was going to survive.

We had launched *Mirabella* in a year when there were a record number of magazine start-ups—605 in all. We'd entered a marketplace that had 16,000 magazines already in publication. Only twenty percent of new magazines were ever expected to survive. Those that made it to four years, the professional wisdom went, could generally be counted to make it in the long term. We'd done stupendously in our first year. We'd been blessed by the addition of a wonderful publisher, Julie Lewit-Nirenberg, a bubbling tiny Hungarian woman who'd turned out to be a godsend. But Julie's most brilliant efforts couldn't fight a bum economy. In 1991 a "seemingly bottomless depression," as *The Washington Post* called it, overcame periodicals publishing. Our ad pages dropped 15.8 percent. *Vogue*'s dropped 14.8 percent. *Elle*'s dropped 23.3 percent.

While our circulation kept growing—upward now of 400,000—our advertising was not keeping pace. In hard times advertisers were opting to stick with "hot" magazines like *Vanity Fair* and old standards like *Vogue*. And the Murdoch crowd, which had never understood very well what we were all about, had done a rather poor job in building up relationships with the fashion community. Our readers understood what *Mirabella* was all about and supported us with enthusiasm, but fashion advertisers didn't, and the greatest circulation growth in the world couldn't keep us solvent without solid advertising.

Adding to our problem of getting advertisers to understand us was the challenge of getting them to trust that we were not constantly about to go out of business. This was a very real and crippling problem. Six months after we began publication, and again at least once every six months afterward, rumors began to circulate that we were going out of business. We were closing on Tuesday, the rumor always went, or on Wednesday or Friday or *last* Monday (we'd missed it), and the minute word got out, our advertisers would call in a panic. Models and photographers too would be scared off of signing with us, fearing their contracts wouldn't be honored if we were to go under. The rumors were widespread, malicious, and utterly mysterious: Rebecca Darwin, our publisher from 1991 to 1994, once went to an awards ceremony on behalf of the magazine and was approached by a colleague who said, "Such a good magazine. I'm sorry to hear you're going out of business." She came back to the office and found two messages waiting, both expressing condolences. I started getting calls too, and we conferred and we realized that we'd gone out of business about an hour earlier. And there was absolutely nothing we could do to stop the rumor before it had run its course.

Once, we managed to trace a rumor back to its source. It turned out to be a limousine driver who happened to overhear Art Cooper, the editor of *GQ*, say to a colleague, "I hear *Mirabella* is going out of business." Well, that driver had a scoop for his next passenger

. . . and the next and the next, all up and down the Condé Nast Building and out onto Madison Avenue.

Another time I discovered that a young Swedish man who had worked for a short and unsuccessful time for us in the art department and then had gone over to *Harper's Bazaar* had called someone at *Mirabella* and said, "I hear Grace is very ill with multiple sclerosis and you're going under." The rumor started making its way around the office, and I found myself having to explain, five times a day, that I was in perfect health.

I was so angry that I called the young man up.

"Please tell me who told you that news," I said. "Because if no one told you and you made it up, I'm telling you right now that Mr. Bennack, the chairman of your company, is a friend of mine, and my next call will be to him."

"Oh, no," he said. "You've got it all wrong."

"Do I really?" I said. "Well, you'll be lucky if you have a job tomorrow."

By the time I got around to thinking of calling Frank Bennack, though, the rumor was over. They were on to the next story already.

One of the worst moments for *Mirabella* rumors came in 1991 when it was announced that Murdoch was shopping around for buyers for his magazines. He was raising cash as part of a restructuring deal he'd worked out with his bankers in an effort to get out from an $8.2 billion debt load, much of which he'd acquired after his satellite service, Sky Television, was launched in Great Britain. Everyone assumed that *Mirabella*, which was projected to lose $12 million in 1991, would be among the first magazines to go. Then, in April, when Murdoch made a deal to sell nine of his magazines—*New York, Seventeen, Premiere, European Travel & Life, Automobile, New Woman, Soap Opera Digest, Soap Opera Weekly*, and the *Daily Racing Form*—for $650 million to KIII Holdings, the communications arm of Kohlberg, Kravis & Roberts Co., a deal which, notably, did *not* include *Mirabella*, the word on the street was that we were sure to fold before the year was out.

"*Mirabella* Is Still Drawing Raves, But Its Survival Remains in Doubt," *The Wall Street Journal* intoned that May. "Mirabelly Up?" asked *Inside Media*. It was particularly painful news at a time when the magazine itself was without question reaching new heights editorially. In the early months of the year we'd run a cover story on the women soldiers in the Gulf War. We'd raised some eyebrows too when, in that profoundly pro-war time, we'd run an anti-war essay by E. L. Doctorow. In May we were nominated for our first National Magazine Award. The Murdoch organization proudly noted that, come September, we were raising our guaranteed circulation base to 500,000. They issued a press release that said he had no intention of selling *Mirabella*. But he said nothing directly to me. And I didn't know what to believe.

The rumors flew thick and fast: We were being shut down. We *were* shut down. We were being sold to Hearst. We were being folded into *Harper's Bazaar*. I began to suspect, after we'd been forced to accept substantial staff layoffs in February, that Les Hinton, the president of Murdoch Magazines, and Marty Singerman, the CEO and president of News America, were skimping on us, letting us limp along because they were hoping to unload us. If I saw Les walking around and smiling I suspected that we'd been sold. I had a nightmare that Si Newhouse had bought *Mirabella* but said he'd take it only without me. I began to pursue the possibility of assembling investors and purchasing the magazine myself.

Through all of this, for the first time, my faith in Rupert Murdoch was deeply shaken. After all, he'd never given me any indication that he intended to sell off *any* of his magazines. Quite the contrary: in November 1990 I'd received a call one morning from his office telling me that Mr. Murdoch was meeting with the editors of his magazines for lunch and requested that I be there. I showed up at 12:30 P.M. at the Murdoch offices at 1211 Sixth Avenue and entered a room with about fifteen other editors. After a good deal of general chitchat, Rupert began very quickly and softly to address us: "I thought we ought to have this talk because I know all of you have been hearing things that are not true and I want to tell you what's going on." He briefly discussed his plans for debt restructuring, then said, "I'm not selling the magazines and news-papers. I know every ten months there are rumors to the contrary, and so I wanted to tell you the truth."

And then he went on to tell some funny stories and contentedly to eat his lunch.

Afterward, as we left the building, Gay Bryant said to me, "What was *that* all about?"

And I said, "I think he's just trying to clear the air."

Less than six months later, we were back, staring at the side-walk on Sixth Avenue with all the other editors and digesting the news that Murdoch was divesting himself of his magazines.

Murdoch kept things so close to his chest that I never knew why. *Mirabella* hadn't been sold, except for what I read in the press—that KIII hadn't wanted it. I probably never would have known otherwise, had I not, about one year later, run into a young man at a media lunch who stopped me and introduced himself. "I'm one of the lawyers who worked on the Murdoch-KIII deal," he said. "And I just think you should know that Murdoch wanted to keep *Mirabella*; he did not want to sell it. They didn't want *Euro-pean Travel & Life* and he insisted that they take it and leave him *Mirabella* instead."

Rumors always fly into a void. They fly faster still when there's a little grist for the mill. That grist was provided, amply, in the spring of 1993, when Amy Gross, after nearly fifteen years of working with me, quit, becoming editorial director of *Elle* and tak-ing three key *Mirabella* editors with her. The loss of these editors shocked me.

"Do you know what you're *doing* to us?" I asked her when she told me of her plans. "This is terrible."

"I hired these people," Amy replied. "I work closely with them and they're my friends."

After that, the rumor instantly started that with no editors we were sure to go out of business. I hadn't appreciated, up until that moment, just how strongly betrayed she'd felt by me. Now, I guessed, we were even.

After Amy left, the Murdoch group stepped in and did something I should have done years earlier, which was to allow Gay Bryant to begin to act like the editor in chief that she was and bring in a stable of editors she knew she could work with. At the same time I started a move toward relinquishing control of the magazine.

It was a process that I was supposed to have begun a year earlier. I had stipulated in my contract with Murdoch that I wanted to be able, after three years, to reduce my work time to three days a week and no longer be involved with the day-to-day running of the magazine. But with all the conflicts between Amy and Gay and the rumors of our being sold, no one felt comfortable letting me do so. Now I realized that no matter how solid we were, the rumors were probably never going to stop. ("I regret when I put together my staff that I didn't ask for an executive to handle rumors," I'd had to quip in 1992 while accepting the magazine industry's highest accolade—a National Magazine Award for General Excellence.) And I'd seen that the magazine could not have two heads. It was time to step back and give Gay Bryant her shot.

I never thought Gay would be the savior the Murdoch men were expecting. She was the kind of editor who walked around with a pen and a notebook, submitting every idea to a quick cost analysis and making the trains run on time. She was intent upon making us more comprehensible to advertisers, more accessible to readers, more eye-catching for newsstand buyers. I felt she had no sense of style and no real convictions about what we were about as a magazine. I was soon proven right.

Instead of getting lighter under Gay, the magazine steadily became terribly gruesome, even bleak. As I protested, it was argued that our content was only a reflection of women's concerns in an angry, frustrated, and frightened time. But I had always hoped that our magazine could transcend the times, to reach to higher, more timeless ideals, to treat the readers intelligently and not pan-

der to them, to entertain as well as to inform. I had been particularly demanding about this as it pertained to our fashion coverage.
Fashion, which was by its very nature once removed from real life,
never *had* to be taken as found, I always felt. Unlike real life, it
could always be edited to remove the negative and unpleasant;
indeed, I believed it had to be. For the first few years of publication, *Mirabella* did so beautifully. But by 1993 this editing wasn't
happening anymore.

As I stepped back, and Gay Bryant became responsible for the
look and content of our fashion pages, the magazine became a
sheer reflection of what was passing for fashion in our time. And it
was the worst of times: the glitz of the eighties had passed, but no
return to simplicity, no concern for women's lives, no real challenge to design, had followed in its wake. Instead, we were given
the waif look. We were given "deconstructed" clothing, a pedo-
philiac "gamine" look and grunge. All of which was followed by a
"return to glamour" that was little more than a rehash of the
vampy Italian jokes of the late 1970s and an extended advertise-
ment for the new Wonderbra.

It was probably the worst moment in fashion that I had ever
seen. The clothing was meaningless, unwearable, undesirable. It
was downright insulting to women. It spoke of an utter void in
design ideas. Deconstructive clothing was almost admirable in that
with its eye-catching seams, rough stitching, hanging hems, and
ripped-out linings, it honestly portrayed its own bankruptcy. The
waif and grunge looks were less honest. They were styling parad-
ing as fashion, the ultimate expression of presentation over design.
Both were trumped up for the runway—combat boots paired with
long skirts, models shown with greasy hair and makeup-induced
pallor—and when the formless clothes were taken off the runway
and shipped into stores, they proved utterly unsalable. The waif
look, so dissected and discussed in the press for all that it did or
didn't mean about infantilizing women, died a very banal death.
All the rationalization in the world couldn't save it from its own
uselessness. Stores were left with merchandise to return, good de-

signers were left with egg all over their faces, and women were left with nothing. And the next year, when the Lolita-esque gamine look hit the runways, it was clear that no one had learned anything. Except, perhaps, for store presidents, who were begging designers to give them something to sell. And, perhaps, for American women, who weren't going shopping anymore.

Under Gay Bryant, *Mirabella* didn't learn anything from the waif debacle, either. The fashion pages I'd once been so proud to show off as real examples of "real life" dressing now hosted pasty, spiritually ugly-seeming girls wearing shapeless, unwearable things. We were trendy; we were "hip." The advertising community was happy; we were showing their clothes. Fashion-y people liked us more: we were becoming "risqué." We were also losing our voice.

In the winter of 1993, when Gay hired a freelance art director who directed Calvin Klein's advertising, we became so "cutting edge that our fashion pages were the antithesis of the vision for *Mirabella*'s style." Our pages looked fuzzy, like a cheap imitation of Calvin and totally inappropriate to the magazine. Another embarrassment came when Gay discovered nudity and ran a couple of half-naked covers and Helmut Newton-esque fashion spreads. When I questioned the pictures, she suggested that they were just "too Helmut Newton-y" for me. I was tempted to retort that she should have *known from* Helmut Newton. She truly couldn't tell the difference. The quality of the pictures was awful and the effect was near disastrous: stores in the Bible Belt embargoed one of our issues, and readers started writing in to complain. When the new art director produced in succession a series of covers featuring models who either screamed their anger behind clenched teeth or seethed, passively, behind half-closed lids, readers began letting their subscriptions expire.

I was caught between biting my tongue and shouting my outrage. Throughout all the years that we'd remained true to our vision, our readership had soared (We'd projected a subscription base of 500,000 readers by our fifth-year anniversary; in 1993 we were up to 620,000 and still going strong) while advertisers and the fashion community had remained tepid. There was a message in that, I knew. Our readers—accomplished, intelligent, highly successful, and educated women—wanted good stories to read and good clothes to wear. And they had the money to buy those clothes; our market research showed that their average yearly household income was $103,000—considerably higher than *Vogue, Harper's Bazaar*, and *Elle*. Our advertisers and erstwhile supporters in the fashion community insisted, however, that we give them what they never knew they wanted: jokes and gimmicks and clothes for nineteen-year-olds. What advertisers wanted was for us to march in lockstep with them down the runway, to prove ourselves "hip," fashion-y, "on the edge." They didn't care that our readers were as far from the edge as anyone could be. They needed to understand us on their own terms—as a traditional, style-oriented fashion magazine.

Mirabella had been created because a certain woman had no magazine, and throughout its glory days it had always been edited to please her—not to placate advertisers or titillate art directors or entertain the very fashion mavens it was created to oppose. But by 1994 the magazine couldn't have come further from its original vision. Not only were we not thinking style instead of fashion, transcending trashiness and trends, we were taking our esthetic cues from advertising. It was one of the worst moments in American fashion history—and we were going with the flow. Doing that, no matter how profitably (which it wasn't), seemed so poor, so empty to me. We were becoming more like any other fashion magazine. We were losing our souls to gain the approval of the advertising community. I didn't want *Mirabella* to be an award-winning magazine that went out of business. But I also didn't want it to be a booming business with no soul.

I tried leaning on Gay to improve the anemic health coverage in the magazine and to relieve the ugliness of our tone. I tried leaning on Jade to control the art department and bring a stronger eye to the fashion pages. She couldn't turn them around and, in the fall of 1994, left us for *New York* magazine. Paul Sinclaire left for Italian men's *Vogue* at the same time. I realized, with a shock, that my entire old crowd was gone. In their place were fashion editors and assistants whom I did not know and who did not recognize me, putting out a magazine in whose pages I could no longer recognize anything approaching my sense of style.

It takes a person with vision to transcend the trends of the times. Gay was not that kind of a person. I felt that something had to change. I felt we needed an editor who really understood that the magazine was not a selling device but a heartfelt thing, a labor of love. We needed an editor with a sense of commitment and who could help the magazine sell.

I'd been writing to Anthea Disney, the editor of *TV Guide* and newly named editorial director of the Murdoch Magazines for some time, voicing in the strongest terms my disappointment with the magazine. She'd asked me to be patient and to give Gay the breathing room to make things better. I tried. And I watched as things went from bad to worse. Finally, as my contract renewal loomed close, in the fall of 1994, I wrote to Rupert Murdoch and said I didn't think I could keep up my association with the magazine anymore. It was getting so that I hung my head when people told me that they missed the old *Mirabella*. I could not defend the new magazine.

Rupert took my letter very seriously. In October he wrote me back an earnest note of his own. "We all feel we would like to keep a very real association with you," he said. "We have all put an immense amount of blood, sweat, money, and patience into this effort . . ." and he promised new changes which, he said, wryly, "will not make you unhappy." Those changes were unveiled two months later: Gay Bryant was out. Dominique Browning was in as our new editor in chief.

Dominique was one of the founding partners of the Edison Project, entrepreneur Chris Whittle's effort to create for-profit schools. She was a smart, energetic, inspiring woman, the first woman to have been named an assistant managing editor of *News-*

week, and a former literary editor at *Esquire*. She was the kind of woman that *Mirabella* was supposed to be all about.

"What I really want to do," Dominique told me in our first meeting, "is to take *Mirabella* back to its founding vision, to its drive for the best of everything. Will you help me?"

"You don't have to ask me for help," I said. "Just tell me when to start."

But Dominique never had a chance. On March 20, 1995, three months after she began, I received a call from Les Hinton's office. Mr. Hinton, I was told, wanted to see me at 11 A.M. the next morning. At 10 A.M. that morning, I looked at Bill.

"I have a feeling," I said, "that this is it."

Les greeted me like an old friend. He ushered me into his office very warmly. Then the ax fell.

"We've decided we can't go on anymore with this," he said. *Mirabella*'s chronic unprofitability had become just too painful, and projected advertising and newsstand sales promised little relief for the near future. News Corp. had decided that the magazine would cease publication after its May issue, which was already en route to the printer.

"We know we've made some mistakes," Les admitted.

"Sure did," I thought, keeping silent. And, as I listened to Les speak—he spoke, with little help from me, for half an hour, hoping, no doubt, to mollify me with his explanations—I realized that, to my surprise, I didn't need soothing at all. I found myself nodding along with Les's account of events. It wasn't so much that I agreed with what he said as that I accepted the endpoint of his arguments. The fashion world had never really embraced *Mirabella*. Our advertisers had never been able to figure out what we were about. We couldn't get by on the esteem of our loyal readers alone. And the magazine wasn't anymore what it had started out to be. It hadn't been that magazine for almost two years. Dominique Browning was less a savior than an afterthought. No matter how much change she might bring, she couldn't shift the perceptions of an entire marketplace.

As soon as I left Les's office, I went to a sidewalk pay phone and called Bill.

"It's over," I said. "It's over."

Before I even had time to get from Les's office to my own, the company publicly announced that the magazine was closing—unless a buyer was found by March 31. The news caught Dominique Browning completely off-guard. When I first saw her, she was in tears. The staff, many of whom had left other jobs to come on board only weeks or months earlier, was hardly in better shape.

A meeting was called for three o'clock. We were told that the offices would close on Friday, March 31. The staff would receive severance pay. No sooner had the news begun to sink in than the phone calls, the requests for newspaper and magazine and television interviews, began. It was all too familiar—the abruptness, the secrecy, the delight of erstwhile "friends" in the industry—all of it. I had been down this road before.

I started coming to the office every day to lend some kind of support to the staff as they packed up their desks and prepared for the unknown. Dominique began making morning visits to Condé Nast—to help the staff find new jobs, it was said. All without a word to me. And, oddly enough, from the time that the closing had first been announced to me, I hadn't had a word from Rupert Murdoch, either. In fact, the last words I'd heard from him on the subject of *Mirabella*'s future had been at the marvelous fifth anniversary party he'd thrown for the magazine at the Museum of Modern Art in June 1994. That anniversary celebration—and the fifth anniversary issue on "fearless women" that had accompanied it—had been a bright spot in an otherwise dreary time. At the dinner with very special guests, Rupert had announced, in a toast to all assembled, that he had no intention of abandoning the magazine.

Finger-pointing is a bad habit, one which I try to avoid. And yet, I cannot help but feel that there must be some accounting for what went wrong with *Mirabella*. Real mistakes were made. Management should not have placed the magazine in the hands of someone who was utterly lacking in experience in the fashion magazine world. It should not have been handed over to someone with no sense of our focus or intent. Despite the lean financial times, some money should have been spent to keep salaries and fees almost commensurate with those paid by other top fashion magazines. We needed talent and we couldn't attract it or keep it. That was a terrible handicap.

I made mistakes, too. I should not have been so eager to get out of the day-to-day running of the magazine. I shouldn't have switched to a three-day-a-week schedule, which made it so easy for the Murdoch group to bring Gay Bryant in over Amy Gross. I shouldn't have allowed myself to be relegated to an ancillary, hands-off position once Amy Gross had left. I should have argued when my monthly editorial comments were renamed from "Mirabella Dictu" to, simply, "Dictu," and when the Hirschfeld caricature of me was deleted from the page. I should have pushed harder, should have followed up more when my story ideas for feature articles were routinely ignored. As I saw myself, under Gay Bryant's tenure, becoming more and more of a figurehead and less and less of a player in the real operations of the magazine, I should have raised my voice higher. I shouldn't just have told Rupert that I found the magazine unreadable and no longer wanted to be part of it, that I didn't want to renew my contract.

As they say in baseball, though, "it ain't over till it's over."

Just one week after Les Hinton had informed me of *Mirabella*'s imminent demise, Murdoch announced his acceptance of an offer by Hachette, the publisher of *Elle*, to buy the magazine. The "new" *Mirabella* would be published just six times a year to start with. I would stay on as a consultant. And the new editor in chief would be Amy Gross, restored to her place at the top of the masthead while maintaining her responsibilities at *Elle*. Dominique Browning, whose final issue of *Mirabella*, perhaps prophetically, had been entirely devoted to gardening, would end up as editor in chief of *HG*, taking Anna Wintour's old job, bringing the defunct magazine back to life and giving our bizarre game of musical chairs one additional twist.

Mirabella was born out of passion. A passion for style, a passion for beauty, a passion for the energy and strength of modern women. It was born out of commitment, a commitment to giving women access to the best style, a commitment to their health and well-being.

Murdoch put up the money. I found the talent. The women were ready and waiting. I thought the rest would be easy. Although Rupert Murdoch had, early on, sent me the message: "Tell Grace that she doesn't have to reinvent the wheel." I really thought that with enough hard work and enough passion and commitment, we could revolutionize fashion magazine publishing overnight.

It wasn't so easy, after all. There *were* great triumphs— particularly, I felt, in the way we were able to position *Mirabella* as *the* premiere women's health advocate in the magazine community, an effort whose greatest moment came when, in 1993, a doctors' panel discussion on women's health that we convened on Capitol Hill drew hundreds of listeners, a broad cross section of women from the House and Senate and Hillary Rodham Clinton as keynote speaker. But there were formidable challenges too, ones which the "new" *Mirabella* still has to face. Yet with the sensibility of Amy Gross and the publishing strength of Hachette and the changed woman reader, ready and waiting, an intelligent magazine can make a niche for itself—without focusing primarily on fashion, as I grew up doing; but, rather, fitting fashion into a thoughtful woman's world. After all, fashion has its wonderful place in life—but so do ideas and good health and an understanding of the larger world.

It's a never-ending drama, this business, with its ins and outs, its flavors of the month, of the day, of the hour. As T. S. Eliot once said, in his poem *Four Quartets*: "to make an end is to make a beginning./The end is where we start from." The story continues. The ending is not yet written.

The former editor in chief of *Vogue* magazine, Grace Mirabella was the founder and publishing director of *Mirabella*. She is a frequent speaker on women's issues and the fashion industry, and she lives in Manhattan with her husband, Dr. William Cahan.